Building Godly Nations

Lessons from the Bible and America's Christian History

Stephen K. McDowell

PROVIDENCE FOUNDATION

CHARLOTTESVILLE, VIRGINIA

Building Godly Nations: Lessons from the Bible and America's Christian History

Copyright © 2003 by Stephen McDowell
First printing, 2004

Published by:
Providence Foundation
PO Box 6759
Charlottesville, VA 22906
434-978-4535
Email: provfdn@aol.com
www.providencefoundation.com

The Providence Foundation is a Christian educational organization whose purpose is to spread liberty, justice, and prosperity among the nations by educating individuals in a Biblical worldview.

Cover Painting: The First Prayer in Congress, September 7, 1774. When the first Continental Congress met in Philadephia, Rev. Jacob Duché led George Washington, John Adams, Patrick Henry, and other of America's Founding Fathers in prayer. This illustrates well the need for civil leaders to seek God, acknowledging His authority and truth, and explains in part why God's blessings were upon the founding of America.

Printed in the United States of America

ISBN 1-887456-15-5

Table of Contents

Building Godly Nations: Lessons from the Bible and America's Christian History

Section I

The Mandate for Building Godly Nations

"Go therefore and make disciples of all the nations."

Matthew 28:18-20

"Be fruitful and multiply, and fill the earth, and subdue it; and rule over . . . every living thing that moves on the earth."

Genesis 1:28

Chapter 1

Fulfilling the Cultural Mandate

How Christians Have Helped Establish God's Kingdom in the Nations

God's plan for mankind

What is man's purpose or mission on the earth? Christians often answer this by referring to the Great Commission (Matthew 28:18-20), and rightly so, but in recent years a large segment of the Church has limited the meaning of this to only personal conversion. Certainly the Great Commission includes the Evangelistic Mandate, to redeem man, but it also includes the Cultural Mandate, to redeem the earth.

God has revealed Himself as both the King of Creation and the Redeemer of mankind. His kingship over creation is depicted in the opening chapters of the Bible. God's purpose for man is also revealed in the book of Genesis. To properly understand God's plan for man, we must understand a fundamental truth declared in Genesis 1:1 — the sovereignty of God. God declares His existence from the beginning. He declares He is the Creator, and hence His Lordship over creation. He rules over all creation. "The heavens are the heavens of the Lord. . . . He does whatever He pleases" (Ps. 115:16, 3). Since He is sovereign, all men are responsible before God.

The first book of Genesis also teaches the distinctiveness of man. Man is made in the image of God (1:26-27), therefore he is unique and distinct. Man displays the principle of individuality — in calling and characteristics. We all have a common general purpose, but each of us has a distinct specific purpose.

God gave a mission to His special creation from the beginning — the Cultural or Dominion Mandate (vs. 28). God gave man an assignment to rule over the earth, to take dominion. Psalm 8:6 says we are made to rule over the works of His hand.

God created man in His own image and likeness as His vice-regent or steward to rule over the earth. Unfortunately, man fell from the purpose for which God created him. Thus, man lost both his intimate relationship with God and his ability to properly govern the earth. Sin not only separated man from God but also brought a curse and great loss. Man was unable to properly fulfill the cultural mandate.

God's redemptive nature is evident early on. Man having fallen from what God made him to be and to do, God planned both to redeem man and to restore man's delegated authority and stewardship over the earth. God promised that the seed of woman would destroy the serpent, Satan (Gen. 3:15). Christ was that seed who came to redeem man and reverse the effects of the fall and the curse. He restored to man the ability to fulfill the mission originally given to Adam, as well as restoring man's relationship to God.

The story of redemption unfolds in the various covenants which God initiated with men. The giving of the law in the Mosaic Covenant was also used by God to further His redemptive program. Of course, God's redemptive purpose has found ultimate fulfillment in the New Covenant through Christ, who was slain and by whose blood God has redeemed men for himself "from every tribe and tongue and people and nation" (Rev. 5:9).

Purpose of salvation in Christ

The complete purpose of salvation in Christ cannot be understood unless we understand the original purpose of man. Salvation goes beyond getting man to heaven. It includes restoring man to his original position. Christ brought to man the restoration of the covenant he had with God, of the glory he had from God, and of the dominion mandate. Jesus also brought His kingdom rule and reign to all creation. He proclaimed and demonstrated the gospel of the Kingdom (that is, the government, righteousness, truth, and peace of God in all areas of life).

His atoning work also reversed the curse due to the fall of man. The curse affects individuals through death, sickness, bondage, etc., and in turn also affects all spheres of life. Christ brought redemption to individuals, but also institutions and all spheres of life (including law, government, education, arts, business). Redemption is as broad as the sweep of sin.

God's desire, as Jesus taught us to pray, is for His kingdom to come and His will to be done on earth as it is in heaven. We have been redeemed for a purpose. In Christ we have been restored to sonship and are now in a position to obey both the Cultural and the Evangelistic Mandates. With respect to the Cultural Mandate, God has restored us to stewardship. Through Christ we are called back to God's original purpose—to live in His image and to "be fruitful and increase in number, fill the earth and subdue it. Rule over . . . every living creature that moves on the ground" (Gen. 1:28). We have been restored to serving God as his vice-regent over the earth.

Nations are also affected by Christ's redeeming work. In Matthew 28:19 Jesus told us to go and make disciples of the nations. Matthew Henry said the intention of this is to admit the nations as Christian nations. Acts 17:26 tells us that God made the nations and determined their appointed times and the boundaries of their habitation, that they should seek God.

Nations have duties to God. George Washington summarized well the duties the nations have to God in a *Proclamation for a Day of Thanksgiving*, observed on Thursday, November 26, 1789: "It is the Duty of all Nations to acknowledge the Providence of Almighty God, to obey his will, to be grateful for his Benefits, and humbly to implore his Protection and Favor."[1]

We need to see that our commission is great and goes beyond converting individuals, though that is of first importance.

Redeeming the earth

The Cultural Mandate calls us to use all our resources to express His image and likeness on the earth. Fulfilling this mandate requires us to discover truth through sciences, apply truth through technology, interpret truth through humanities, implement truth through commerce and social action, transmit truth through education and arts, and preserve truth through government and law.

Historically, Christians have led the way in each of these areas. As these men and women have been faithful to fulfill the call on their lives and utilize the talents God gave them, they have contributed greatly in taking dominion over the earth and extending God's purposes and government in this world.

In the parable in Luke 19:11-27 Jesus instructs us in how we should live on the earth as we wait for, and assist in bringing forth, His kingdom. He told us to "do business with this until I come back" (vs. 13). The *this* are minas, which certainly speak of wise money usage, but in a broader sense represent the talents, skills, and abilities God has given each of us. God created us for a purpose. He wants us to work as partners with Him to take dominion over the earth by using the talents He has given us. These talents express themselves in the business or work He has called us to. Our work is a vital part of God's plan for us and the nations. As we are faithful to labor hard and multiply what He has given us, we will be taking part in bringing forth His Kingdom on earth and being a blessing to the nations.

We can learn much in how to disciple the nations today from the examples of Christians God has used throughout history. Following are listed some Christians who have contributed to fulfilling the cultural mandate by doing business with the talents God gave them in various fields. A few of these pioneers are briefly examined so that we may learn from and be inspired by their examples.

Fulfilling the Cultural Mandate Requires Us to:

1. Discover truth through sciences

- Scientists/inventors — Johann Kepler, William Herschel, Isaac Newton, James Maxwell, Francis Bacon, Carolus Linneaus, Blaise Pascal, James Joule, Michael Faraday, John Herschel, Robert Boyle, Louis Agassiz, Lord Kelvin

James Maxwell (1831-1879), Scottish Physicist and Mathematician, reflected the proper view scientists should have when they approach the study of the universe from God's perspective in his following prayer:

> Almighty God, Who has created man in Thine own image, and made him a living soul that he might seek after Thee, and have dominion over Thy creatures, teach us to study the works of Thy hands, that we may subdue the earth to our use, and strengthen the reason for Thy service.[2]

Isaac Newton (1642-1727), who discovered the Law of Gravity and the Laws of Motion, developed calculus and the particle theory of light, and invented the first reflecting telescope, was probably the greatest scientist of all time. He wrote more about God than science. In his *Philosophy of Nature* he wrote:

> We are to . . . acknowledge one God, infinite, eternal, omnipresent, omniscient, omnipotent, the Creator of all things, most wise, most just, most good, most holy. We must love him, fear him, honor him, trust in him, pray to him, give him thanks, praise him, hallow his name, obey his commandments, and set times apart for his service, as we are directed in the Third and Fourth Commandments, for this is the love of God that we keep his commandments, and his commandments are not grievous (1 John 5:3).

2. Apply truth through technology

- <u>Colonizers/Explorers</u> — Christopher Columbus, Richard Hakluyt, The Pilgrims, Roger Williams, Thomas Hooker, William Penn, Marcus Whitman, Jason Lee, Jedidiah Smith, Johnny Appleseed

Christopher Columbus wrote in his *Book of Prophecies*, 1502: "It was the Lord who put into my mind, I could feel His hand upon me, the fact that it would be possible to sail from here to the Indies."[3]

The person most responsible for the colonization of America by England was a minister, Richard Hakluyt. He wrote of the providential purposes of American in *Discourse of Western Planting*, 1584:

> Wee shall by plantinge there inlarge the glory of the gospell and provide a safe and a sure place to receave people from all partes of the worlds that are forced to flee for the truthe of Gods worde.[4]

William Bradford, the governor of the Pilgrims for 33 years wrote and author of a history of the Pilgrims, *Of Plimouth Plantation*, wrote of one reason for their starting a new colony:

> A great hope and inward zeal they had of laying some good foundation, or at least to make some way thereunto, for the propagating and advancing of the Gospel of the kingdom of Christ in those remote parts of the world.[5]

The founder of Pennsylvania, William Penn, said after receiving a charter for land in America: "My God that has given it to me ... will, I believe, bless and make it the seed of a nation."[6]

When missionaries, Marcus and Narcissa Whitman, reached the Continental Divide on July 4, 1836, they claimed the Oregon Territory for God and the United States. Rev. Spalding wrote:

> They alighted from their horses and kneeling on the other half of the continent, with the Bible in one hand and the American flag in the other, took possession of it as the home of American mothers and of the Church of Christ.[7]

- <u>Inventors</u> — Johann Gutenberg, Robert Fulton, Cyrus McCormick, Samuel F.B. Morse, R.G. LeTourneau

Samuel F. B. Morse' s Invention Shrunk the World

Samuel F. B. Morse invented the telegraph in 1832 and worked during the next decade to improve it. The first inter-city line was tested in 1844, when a message was sent from the Capitol Building in Washington to Baltimore.

The invention of the telegraph was one of the most significant technological discoveries in history. It ranks with the printing press in its impact in the area of communication. The message from Washington to Baltimore took a few minutes, which before would have taken about a day. When cables were laid across the Atlantic and across the continent, messages that would have taken days and weeks, now took just a moment.

The New York Herald declared Morse's telegraph "is not only an era in the transmission of intelligence, but it has originated in the mind . . . a new species of consciousness." Another paper concluded that the telegraph is "unquestionably the greatest invention of the age."[8]

Morse was a Christian who believed he had been chosen by God to make this discovery—a discovery that would lead to the advancement of man and the fulfilling of God's purpose for mankind. Annie Ellsworth, a friend of Morse's, composed the first message sent over the Washington-Baltimore line on May 24, 1844. She "selected a sentence from a prophecy of the ancient soothsayer Balaam" — "What hath God wrought!"[9] Of this message Morse wrote:

> Nothing could have been more appropriate than this devout exclamation, at such an event, when an invention which creates such wonder, and about which there has been so much scepticism, is taken from the land of visions, and becomes a reality.[10]

Morse considered it remarkable that he, an artist, "should have been chosen to be one of those to reveal the meaning of electricity to man! How wonderful that he should have been selected to become a teacher in the art of controlling the intriguing 'fluid' which had been known from the days when the Greeks magnetized amber, but which had never before been turned to the ends of common man! 'What hath God wrought!' As Jehovah had wrought through Israel, God now wrought through him."[11]

Morse wrote to his brother:

> That sentence of Annie Ellsworth's was divinely indited, for it is in my thoughts day and night. "What hath God wrought!" It is His work , and He alone could have carried me thus far through all my trials and enabled me to triumph over the obstacles, physical and moral, which opposed me.
>
> "Not unto us, not unto us, but to Thy name, O Lord, be all the praise."
>
> I begin to fear now the effects of public favor, lest it should kindle that pride of heart and self-sufficiency which dwells in my own as well as in others' breasts, and which, alas! is so ready to be inflamed by the slightest

spark of praise. I do indeed feel gratified, and it is right I should rejoice with fear, and I desire that a sense of dependence upon and increased obligation to the Giver of every good and perfect gift may keep me humble and circumspect.[12]

Morse would remark in a speech many years later:

> If not a sparrow falls to the ground without a definite purpose in the plans of infinite wisdom, can the creation of an instrumentality, so vitally affecting the interests of the whole human race, have an origin less humble than the Father of every good and perfect gift? I am sure I have the sympathy of such an assembly as is here gathered, if in all humility and in the sincerity of a grateful heart, I use the words of inspiration in ascribing honor and praise to him to whom first of all and most of all it is pre-eminently due. "Not unto us, not unto us, but to God be all the glory." Not what hath man, but "What hath God wrought!"[13]

- Scientists — Jedediah Morse, John Fleming, Joseph Lister, James Simpson, Matthew Maury, Nathaniel Bowditch, Ephraim McDowell, George W. Carver, Crawford W. Long

An engraving on the base of a statue in United States Capitol of Dr. Crawford W. Long says:

> Discoverer of the use of sulphuric ether as an anaesthetic in surgery on March 30, 1842 at Jefferson, Jackson County, Georgia U.S.A. "My profession is to me a ministry from God."

George Washington Carver Applied the Truth and Transformed the Economy of the South

George W. Carver was born into slavery just before the close of the Civil War. His mom was a slave, but after emancipation she stayed with the family in Missouri who had owned her. George and his mom were carried off from the Carver family by raiders when he was just a baby. Mose Carver offered 40 acres and a horse (since he had no cash) to a man to find the mom and child. He brought back George, but was unable to find the mother. George, therefore, grew up on the Carver farm, but in relative poverty.

As a child he loved the woods and plants and things related to botany. He was very observant of nature and always asked questions. He also enjoyed using his hands. At about age 10 he left the farm and worked his way through high school. As a young man he worked hard and saved money to go to a certain college, but was not allowed to attend. A couple helped him to go to an artist school, but he found there were no jobs for an artist. He eventually was able to study his first love, agriculture.

After obtaining his university degree, Carver was invited by Booker T. Washington to come and teach at his newly formed Tuskegee Institute in Alabama. His work while here transformed the economy of the South and affected many nations as well.

Carver would rise every morning at 4:00 AM, read the Bible, and seek God concerning what He wanted him to do. Toward the end of his life Carver remarked: "The secret of my success? It is simple. It is found in the Bible, 'In all they ways acknowledge Him and He shall direct thy paths.'"[14]

One thing he sought God concerning was how to improve the economy of the southeastern part of the United States. Continual planting of cotton had depleted the soil and the invasion of the boll weevil was destroying much of the cotton crop.

Biographer Rackham Holt wrote that, "He devoutly believed that a personal relationship with the Creator of all things was the only foundation for the abundant life. He had a little story in which he related his experience:"

> I asked the Great Creator what the universe was made for.
> "Ask for something more in keeping with that little mind of yours," He replied.
> "What was man made for?"
> "Little man, you still want to know too much. Cut down the extent of your request and improve the intent."
> Then I told the Creator I wanted to know all about the peanut. He replied that my mind was too small to know all about the peanut, but He said He would give me a handful of peanuts. And God said, "Behold, I have given you every herb bearing seed, which is upon the face of the earth . . . to you it shall be for meat. . . . I have given every green herb for meat: and it was so."
> I carried the peanuts into my laboratory and the Creator told me to take them apart and resolve them into their elements. With such knowledge as I had of chemistry and physics I set to work to take them apart. I separated the water, the fats, the oils, the gums, the resins, sugars, starches, pectoses, pentosans, amino acids. There! I had the parts of the peanuts all spread out before me.

This story of Carver's teaches us the importance of preparation in fulfilling God's plan for our lives. Carver had labored hard to develop his skills of chemistry. Consequently, God could answer the question Carver posed to Him. God could not reveal the answer to this question to me today;

I would need much preparation before I would be in a position to understand and act upon the answer. This is true in many areas of our lives. God is not able to answer many of our inquiries or lead us deeper into our providential purpose for we have not learned enough or been properly prepared to hear and understand what He may say. This is an important lesson to learn. To continue with Carver's story, he relates:

> I looked at Him and He looked at me. "Now, you know what the peanut is."
>
> "Why did you make the peanut?"
>
> The Creator said, "I have given you three laws; namely, compatibility, temperature, and pressure. All you have to do is take these constituents and put them together, observing these laws, and I will show you why I made the peanut."
>
> I therefore went on to try different combinations of the parts under different conditions of temperature and pressure, and the result was what you see.[15]

The results: Carver discovered over 300 uses for the peanut. Food items included nuts, soup, a dozen beverages, mixed pickles, sauces, meal, instant and dry coffee. Other items included: salve, bleach, tan remover, wood filler, washing powder, metal polish, paper, ink, plastics, shaving cream, rubbing oil, linoleum, shampoo, axle grease, synthetic rubber.

He produced milk which would not curdle in cooking or when acids were added. Long-lasting cream and cheese could be made from this milk. "This milk proved to be truly a lifesaver in the Belgian Congo. Cows could not be kept there because of leopards and flies, so if a mother died her baby was buried with her; there was nothing to nourish it. Missionaries fed the infants peanut milk, and they flourished."[16]

George worked with many other plants and items — making 107 products from sweet potatoes; making synthetic marble from sawdust; and making wallboard from many different Southern plants.

For his work, Carver received many awards and became the advisor to many world leaders, including President Franklin Roosevelt, Mahatma Gandhi, and Thomas Edison. In all his work he never failed to acknowledge God. In 1921 when he testified before a committee of Congress, he was asked by the Chairman:

> "Dr. Carver, how did you learn all of these things?"
>
> Carver answered:
>
> "From an old book."
>
> "What book?" asked the Senator.

Carver replied, "The Bible."

The Senator inquired, "Does the Bible tell about peanuts?"

"No Sir" Dr. Carver replied, "But it tells about the God who made the peanut. I asked Him to show me what to do with the peanut, and he did."[17]

Carver looked for divine direction and saw God as the revealer of truth. He said:

> I discover nothing in my laboratory. If I come here of myself I am lost. But I can do all things through Christ. I am God's servant, His agent, for here God and I are alone. I am just the instrument through which He speaks, and I would be able to do more if I were to stay in closer touch with Him. With my prayers I mix my labors, and sometimes God is pleased to bless the results.[18]

He knew his purpose in life: "My purpose alone must be God's purpose — to increase the welfare and happiness of His people."[19] This, not money or fame, was his primary motivation. In fact, Edison offered him a job with a six-figure income, a fortune in those times, but he turned it down so he could continue his agricultural work in his laboratory that he called "God's little workshop." "George Washington Carver worked for the riches of God rather than the wealth of this world."[20]

Carver helped transform the economy of the South, and affected agriculture all over the world. Carver had to overcome all kinds of obstacles to fulfill his destiny (only a few have been mentioned here). In all of these he persevered, labored hard, and pursued the desires in his heart. He had a great impact upon many people and upon agriculture and the economy at large.

Like Carver, you can do great things for God. In fact, whatever He has called you to do is great, whether small or large in your eyes or the eyes of man. Carver can inspire you to not limit what God can do through you, regardless of your situation in life. Find out His plan and develop the talents and abilities He has given you.

3. Interpret truth through humanities

- Historians — William Bradford, Cotton Mather, Charles Rollin, David Ramsay, Mercy Otis Warren, Daniel Neal, George Bancroft, Noah Webster

- Authors — Geoffrey Chaucer, Lew Wallace, Daniel Defoe, John Bunyan, John Milton, Charles Dickens, John Whittier, Henry Longfellow, Samuel Coleridge

There is a statue in the United States Capitol of Lew Wallace, honored as an author and General in the Civil War. He was converted to Christianity during research for his great Christian classic, *Ben Hur*, one of the best sellers of all time.

- Theologians/Religious Leaders — John Wycliffe, Martin Luther, William Tyndale, John Calvin, John Knox, Cotton Mather, John Wesley, George Whitefield, Jonathan Edwards

Jonathan and Sarah Edwards are a great example of passing the torch to future generations by faithfully and educating their eleven children. Their children, in turn, passed on to future generations the vision for advancing liberty and building up their nation. A study was done of 1400 descendants of Jonathan and Sarah. Of these 13 were college presidents, 65 were professors, 100 lawyers, 30 judges, 66 physicians, and 80 holders of public office including 3 senators, 3 governors, and a vice president of the United States.[21] Their training not only benefitted their children, but thousands of their descendants, and the nation at large.

The seeds we plant today through education of our children (and others) have impact beyond measure in the future. After all, you can count how many seeds are in an apple, but you cannot count how many apples are in a seed.

- Political, Governmental, and Economic Philosophers — John Calvin, Samuel Rutherford, John Locke, Adam Smith, Hugo Grotius, John Wise, William Blackstone

William Blackstone (1723-1780) was an English jurist and writer of *Commentaries on the Laws of England*, which was the primary source for legal studies in the U.S. until this century. In this work he wrote:

> Man, considered as a creature, must necessarily be subject to the laws of his Creator, for he is entirely a dependent being. . . . And consequently, as man depends absolutely upon his Maker for everything, it is necessary that he should in all points conform to his Maker's will. This will of his Maker is called the law of nature. . . . These laws laid down by God are the eternal immutable laws of good and evil. . . . This law of nature . . . dictated by God himself, is of course superior in obligation to any other. It is binding over all the globe, in all countries, and at all times: no human laws are of any validity, if contrary to this.[22]

4. Implement truth through commerce and social action

- Businessmen — Cyrus McCormick, Cyrus Field, George Pullman, Peter Cooper, John Wanamaker, Jack Eckard

Cyrus McCormick, the inventor of the reaper, was a great example of a Christian inventor and businessman. He was a reaper in the Kingdom of God who instituted many new principles of business which reflected his Biblical view of life. He advanced civilization and destroyed famine by fulfilling his Kingdom business.

His invention of the reaper, and the ensuing business of making and selling reapers, lay the foundation for the advancement and prosperity of America, for it enabled one man to do the work of many, increasing his productivity many fold.

One biographer wrote:

> He instructed the wheat-eating races how to increase the 'seven small loaves' so that the multitudes should be fed. He picked up the task of feeding the hungry masses – the Christly task that had lain unfulfilled for eighteen centuries, and led the way in organizing it into a system of international reciprocity.[23]

- Social Reformers — William Wilberforce, John Eliot, Samuel Adams, Frances Willard, Charles Finney, Francis Makemie

Rev. Francis Makemie and Religious Liberty

In 1680 Colonel William Stevens and a number of Presbyterians in Maryland asked the Presbytery of Laggan in Ireland to send a Godly minister to help them form a church. In response Francis Makemie was sent and under his leadership the first Presbyterian Church in America was organized and was called Rehoboth Church. For many years Makemie traveled and preached and organized churches. Though he had a certificate from the court to preach in Maryland, he still faced many trying times. His greatest trial, though, occurred in New York.

His arrest and subsequent trial in 1707 link him as a leader in the struggle for religious liberty. After preaching in the city of New York, a warrant was issued for his arrest. The charge, signed by Lord Cornbury, said that he had taken upon himself "to Preach in a Private House, without having obtained My Licence for so doing, which is directly contrary to the known Laws of England."[24]

When brought before Lord Cornbury, Makemie said:

> We have Liberty from an Act of Parliament, made the first year of the Reign of King William and Queen Mary, which gave us Liberty, with which Law we have complied.

But Lord Cornbury replied:

> No one shall Preach in my Government without my Licence. . . . That Law does not extend to the American Plantations, but only to England. . . . I know, for I was at Making thereof. . . . That Act of Parliament was made against Strowling Preachers, and you are such, and shall not Preach in my Government.[25]

Makemie refused to pay bail and to agree to preach no more, so he was imprisoned. He defended himself at the trial and was found "not guilty," but was forced to pay all court costs, more than 80 pounds (a tremendous sum).

The great burden of the arrest and trial hastened his death a few months later. But he had not suffered in vain, for his struggles for religious liberty were to bear much fruit in the years to come. It was another dissenting minister, John Leland of Virginia, who played an important role in the proposal and approval of the *Virginia Statute for Religious Freedom* (1786), which was a culminating event in the development of religious freedom.

5. Transmit truth through education and arts

- Educators — John Harvard, John Cotton, John Witherspoon, Noah Webster, Emma Willard, William McGuffey, Booker T. Washington

Noah Webster, the father of American Education, wrote in 1836:

> In my view, the Christian religion is the most important and one of the first things in which all children, under a free government, ought to be instructed. . . . No truth is more evident to my mind than that the Christian religion must be the basis of any government intended to secure the rights and privileges of a free people.[26]

Witherspoon Disciples a Nation

John Witherspoon educated young men in a Biblical manner. He was "the man who shaped the men who shaped America." Witherspoon was a Presbyterian minister who came from Scotland in 1768 to serve as President of the College of New Jersey. During Witherspoon's tenure there were 478 graduates of what is now known as Princeton University. Of these, at least 86 became active in civil government and included: one president (James Madison), one vice-president (Aaron Burr), 10 cabinet officers, 21

senators, 39 congressmen, 12 governors, a Supreme Court justice
(Brockholst Livingston), and one attorney general of the United States
(William Bradford).

> Nearly one-fifth of the signers of the Declaration of Independence,
> one-sixth of the delegates of the constitutional Convention, and one-fifth
> of the first Congress under the Constitution were graduates of the College
> of New Jersey. [27]

Here was a man who literally discipled his nation. Those with a vision
for Biblical education have the same opportunity to disciple the nations today.

- Artists, Musicians, Newsmen — Leonardo da Vinci, Isaac Watts,
  Charles Wesley, Benjamin West, Peter Zenger, Horace Greeley, J. S.
  Bach, George F. Handel

Peter Zenger and Freedom of the Press

Lee Grady writes of Peter Zenger's contribution to freedom of the
press:

> In the 1730s, a Dutch Reformed journalist named John Peter Zenger
> became the editor of the New York Weekly Journal. During his day, jour-
> nalists were expected to speak favorably of the king and the governor or
> risk charges of sedition, but Zenger could not keep quiet when it became
> apparent that William Cosby, New York's royal governor, had stolen land
> from some Indians and then burned the deed. Zenger exposed the crime in
> his newspaper and expressed his own disgust over the matter in an edito-
> rial statement.
>
> At that time, English law dictated that a person could be found guilty
> of libel regardless of whether the statements published were true or false.
> The jury could only determine whether the statements had actually been
> printed. At Zenger's famous trial in 1735, his lawyer, Andrew Hamilton,
> risked his own life by declaring in court that Zenger should be cleared of
> charges because he had exposed evil. "Nature and the laws of our country
> have given us a right — the liberty — both of exposing and opposing arbi-
> trary power by speaking and writing Truth!" Hamilton exclaimed in the
> courtroom. [28]

Hamilton continued his appeal to the jury by saying:

> The question before you is not the cause of a poor printer, nor of New
> York alone; it is the cause of liberty . . . the liberty of opposing arbitrary
> power by speaking and writing truth. [29]

The jury found him not guilty and Zenger was released from his imprisonment of 35 weeks. This event has been termed "the morning-star of that liberty which subsequently revolutionized America."[30] Zenger became a hero of American journalism.

6. Preserve truth through government and law

- Political and Legal Leaders — Thomas Hooker, Patrick Henry, George Mason, William Penn, John Winthrop, James Madison, Samuel Adams, John Marshall, Daniel Webster, George Washington, Abraham Kuyper

George Washington, the World's Apostle of Liberty

One biographer wrote that "Washington was without an equal, was unquestionably the greatest man that the world has produced in the last one thousand years." This is quite a statement. Is there justification for it? Thomas Paine wrote: "By common consent, Washington is regarded as not merely the Hero of the American Revolution, but the World's Apostle of Liberty."

The above statements have validity when we consider the central role that Washington played in the establishment of the United States:

- Without Washington we would not have won the American Revolution. He provided the leadership necessary to hold the troops together, even in the most difficult situations, as at Valley Forge.
- Due to Washington's influence we did not set up a monarchy or military rule. (He rebuffed an attempt to make him King; he thwarted a military coup; he set an example of civilian rule by resigning as commander in chief.)
- We would never have completed the Constitutional Convention without Washington and his role as President of the Convention.
- We may never have set into motion our constitutional form of government, with a limited role of the President, without his example. (Washington was elected unanimously and modeled how the President was to govern.)
- Washington also set the standard for international relations in his *Farewell Address*.

Washington's Christian faith was key to his character, career, and accomplishments. His faith is revealed in a Circular Letter he sent to all the Governors of the states in 1783:

> I now make it my earnest prayer, that God would have you, and the State over which you preside, in his holy protection . . . that he would most

graciously be pleased to dispose us all to do justice, to love mercy, and to demean ourselves with that charity, humility, and pacific temper of mind, which were the characteristics of the Divine Author of our blessed religion, and without an humble imitation of whose example in these things, we can never hope to be a happy nation.[31]

America set into motion a new example of civil liberty that the nations have attempted to embrace during the last two centuries. The advancement of civil liberty in the world is directly related to the establishment of liberty in America, which owes its beginnings in large part to Washington. This is why Paine called him the World's Apostle of Liberty.

Christians have led the way in the advancement of mankind in every sphere of life. This is how it should be. Since Christians have encountered the Truth, in their hearts and minds, they should best be able to discover and apply the Truth in all areas. The world desperately needs Christians today to understand their God-given purpose and once again assume the leading role in the advancement of mankind through extending God's truth. Jesus told us to "go and make disciples of all the nations." Commenting on this, Matthew Henry said that "the principal intention of this commission" is clear; it is to "do your utmost to make the nations Christian nations." The New English Bible states that we are to "make all nations disciples."

We can fulfill Christ's commission to disciple the nations by using the talents and skills God has given us and doing business with them (in a Biblical manner) until He comes.

Patrick Transforms the Nation of Ireland

Patrick of Ireland was an outstanding example of a man who discipled a nation. He was a world figure; one of the very great among men; "one of the dominant personalities of world history."[32] He completely transformed a nation in his lifetime and set Ireland on its destiny. His work in Ireland was a world event. Historian Seumas MacManus writes:

All histories of all countries probably could not disclose to the most conscientious searcher another instance of such radical change in a whole nation's character being wrought within the lifespan of one man.[33]

There was a complete transformation of Ireland from the time before and after Patrick. The people before Patrick were worshiping idols and "were carrying the ruthless law of the sword far over sea and land" enslaving those they encountered. After Patrick the worship of the living God was predominant throughout the nation and the Irish people "left the conquering sword to be eaten by rust, while they went far and wide again over sea and land, bearing now to the nations—both neighbouring and far off—the healing balm of Christ's gentle words."[34]

Patrick's providential preparation is an amazing story. At the age of 15 or 16 Patrick was captured and enslaved by Irish marauders. He spent six years as a slave in Ireland during his impressionable years. He learned the language, religion, and culture and became an Irishman in many ways. Most importantly, he was converted, remembering his Christian upbringing, and had the seeds of his life work planted in him. His life of a shepherd gave him much time to pray and seek God. He eventually escaped Ireland, acting upon a vision from the Lord, and would not return for over 35 years.[35]

Patrick was about 58 years old when God sent him back to Ireland to fulfill his destiny. He labored about 28 years in Ireland and transformed the nation in a greater way than did any man transform any nation in history.

He worked at all levels:

- He saw untold thousands converted
- He founded 700 churches
- He trained and set in place Church leadership — 700 bishops and 3000 ministers
- He set up training centers to educate thousands
- He transformed civil government, working with kings to establish godly laws. He wrote *Liber Ex Lege Moisi,* which were extracts from the Laws of Moses used as the basis for civil law in Ireland.

Many other nations were impacted through those who were trained in the churches, seminaries, and schools Patrick started. The apostle to the Picts, Columba, was a product of one of these training centers.

Everyone will not be a Patrick, but we all have an important mission to fulfill. God is orchestrating all events and knows how everything fits together. We can never tell what impact one seed we plant may have in God's great plan. So we must be faithful in every little thing. Seemingly small incidents can have great effect upon our lives and others.

As we each cultivate and use the talents and skills God has given us and fulfill our divine purpose, we will be taking part in discipling the nations and seeing His kingdom come to earth as it is in heaven.

End Notes

1. *A Compilation of the Messages and Papers of the Presidents, Vol. 1,* James D. Richardson, ed., New York: Bureau of National Literature, Inc., 1897.

2. James Rose, *A Guide to American Christian Education,* Camarillo, CA: American Christian History Institute, 1987, 455.

3. Christopher Columbus' *Book of Prophecies*, reproduction of the Original Manuscript with English Translation by Kay Brigham, Fort Lauderdale: TSELF, 1991, pp. 178-179.

4. E.G.R. Taylor, editor, *The Original Writings and Correspondence of the Two Richard Hakluyts,* Vol. 2, London: Hakluyt Society, 1935, p. 318.

5. William Bradford, *Of Plymouth Plantation,* 1620-1647, a New Edition of the Complete Text, with notes and an Introduction by Samuel Eliot Morison, New York: Alfred A. Knopf, 1952, p. 25.

6. *Remember William Penn,* compiled by the William Penn Tercentenary Committee, Harrisburg, Penn.: Commonwealth of Pennsylvania, 1945, p. 74.

7. William A. Mowry, *Marcus Whitman and the Early Days of Oregon,* New York: Silver, Burdett and Company, 1901, p. 72.

8. Carleton Mabee, *The American Leonardo, A Life of Samuel F. B. Morse,* New York: Alfred A. Knopf, 1943, 279.

9. Ibid., p. 275.

10. Ibid., p. 276.

11. Ibid., p. 280.

12. Ibid.

13. Ibid., p. 369.

14. William J. Federer, *America's God and Country,* Coppell, Tex: FAME Publishing, Inc., 1994, 98.

15. Rackham Holt, *George Washington Carver, An American Biography,* Garden City, N Y: Doubleday, Doran, and Co., Inc., 1943, 226-227.

16. Ibid., p. 229.

17. Charles E. Jones, *The Books You Read,* Harrisburg, PA: Executive Books, 1985, 132. Quoted in Federer, p. 96.

18. Holt, p. 220.

19. Federer, p. 97.

20. James Manship, "George Washington Carver," notes of speech, 1998.

21. William J. Petersen, *Martin Luther Had a Wife,* Wheaton, Ill.: Tyndale House, 1983, 75.

22. Sir William Blackstone, *Commentaries on the Laws of England,* Philadelphia: Robert Bell, Union Library, 1771, Vol. 1, 39-42.

23. *Cyrus Hall McCormick, His Life and Work,* Herbert N. Casson, Chicago: A.C. McClurg & Co., 1909, 202. For more on McCormick see Chapter 14.

24. John T. Faris, *Historic Shrines of America,* New York: George H. Doran, 1918, 213.

25. Ibid., p. 214.

26. Letter to David McClure, October 25, 1836. *Letters of Noah Webster,* Harry R. Warfel, ed., New York: Library Publishers, 1953, 453.

27. Mary-Elaine Swanson, *The Education of James Madison, A Model for Today,* Montgomery: The Hoffman Education Center, 1992, 53.

28. J. Lee Grady, "Journalism and the Gospel," *Providential Perspective,* Nov. 1991, pp. 2-3.

29. *Appletons' Cyclopedia of American Biography,* Vol. 6, edited by James Wilson & John Fiske, New York: D. Appleton & Co., 1893, 659.

30. Ibid.

31. *Circular Letter Addressed to the Governors of all the States on Disbanding the Army,* 1783, Old South Leaflets, No. 15.

32. Seumas MacManus, *The Story of the Irish Race,* New York: The Devin-Adair Co., 1967, 124.

33. Ibid., p. 126.

34. Ibid.

35. See MacManus, pp. 111 ff.

Chapter 2

God's Sovereignty Over the Nations
God Governs in the Affairs of Men

On June 28, 1787, Benjamin Franklin, who was 81 years old and in poor health, called the Constitutional Convention to prayer when they were on the brink of breaking up. He declared:

> I have lived, Sir, a long time, and the longer I live, the more convincing proofs I see of this truth—that God Governs in the affairs of men. And if a sparrow cannot fall to the ground without His notice, is it probable that an empire can rise without His aid? We have been assured, Sir, in the sacred writings, that "except the Lord build the House they labour in vain that build it." I firmly believe this; and I also believe that without His concurring aid we shall succeed in this political building no better, than the Builders of Babel.[1]

Franklin proclaimed a truth that must be restored to the Church today; that is, that God governs in the affairs of men. There are three aspects of this governance that we must see.

God Governs in the Affairs of His Children

During the time of the prophet Elisha, Israel was at war with Syria. The king of Syria would make secret plans for his army to surprise the army of Israel, but God would reveal these plans to Elisha who in turn warned the Israelites to avoid the area. After this happened a number of times, the king of Syria became enraged and gathered his men to interrogate them, thinking one of them must be a spy. However, his servants informed him that they had nothing to do with the leaks, but "Elisha, the prophet who is in Israel, tells the king of Israel the words that you speak in your bedroom" (2 Kings 6:12). The Syrian king then sent a whole army to capture Elisha. 2 Kings 6:15-17 relates what happens:

> Now when the attendant of the man of God had risen early and gone
> out, behold, an army with horses and chariots was circling the city. And
> his servant said to him, "Alas, my master! What shall we do?"
> So he answered, "Do not fear, for those who are with us are more than
> those who are with them."
> Then Elisha prayed and said, "O Lord, I pray, open his eyes that he
> may see." And the Lord opened the servant's eyes, and he saw; and be-
> hold, the mountain was full of horses and chariots of fire all around
> Elisha."

Elisha's servant's eyes were opened so that he could see. But what did
he need to see? Yes, he needed to see the armies of the Lord surrounding
the armies of their enemy; but in a broader sense, he needed to have his
eyes opened to see that God governs in the affairs of men, that God is sovereign over men, nations, and history, and He moves in supernatural ways
to accomplish His purposes.

Just like Elisha's servant, we need our eyes to be opened to see that
God governs in the affairs of men. God watches over His children. As we
trust in the Lord with all our heart, and do not lean on our own understanding, but acknowledge Him in all our ways, He will direct our paths (Proverbs 3:5-6). The Bible teaches that the steps of a good man are ordered or
established by the Lord (Ps. 37:23).

God Governs in the Affairs of the Ungodly

God not only governs in the affairs of His children, but He also governs
in the affairs of the ungodly. The life of King Nebuchadnezzar illustrates
this well.

Nebuchadnezzar was king of the Babylonian empire during the time of
Daniel. He built Babylon into a mighty city, and his empire was the greatest
the world had seen. One night he had a very disturbing dream that he asked
all of the wise men of Babylon to interpret. None of the "magicians, the
conjurers, the Chaldeans, and the diviners" could make the interpretation
known, but finally Daniel, "in whom is a spirit of the holy gods," was
brought before the king and he was able to interpret it, though he was
alarmed for the dream applied to the king. Daniel said:

> The tree that you saw, which became large and grew strong, whose
> height reached to the sky and was visible to all the earth, and whose foliage
> was beautiful and its fruit abundant, and in which was food for all, under
> which the beasts of the field dwelt and in whose branches the birds of the
> sky l odge — it is you, O king; for you have become great and grown

strong, and your majesty has become great and reached to the sky and your dominion to the end of the earth (Daniel 4:20-22).

Then in the dream an angelic watcher came and declared that the tree would be cut to a stump. Daniel's interpretation proclaimed God's judgment against Nebuchadnezzar for his sins and pride, revealing God's sovereign hand in removing the kingdom from him for a period of seven years, during which time Nebuchadnezzar would dwell with animals and eat grass like cattle and be drenched with the dew. At the end of this time, his kingdom would be restored to him, after he recognized "that it is Heaven that rules" (Dan. 4:26).

Daniel advised the king to break away from his sin and turn to God, but he did not listen. Twelve months later, while walking upon the walls of the city, he began to think of how great he was and how his empire was built by his power and for his glory. At this very moment a voice came from heaven telling King Nebuchadnezzar that "sovereignty has been removed from you." According to the word of the Lord in the dream, Nebuchadnezzar was driven from mankind and dwelt among the beasts of the field, eating grass, being drenched with dew, and having his hair and nails grow long, for seven years until he recognized "that the Most High is ruler over the realm of mankind, and bestows it on whomever He wishes" (Dan. 4:31-32).

God Governs in the Affairs of Nations

Nebuchadnezzar learned the hard way that God not only governs in the affairs of men, but He is also sovereign over the nations — that "the Most High is ruler over the realm of mankind, and bestows it on whom He wishes. . . . It is Heaven that rules" (Dan. 4: 17, 25, 26, 32).

After seven years of living like an animal (which occurs when man rejects God), Nebuchadnezzar's reason returned to him and he "blessed the Most High and praised and honored Him who lives forever." Nebuchadnezzar learned and declared what all men and nations should declare:

> His dominion is an everlasting dominion, and His kingdom endures from generation to generation. And all the inhabitants of the earth are accounted as nothing, but He does according to His will in the host of heaven and among the inhabitants of earth (Daniel 4:34-35).

The Book of Daniel is a great example of the sovereignty of God. It shows how He sovereignly watched over and directed the events in the lives of His children (Daniel, Shadrach, Mesach, and Abednego), in the lives of ungodly kings, and in the history of the nations. It presents a Christian philosophy, or providential view, of history.

The Bible clearly teaches the providence and sovereignty of God. "He rules over the nations" (Psalms 22:28). "He makes the nations great, then destroys them; He enlarges the nations, then leads them away" (Job 12:23). "It is He who changes the times and the epochs; He removes kings and establishes kings" (Daniel 2:21). "The God who made the world . . . gives to all life and breath and all things; and He made from one, every nation of mankind to live on all the face of the earth, having determined their appointed times, and the boundaries of their habitation, that they should seek God" (Acts 17:24-27). As these Scriptures teach, God is the one who raises up nations. He determines their time of existence and even their boundaries. Though men in rebellion to God have formed their own cities and nations, God is still sovereign over them. He has demonstrated that sovereignty in different ways as He set about accomplishing His plan in history. He deals with nations in a way that is based on the heart of the inhabitants.

Historian Charles Rollin wrote that history proclaims "that God disposes all events as Supreme Lord and Sovereign; that He alone determines the fate of kings and the duration of empires; and that he transfers the government of kingdoms from one nation to another because of the unrighteous dealings and wickedness committed therein."[2]

Historian George Bancroft eloquently spoke of God's sovereignty and providence in an address to Congress in 1866. He begins his oration:

> Senators, Representatives of America: That God rules in the affairs of men is as certain as any truth of physical science. On the great moving power which is from the beginning hangs the world of the senses and the world of thought and action. Eternal wisdom marshals the great procession of the nations, working in patient continuity through the ages, never halting and never abrupt, encompassing all events in its oversight, and ever effecting its will, though mortals may slumber in apathy or oppose with madness. Kings are lifted up or thrown down, nations come and go, republics flourish and wither, dynasties pass away like a tale that is told; but nothing is by chance, though men, in their ignorance of causes, may think so. The deeds of time are governed, as well as judged, by the decrees of eternity. The caprice of fleeting existences bends to the immovable omnipotence, which plants its foot on all the centuries and has neither change of purpose nor repose. Sometimes, like a messenger through the thick darkness of night, it steps along mysterious ways; but when the hour strikes for a people, or for mankind, to pass into a new form of being, un-

seen hands draw the bolts from the gates of futurity; an all-subduing influence prepares the minds of men for the coming revolution; those who plan resistance find themselves in conflict with the will of Providence rather than with human devices; and all hearts and all understandings, most of all the opinions and influences of the unwilling, are wonderfully attracted and compelled to bear forward the change, which becomes more an obedience to the law of universal nature than submission to the arbitrament of man.[3]

In early America the doctrine of Providence was widely embraced — "that God rules in the affairs of men is as certain as any truth of physical science," as stated by Bancroft. This was true even of non-Christians, as evidenced in Franklin's statement calling the Constitutional Convention to prayer.

Nations, as well as men, are accountable to God. While both the just and the unjust will give an account on the final judgment day, and receive corresponding rewards and punishments, nations will be accountable in history, receiving recompense for national virtues and sins. The history of Babylon is a good example of this.

Babylon began as a city built by men for the glory of men in disobedience to God's command to spread out and fill the earth (see Genesis 10:8-12; 11:1-9). God thwarted this attempt by man to set up a secular civilization by confusing the language of those at Babel, which led to the scattering of these people throughout the earth (Genesis 11:8-9). But worldly people do not give up easily, and so at a later time under the leadership of King Nebuchadnezzar the city of Babylon was refounded and built into the mightiest city on earth. It was this empire that eventually destroyed Jerusalem in 586 B.C. and carried many into exile, including Daniel.

Babylon was a truly "golden" city. (Nebuchadnezzar, who represented the city, was depicted as a gold head in the dream God gave to the King [see Daniel 2].) It was called "the beauty of kingdoms, the glory of the Chaldean's pride" (Is. 13:19). The walls that surrounded the city were 60 miles in circumference, 300 feet high, and at places 75 feet wide. A moat surrounded the walls and there were 25 brazen gates in each of the four sides. Inside the city was Nebuchadnezzar's palace which was enclosed by walls six miles in circumference. This contained the famous "hanging gardens" which were sustained by arches upon arches, mounding up to 400 feet in height. Babylon was known for learning, for skill in many arts, and for great wealth. Hence, it was called "the great" (Dan. 4:20) and "the praise of the whole earth" (Jer. 51:41). However, the inhabitants were corrupt, licentious, and extremely immoral, worshiping idols and rejecting the true God.[4]

While God used Babylon to execute His judgment against Judah and His people, He did not leave Babylon unpunished for its many sins. The judgment of God against Babylon is spoken of many times in the Scriptures (see Isaiah 13; 14:22; 21:9; 47; Jeremiah 25; 50; 51). During the reign of Belshazzar, Nebuchadnezzar's grandson, the city was besieged and taken over by Cyrus (just as Daniel predicted the handwriting on the wall foretold, see Daniel 5). This was the beginning of the decline of Babylon. In the centuries that followed the once mighty city was utterly abandoned and lost. Isaiah predicted that Babylon would be completely destroyed and never inhabited — "It will never be inhabited or lived in from generation to generation" (Is. 13:20). This remains true even until today.

God is truly sovereign over the nations. He raises up and puts down nations in accordance with His plans and purposes for mankind.

How Nations Are Built

As is generally the case throughout history, God in His sovereignty uses the actions of men (both sinful and righteous) to bring about His purposes. Nations have been raised up in different ways in history, but in them all the "eternal wisdom" works "in patient continuity through the ages, never halting and never abrupt, encompassing all events in its oversight, and ever effecting its will, though mortals may slumber in apathy or oppose with madness." [5]

There are at least four different ways that nations have been built. [6]

1. Conquest with enslavement

As a people grow in strength, they conquer surrounding peoples or tribes or nations, annexing them under their governance but without allowing them to share in the political life of the growing nation. Those conquered become, in essence, slaves. The nation-empires of Babylon and the Medo-Persians are examples.

2. Conquest with incorporation, but without representation

Rome is a good example of this method of nation making. While Rome did enslave some of the people she conquered, there were many vanquished peoples that she incorporated into her own body politic. These peoples became part of the union of the Roman Empire and retained much liberty. They were protected by Roman law and benefitted by sharing in the material wealth of the Empire. They could also look to Roman military might for protection from outside enemies. However, the "essential vice of the Roman system was that it had been unable to avoid weakening the spirit of personal independence and crushing out local self-government among the peoples to whom it had been applied."[7] It joined liberty with union, but as time passed, liberty had to be sacrificed to preserve the union. The primary reason for this was that the Roman system lacked the principle of representation.

3. The English method

This method of nation-making is different than the first two in that it contains the principle of representation. In addition, unlike the first two, it does not necessarily require war in the early stages. John Fiske explains: "where representative government is once established, it is possible for a great nation to be formed by the peaceful coalescence of neighbouring states, or by their union into a federal body."[8] Over many centuries the representative principle worked itself out in England (hence the name English method), locally through county-meetings and on the national level in parliament, showing that it was possible for a nation to grow large without centralized despotism. This method has been worked out even more completely in America, but with an added ingredient.

4. Covenant

While adhering to the important principle of representation, the founders of America also built their nation upon the principle of covenant. Many of the early colonies began with a group of people covenanting together under God to live in a civil society in accordance with His will and purpose. The founders of the Plymouth Colony agreed in 1620 to "solemnly and mutually, in the Presence of God and one another, covenant and combine ourselves together in to a civil Body Politick."[9] The first settlers of New Hampshire declared: "Wee . . . considering wth ourselves the holy will of god and our owne necessity, that we should not live whout wholsome lawes & government amongst us . . . doe in the name of Christ & in the sight of God combine ourselves together, to erect & set up amongst us such government as shall be to our best discerning, agreeable to the will of god."[10] Scores of other covenant like documents were agreed to during the colonial period of American history. The covenantal ideas in these seminal documents were reflected in the Declaration of Independence, the founding document of the United States of America.

The nation of Israel also began as a covenant nation, but it was different than the United States in that God initiated the covenant with Abraham and Moses and the people — He entered into a covenant with them. With

America the people initiated the covenant with one another under God. Both experienced the covenant blessings of God as they walked in obedience to Him.

What Responsibilities Do Nations Have to God?

Acts 17:26-27 reveals that God created the nations and that they should seek for Him. Jesus instructed us to make disciples of the nations (Matthew 28:19). Bible commentator Matthew Henry said that "the principal intention of this commission" is clear; it is to "do your utmost to make the nations Christian nations."[11] Psalm 102:15 informs us that the nations should fear the Lord. Nations have responsibilities to God. George Washington summarized well the duties the nations have to God in a Proclamation for a Day of Thanksgiving, observed on Thursday, November 26, 1789: "It is the Duty of all Nations to acknowledge the Providence of Almighty God, to obey his will, to be grateful for his Benefits, and humbly to implore his Protection and Favor."[12]

It is our task to work to see that the nations fulfill their duties and responsibilities to God — to obey His will and reflect His glory; to operate in such a way that there be peace, order, justice, and freedom within society; and that the laws and institutions reflect His truth and principles. Such a civil society will be a means of provoking others to follow after Him. This was the vision of the early settlers of America. The Charter of Massachusetts Bay (1629) had provisions for establishing laws, electing representatives, and punishing offences "whereby our said People, Inhabitants there, may be soe religiously, peaceablie, and civilly governed, as their good Life and orderlie Conversacon, maie wynn and incite the Natives of Country, to the Knowledg and Obedience of the onlie true God and Sauior of Mankinde, and the Christian Fayth, which . . . is the principall Ende of this Plantacion."[13]

Our task is to disciple the nations, but how is this to be accomplished? This question is addressed in Chapter 3 and elsewhere in this book, but to answer briefly: God created individuals and three divine institutions (the family, the church, and the state or civil government). The Scriptures reveal specific purposes and responsibilities for each of these. Our task is to find out to whom God has given authority to do what, and then implement this in the nations. Comprehending this jurisdictional authority and working to educate and organize society such that no usurpation by one institution of another occurs, is key to discipling the nations.[14]

God' s Purposes for Governing in the Affairs of Men

We have seen that God is sovereign over men and nations and that He has providentially directed history from the beginning. What does God accomplish in governing in the affairs of men? What is He doing through His sovereign acts in history? Following are three things that He is accomplishing through governing in the affairs of men and nations.

1. Preparation of His people, both individually and corporately

God is preparing His people to fulfill His purposes in the earth. As fallen and feeble people, we have need of much—including Christian character, a Biblical worldview, skills and talents —to effectively carry out his plan. Daily devotion to His many means of grace is of primary importance for that preparation. But, in addition, God often providentially moves in our lives to prune us and equip us that we might bear much fruit. In John 15, Jesus instructs us that every branch in Him that does not bear fruit is pruned and burned (see verses 2, 6). Every branch that does bear fruit is also pruned. So no matter what we do, we are going to get cut. However, the pruning God does for the fruitful is for the purpose of producing fruit of greater quantity and quality. God's pruning work often occurs through providentially arranged events in our lives.

God is not only preparing individuals for a personal destiny; He is also preparing peoples and nations in order for them to fulfill their corporate destiny. This can be seen in His dealings with the nation of Israel. The Rechabites (see Jeremiah 35) are another Biblical example of a corporate people prepared by God to fulfill a unique purpose. The preparation of the seed of the American republic is an excellent modern example of how God prepares a people through His providential governance in order to fulfill His plan and purpose for mankind. Another example of God's corporate preparation, and the subsequent influence on the course of history, is seen in the Dutch people.

The Siege of Leyden (1574)

The Dutch have been in a continuous battle for centuries — a battle not against men, but against the sea. They have wrestled almost half of their nation from the water by building a series of dykes to keep out the sea; and they have built many windmills to continue to pump out the water.

The country has been inundated by storms many times. During one devastating storm a hundred thousand people lost their lives when the lands were flooded. Crops have been destroyed and animals killed. But in the midst of all these devastations, the Dutch did not give up and move to higher ground. This fight against nature helped develop their character to persevere and never give up. This proved of great value as they faced human enemies who threatened them with not only lose of life but also lose of liberty, both civil and religious.

One such fight occurred in 1574 when they were at war with Spain. The city of Leyden was laid siege to by the Spanish army. Unable to penetrate the walls of the city, the Spanish attempted to starve the inhabitants of Leyden, patiently waiting until they ran out of food. As the food supply dwindled, the Dutch began to eat whatever they could find, including rats and dogs and even leaves off the trees. From six to eight thousand people died from hunger and disease, "yet the people resolutely held out — women and men mutually encouraging each other to resist the entrance of their foreign foe — an evil more horrible than pest or famine."[15]

To undermine morale, the Spanish taunted them with shouts from outside the walls: "Ha! How are you rat-eaters getting along?" The response of the Dutch reflect their great resolve:

> "Ye call us rat-eaters and dog-eaters," they cried, "and it is true. So long, then, as ye hear dog bark or cat mew within the walls, ye may know that the city holds out. And when all has perished but ourselves, be sure that we will each devour our left arms, retaining our right to defend our women, our liberty, and our religion, against the foreign tyrant. Should God, in his wrath, doom us to destruction, and deny us all relief, even then will we maintain ourselves for ever against your entrance. When the last hour has come, with our own hands we will set fire to the city and perish, men, women, and children together in the flames, rather then suffer our homes to be polluted and our liberties to be crushed."

Such words of defiance came daily from the starving citizens of Leyden, as well as from Hollanders throughout the nation. The Prince of Orange expressed their sentiment: "As long as there is a living man left in the country, we will contend for our liberties and our religion." Such resolve would indicate the great difficulty of defeating these people. To add to this, God providentially moved on their behalf. During the night one wall of the city collapsed, leaving an opening for the Spanish to easily enter the city; "but the hand of God . . . had struck her enemies with terror." Fearing the unknown events of the night, the Spanish leader had ordered the retreat of the troops. "Thus, the Spaniards had retreated at the very moment that an extraordinary accident had laid bare a whole side of the city for their entrance."

When food came to relieve their starvation, before eating a morsel, "nearly every living person within the walls, all repaired without delay to the great church. . . . The starving and heroic city, which had been so firm in its resistance to an earthly king, now bent itself in humble gratitude before the King of kings."

Holland would eventually drive out the Spanish. The history of America and the advancement of liberty would have been much different if not for the courage and determination of the Dutch people. Their resistance strengthened Christian freedoms, not only in Holland, but in other European nations as well. All types of religious dissenters found refuge in Holland. It was in the very city of Leyden that our Pilgrim fathers lived for about eleven years (1609-1620), as God was preparing them to become the "parents" of the world's first Christian republic.

The events of history reveal that God governs in the affairs of men, and He moves on behalf of His people as they trust in Him. The providence of God in the siege of Leyden is not unique, for God has continually moved throughout history to assure that His purposes are fulfilled.

2. Revelation of His power and Person

During the normal course of our lives, God will often use us to reveal Himself to others. At times He moves in extraordinary ways to arrange divine appointments for us so that He can reveal His person, power, presence, and salvation to individuals. Likewise, through intervention in the events of history, God reveals His power to the nations. This is readily seen in the defeat of the Spanish Armada.

The Spanish Armada (1588)

In 1588, Philip II of Spain sent the Spanish Armada to bring England and the Low Countries (the Netherlands) again under the domination of the Holy Roman Empire. One-half century before, under Henry VIII, England had split from Rome and established her own church, the Church of England. Holland had also separated from Catholic control and had already been engaged with the Spanish in many battles. Those faithful to Rome had not appreciated the direction these two countries were taking and had sought for ways to bring them back into the fold of the Catholic religion. With the rise of Puritanism and Separatism in England and Holland, these renegades were straying even further from the established religion. With the build-up of the massive Spanish fleet, there was now a way to bring these nations back to the true faith. King Philip had amassed a mighty Navy "as never the like had before that time sailed upon the Ocean sea."[16] It was comprised of 134 ships and about 30,000 men; Spain considered it invincible.

When the English got word that the Armada was being assembled to be sent against them, they began to prepare as best as they could, but they had fewer ships that were smaller and not nearly as well armed. Their only hope was for a miracle to occur. People gathered throughout England to pray for such a miracle — especially those of the reformed faith because the Spanish specifically mentioned them as a target of their attack, for they knew these reformers were the major threat to the re-establishment of the Catholic religion in England.

Richard Hakluyt records:

> [I]t is most apparant, that God miraculously preserved the English nation. For the L. Admirall wrote unto her Majestie that in all humane reason, and according to the judgement of all men (every circumstance being duly considered) the English men were not of any such force, whereby they might, without a miracle, dare once to approch within sight of the Spanish Fleet: insomuch that they freely ascribed all the honour of their victory unto God, who had confounded the enemy, and had brought his counsels to none effect.
>
> While this woonderfull and puissant Navie was sayling along the English coastes, and all men did now plainely see and heare that which before they would not be perswaded of, all people thorowout England prostrated themselves with humble prayers and supplications unto God: but especially the outlandish Churches (who had greatest cause to feare, and against whom by name, the Spaniards had threatened most grievous torments) enjoyned to their people continuall fastings and supplications, that they might turne away Gods wrath and fury now imminent upon them for their sinnes: knowing right well, that prayer was the onely refuge against all enemies, calamities, and necessities, and that it was the onely solace and reliefe for mankinde, being visited with affliction and misery. Likewise such solemne dayes of supplication were observed thorowout the united Provinces.[17]

Here is what happened: As the Spanish fleet sailed up the English Channel, they were met by the much smaller English and Dutch navies. In the natural, the English had little hope, yet England and Holland had been fasting and praying. A series of storms caused many of the Armada ships to sink, disease wiped out many of the Spanish troops, and other providential occurrences resulted in a resounding defeat of the invincible Armada. Of the original force only 53 ships returned to Spain with less than half of the original 30,000 men. It seemed apparent to those delivered that "God. . . fought for them in many places with his owne arme."

After this miraculous defeat, Holland minted coins as a perpetual memory. Of one coin Hakluyt recorded: "on the one side contained the armes of Zeland, with this inscription: GLORY TO GOD ONELY: and on the other side, the pictures of certeine great ships, with these words: THE SPANISH FLEET: and in the circumference about the ships: IT CAME, WENT, AND WAS. Anno 1588. That is to say, the Spanish fleet came, went, and was vanquished this yere; for which, glory be given to God onely." They minted another coin that "upon the one side whereof was represented a ship fleeing, and a ship sincking: on the other side foure men making prayers and giving thanks unto God upon their knees; with this sentence: Man purposeth; God disposeth. 1588."

England and Holland marked the victory with a public day of fasting and prayer. Hakluyt writes:

> Also a while after the Spanish Fleet was departed, there was in England, by the commandement of her Majestie [Elizabeth], and in the united Provinces, by the direction of the States, a solemne festivall day publikely appointed, wherein all persons were enjoyned to resort unto the Church, and there to render thanks and praises unto God: and the Preachers were commanded to exhort the people thereunto. The foresayd solemnity was observed upon the 29 of November; which day was wholly spent in fasting, prayer, and giving of thanks.

The Queen rode into London in great triumph and fanfare and all the people turned out with banners and ensignes heralding the event. "Her Majestie being entered into the Church, together with her Clergie and Nobles gave thanks unto God, and caused a publike Sermon to be preached before her at Pauls crosse; wherein none other argument was handled, but that praise, honour, and glory might be rendered unto God, and that Gods name might be extolled by thanksgiving."

3. Consummation of His purpose

History is the outworking of God's purpose and plan for mankind. God created man in His own image and likeness as His vice-regent or steward to rule over the earth. Unfortunately, man fell from the purpose for which God created him — to rule and to cultivate the garden (Gen. 1:26-28; 2:15). Thus, man lost both his intimate relationship with God and his ability to properly govern the earth. Sin not only separated man from God but also brought a curse and great loss. Man was unable to properly fulfill the cultural mandate.

God's redemptive nature is evident early on. Man having fallen from what God made him to be and to do, God planned both to redeem man and to restore man's delegated authority and stewardship over the earth. God promised that the seed of woman would destroy the serpent (Satan; Gen. 3:15). Christ was that seed who came to redeem man and reverse the effects of the fall and the curse. He restored to man the ability to fulfill the mission originally given to Adam, as well as restoring man's relationship to God.

The story of redemption unfolds in the various covenants which God initiated with men. The giving of the law in the Mosaic Covenant was also used by God to further His redemptive program. Of course, God's redemptive purpose has found ultimate fulfillment in the New Covenant through Christ, who was slain and by whose blood God has redeemed men for himself "from every tribe and tongue and people and nation" (Rev. 5:9).

The purpose of salvation in Christ is multi-faceted. Through Christ man is restored to his original position. There is a restoration of the covenant he had with God, of the glory he had from God, and of the dominion or cultural mandate. His desire is for us to rule over the earth — to bring His kingdom rule and reign to all creation. Jesus also reversed the curse due to the fall of man (Gal. 3:13). The curse affects individuals through death, sickness, bondage, etc., and in turn also affects all spheres of life (Rom. 8:22). Christ brought redemption to individuals, but also institutions and all spheres of life (including law, government, education, arts, business, etc.). Redemption is as broad as the sweep of sin (Rom. 5:19-21). God's desire, as Jesus taught us to pray, is for His kingdom to come and His will to be done on earth as it is in heaven (Matt. 6:10).

We have been redeemed for a purpose. In Christ we have been restored to sonship and are now in a position to obey both the Cultural and the Evangelistic Mandates. With respect to the Cultural Mandate, God has restored us to stewardship. Through Christ we are called back to God's original purpose — to live in His image and to "be fruitful and multiply, and fill the earth, and subdue it; rule over . . . every living thing that moves on the earth" (Gen. 1:28). We have been restored to serving God as his vice-regent over the earth.

As part of this larger purpose, we each have a distinct specific calling in God. God in His providence gives us the characteristics, talents, skills, abilities, and interests we need, and directs our steps and arranges events in our lives to see His purpose for us fulfilled. We can each look back on our lives and recognize the hand of God orchestrating events that affect our destiny.

God not only sovereignly moves in the lives of individuals to fulfill their individual purpose, but He also governs in the affairs of men to fulfill His overall purpose for mankind. Events of history have not happened by chance but by God's choice to fulfill His plan for the nations. Our personal destiny is part of God's overall plan and what happens in the lives of individuals often has great effect on the course of history.

George Washington impacted the history of America and the advancement of liberty in the world. God's providential care can be seen in an incident that occurred in Washington's life during the French and Indian War in 1755.

Washington was second in command to British General Braddock as the British and Colonial troops marched out into the wilderness to drive the French off British territory. Washington tried to warn Braddock that European military tactics would not work in the American frontier, but the General wouldn't listen and they marched right into an ambush, where they were soundly defeated. Only Washington's fearlessness and leadership saved the day.

During the battle Gen. Braddock was mortally wounded. Washington had four bullets pass through his coat and two horses shot from under him, yet escaped unhurt. He was fired upon numerous times from near point-blank range and remained unharmed. An Indian chief singled him out and told his braves to do the same, "but after striving in vain to hit him, became alarmed, and told his men to desist from firing at one who was plainly under the care of the great Manitou."[18]

Years later a chief who took part in this battle made a special effort to visit Washington, where he spoke to him of this battle and how they attempted to shoot him. The chief said:

> Our rifles were levelled, rifles which, but for him, knew not how to miss—'t was all in vain, a power mightier far than we, shielded him from harm. He can not die in battle. I am old, and soon shall be gathered to the great council-fire of my fathers. . . but ere I go, there is a something, bids me speak, in the voice of prophecy. Listen! *The Great Spirit protects that man, and guides his destinies—he will become the chief of nations, and a people yet unborn, will hail him as the founder of a mighty empire!*[19]

In a letter to his brother, Washington spoke of God's protection:

> But by the all-powerful dispensations of Providence, I have been protected beyond all human probability or expectation; for I had four bullets

through my coat, and two horses shot under me, yet escaped unhurt, although death was levelling my companions on every side of me.[20]

Rev. Samuel Davies preached a sermon on August 17, 1755, wherein he cites the preservation of young Washington. He spoke of "that heroic youth, Colonel Washington, whom I cannot hope but Providence has hitherto preserved in so signal a manner for some important service to his country."[21] In accordance with God's plan, Washington did play an extremely important role in the establishment of America as a nation.

Multitudes of examples could be given from history that reveal God's sovereign hand directing events to assure a specific outcome in accordance with His purposes in the earth. In fact, while His hand may be more obvious in certain events, He is directing them all.

Knowledge of God's Sovereignty Produces Great Confidence

Just like Elisha's servant, we need to have our eyes opened to see that God governs in the affairs of men, that God is sovereign over the nations. An understanding of God's sovereignty will produce a great confidence in us.

1. Confidence in His continual care

After Elisha's servant's eyes were opened and he saw God's horses and chariots all around, his confidence in God's care must have increased greatly. When God delivered the entire army into Elisha's hands (2 Kings 6:18-23), his servant must have embraced more of the faith of Elisha who had confidently proclaimed that "those who are with us are more than those who are with them." Just as knowing God as sovereign gave Shadrach, Meshach, and Abednego the ability to stand firm and not bow down to the statue, so too can we stand firm when faced with trials if we have a firm understanding of God's providence and sovereignty.

2. Confidence in His coming Kingdom

Knowing God governs in the affairs of men will assure us that God will build His kingdom in us (Phil. 1:6), and also that He will bring His kingdom to earth. Speaking of the Messiah, Isaiah said "there will be no end to the increase of His government" (or kingdom; Is. 9:6). From the time Jesus set foot upon earth, there has been a continual increase of His kingdom or government. Viewing history from a providential perspective affirms this.

In recent years, many Christians have lost an understanding of the sovereignty of God — that He governs in the affairs of men — and, consequently, have viewed the world under the control of Satan. They have looked at the world as a sinking ship, where all the church can do is get a few people saved before it goes under. However, as we recognize that God governs in the affairs of men, we will gain confidence in a victorious future. We will have great confidence that He is establishing His kingdom (government) in the earth and that "all the earth will be filled with the glory of the Lord" (Num. 14:21).

3. Confidence in His conquering Christ

Elisha and his servant saw that God can deliver by a few as easily as He can deliver by many. When the army of the Syrians was struck with blindness and God delivered them into Elisha's hand, their confidence in the Lord as the conquering King must have increased greatly. Realizing that God is sovereign would eliminate all fear in the battle that Elisha faced.

Christ is a conquering King. He first triumphed over sin with His death and resurrection, and will ultimately triumph over all his enemies, putting them under His feet (1 Cor. 15:25). In the past two millennium, His truth has marched throughout the world, triumphing over sin and Satan, but also over vain philosophies and the contrary ideas of man (2 Cor. 10:5). We can see the victory of Christ in our lives and in society, now, while living on earth. We do not have to wait until He returns.

We are in a battle today, not of guns and bullets, but a battle of ideas. To win, we need confidence that we will conquer, knowing that God is in control and that His truth is powerful. Lack of knowledge of God's sovereignty and providence is one reason why the church has been losing in the battle of ideas in recent years. Consequently, the enemies of Christ have grown confident in their victory. An episode from the life of Captain John Paul Jones will serve as an example to us today.

During the war for American independence, Captain Jones was commanding a colonial ship, the *Bonhomme Richard*, that was engaged in battle with a superior British ship. Before Jones could take action in his smaller and slower ship the British frigate had blasted holes throughout his ship. Jones managed to grapple the two ships together with the intention of climbing aboard and overtaking the British. But when he did the British ship continued to unload her guns into the *Bonhomme Richard* . . . All looked lost.

The British captain called out, "Do you surrender?"

Amidst the smoke and fire and cannon-racked ship, Jones' answer rang out: "Surrender?!! Sir, I have not yet begun to fight!"

The men of the *Bonhomme Richard*, inspired by their commander, began to fire upon the British ship and entered into hand to hand combat and soon defeated the enemy in one of the greatest naval victories of our history.[22]

We as Christians are in a battle today and our ship has had many holes blown in it. The humanistic, anti-God forces have blasted holes in the Christian foundation of our civil government and of our educational system. They have tried to destroy our Christian heritage, our system of values, our godly heroes and even our families. Many are confident in their victory and have called out as the British captain, "Christians, do you surrender?"

As we come to understand that God is sovereign over the nations, that He governs in the affairs of men, then we can assuredly say with Captain Jones: "Surrender?!! We have not yet begun to fight!"

Some who have entered the battle may be discouraged and feel overwhelmed at the shear number of the enemy. They say that those who oppose God seem to be everywhere, especially in positions of influence and authority. Colonel Chesty Puller, during the Korean War, provides the appropriate attitude we should have as Christians who serve an all-powerful God. Col. Puller was sent behind the enemy position to attempt to cut off the supply line for the army. While there, a huge number of Chinese soldiers swarmed over from North Korea. Col. Puller and his men found themselves completely surrounded by the enemy. Communicating with his superiors, Puller related their situation: "The enemy is in front of us, behind us, to the left of us, and to the right of us. They won't escape this time!"

No matter how many oppose us, we can have confidence that God will be victorious as long as we recognize that God is sovereign, that God governs in the affairs of men and nations, that God is directing the course of history, and that He is, and will, fulfill His purposes in the earth.

End Notes

1. *Notes of Debates in the Federal Convention of 1787*, reported by James Madison, New York: W.W. Norton & Co., 1987, 209-210.

2. From Charles Rollin's *Ancient History*, quoted in "The Education of John Quincy Adams," by Rosalie J. Slater, in *The Christian History of the American Revolution*, Verna M. Hall, compiler, San Francisco: Foundation for American Christian Education, 1976, 605.

3. George Bancroft, *Memorial Address on the Life and Character of Abraham Lincoln*, Delivered at the Request of Both Houses of the Congress of America, Before Them in the House of Representatives at Washington, on the 12th of February, 1866, Washington: Government Printing Office, 1866, 3-4.

4. *International Bible Dictionary*, Plainfield, New Jersey: Logos International, 1977, 49.

5. Bancroft, p. 3.

6. The first three ways are from John Fiske, *The Beginnings of New England*, Boston: Houghton, Mifflin and Company, 1902, pp. 11 ff.

7. *Ibid.*

8. *Ibid.*

9. "The Mayflower Compact", November 11, 1620, in *Sources of Our Liberties*, Richard L. Perry, ed., New York: American Bar Foundation, 1959, 60.

10. "Agreement of the Settlers of Exeter in New Hampshire", July 5, 1639, in *Colonial Origins of the American Constitution*, Donald S. Lutz, ed., Indianapolis: Liberty Fund, 1998, 3-4.

11. Mark A. Beliles & Stephen K. McDowell, *America's Providential History*, Charlottesville, Vir.: Providence Foundation, 1996, 3.

12. *A Compilation of the Messages and Papers of the Presidents*, Vol. 1, James D. Richardson, ed., New York: Bureau of National Literature, Inc., 1897.

13. "The Charter of Massachusetts Bay" in *Sources of Our Liberties*, 94.

14. For more on this see Chapters 3 and 1 and Bruce Anderson, Mark Beliles, and Stephen McDowell, *Watchmen on the Walls*, and McDowell and Beliles, *Liberating the Nations*, both published by the Providence Foundation.

15. This and the following quotes on the Siege of Leyden are from John Lothrop Motley, *The Rise of the Dutch Republic, Vol. 2*, New York: Harper & Brothers, 1883, 551-582.

16. Richard Hakluyt, *A Selection of The Principal Voyages, Traffiques and Discoveries of the English Nation*, compiled by Laurence Irving, New York: Alfred A. Knopf, 1926, 260.

17. This and the following quotes on the Spanish Armada are from Hakluyt, pp. 285-292.

18. J.T. Headley, *The Illustrated Life of Washington*, New York: G. & F. Bill, 1859, 59.

19. *Recollections and Private Memoirs of Washington*, by George Washington Parke Custis, edited by Benson J. Lossing, 1860. p. 304.

20. Washington Irving, *The Life of Washington*, Vol. 1, New York: G.P. Putnam's Sons, 1857, 259.

21. Ibid., pp. 268-269.

22. Iris Vinton, *The Story of John Paul Jones*, New York: Gosset and Dunlap, 159-167.

Chapter 3

How to Disciple the Nations

Jesus said, "All authority has been given to Me in heaven and on earth. Go therefore and make disciples of all the nations, baptizing them in the name of the Father and the Son and the Holy Spirit, teaching them to observe all that I commanded you; and lo, I am with you always, even to the end of the age" (Matt. 28:18-20).

We have been given a clear commission to disciple the nations. Many modern Christians have relegated this command of Jesus in the Great Commission to only converting individuals. Christians in the past had a much broader view of this commission. Matthew Henry said that "the principal intention of this commission" is to "do your utmost to make the nations Christian nations."

What does it mean "to make the nations Christian nations"? What is a Christian nation? Simply stated, a Christian nation is one built upon the principles of God's word, and infused with the presence of God. Deuteronomy 4:5-8 reveals that for a nation to be great it needs the **Spirit of God** and the **Law of God**. This is what made Israel great among the nations.

The fruit of such a nation is liberty, both internal and external, personal and civil. The Bible teaches that "where the Spirit of the Lord is, there is liberty" (2 Cor. 3:17). Proverbs 29:18 tells us that "Where there is no vision, the people are unrestrained [perish; run wild], but happy is he who keeps the law." The Spirit and law/word of God are essential for liberating our nation. We must apply His entire word to our entire society through the Holy Spirit. Without that the people will run wild and our nation will perish.

Discipling nations begins in the heart.

The discipling of nations begins with the regeneration of individuals. All Godly change in society begins in the heart of man, and since only God can change the heart, all change for good begins with God. This is why Christianity must be introduced into any nation that desires liberty, justice, and prosperity. Fallen, sinful man must be transplanted from the kingdom of darkness, by the power and grace of God, into the Kingdom of light. Men need a new heart, but Christianity does not stop there. Men also need a new mind; they need to learn how to think Biblically and apply all of God's word to all areas of life.

Loving God with All Our Minds

The Bible teaches that we are to love the Lord our God with all our heart, all our soul, all our mind, and all our strength (Mark 12:30). To live as God desires, and to disciple our nation as Christ commands, we must have a passionate heart and soul for Him, willing to do anything He asks and to follow Him anywhere. But we must also love God with all our mind and strength. We must exert energy to develop a Biblical worldview.

Jesus said that we will "make disciples of all the nations" by "teaching them to observe all that I commanded you." We need to learn all that the Bible teaches in regard to personal and civil life. We must learn to think as Jesus thinks, to have a Biblical worldview. We must cultivate a passionate mind. The Bible instructs us that:

- We are to have knowledge with our zeal (Rom. 10:2).
- We are transformed by renewing our mind (Rom. 12:2). Our worldview (how we think) determines our actions. We love God with our minds when we think Biblically. We must bring the mind of Christ to bear upon our thoughts (which will affect our actions).
- We are to study to show our self approved and handle accurately the Word of Truth (2 Tim. 2:15).
- We must search the Scriptures daily (Acts 17:11).
- Our battle is not only in the spiritual but also the mental realm. 2 Corinthians 10:5 says "we are destroying speculations and every lofty thing raised up against the knowledge of God, and we are taking every thought captive to the obedience of Christ." We must prepare in knowledge; for truth is a weapon and we need to learn to handle it accurately (2 Tim. 2:15).

Our growth and preparation as Christians includes the spiritual, mental, and physical arena. We must prepare in character **and** thought if we truly hope to see God's purposes fulfilled for us, and if we desire to see Godly revival and reformation occur — to see the nations become Christian nations. In fact, the extent and quality of reformation will be determined by how believers view all of life from the Bible's perspective.

Therefore, to disciple nations, we must understand what the Bible teaches regarding personal growth and discipleship, and we must introduce the lost to these things. In addition, we must grow in a Biblical worldview, especially in the knowledge of how the nations can align themselves with the precepts of Godly government.

What is needed to disciple the nations?

Three general components needed to disciple a nation include:

1. Prayer — bringing God's grace and presence to man and society. Prayer undergirds and gives power to education and action.

2. Education — bringing God's truth to the mind. It gives us a standard by which to live and structure society. It is how we plants seeds of change.

3. Action — infusing God's truth and presence in society. This is the natural outworking of prayer and education; we should apply what we learn. As we act, the seeds will grow and produce fruit to be harvested.

Jesus said that we will "make disciples of all the nations" by "teaching them to observe all that I commanded you." We will not attempt to look at all He commanded, but we will examine a few key areas we must understand if we hope to disciple the nations.

Key civil teachings of Jesus necessary for the discipling of nations

I. Jurisdictional authority

In Matthew 12:17-21 Jesus said: "Then render to Caesar the things that are Caesar's; and to God the things that are God's." Jesus is teaching an extremely important concept here — that of jurisdictional authority. Jesus used a coin with Caesar's image upon it to illustrate that civil government does indeed have certain jurisdictional authority, such as in the area of taxation. However, Christ went on to pronounce that the state's jurisdiction is limited when He said that we are to render "to God the things that are God's." The inference is that there is a sphere of life where civil government (i.e. Caesar) has no jurisdiction at all. That sphere is implied here as involving the soul and mind of men, being made, not in Caesar's image, but in the image of God. Jesus was affirming that religious worship and opinions, and any endeavor relating to thoughts or speech, must remain completely free from government control.

This is the Biblical idea of the separation of church and state. It is not like the modern idea, which says we must remove God from public life. The principle of separation of church and state, the separation of school and state, and the separation of the press and speech from the control of the state, which are articulated in the First Amendment of the Constitution, are rooted in this historic political teaching of Christ. Before Christianity, the pagan world always included religion and education under the jurisdiction of the state. It was a radical political concept for Christ to declare that Caesar's power should be limited and, therefore, was used against Jesus when He was convicted of treason and crucified under Roman law. Christ's teaching has since changed the western world.

The responsibilities of the state are to be distinguished from that of the individual, family, and church. Usurpation of authority occurs when one jurisdiction encroaches upon another jurisdiction. The result is tyranny. Usurpation is exercising authority or power that belongs to another. It is "the act of seizing or occupying and enjoying the property of another, without right."

What jurisdictions has God established and what authority and responsibility has He given them?

All authority comes from God. He has established several divine institutions and jurisdictions on the earth through which authority is to flow. Our task is to find out **to whom God has commissioned to do what.** When one jurisdiction usurps the authority of another, the result is tyranny. The history of liberty is intertwined with the usurpation of power of one institu-

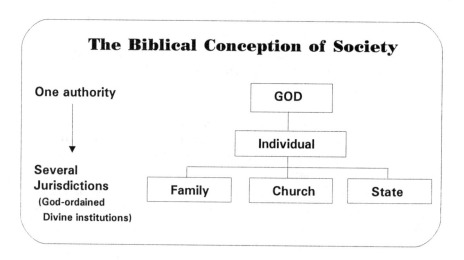

The Biblical Conception of Society

One authority → Several Jurisdictions (God-ordained Divine institutions)

GOD → Individual → Family, Church, State

tion over another. The more a nation operates according to Godly jurisdictional authority, the freer that nation will be.

The diagram on the previous page depicts "The Biblical Conception of Society," with the divine institutions. There are other jurisdictions where authority flows (that is, other spheres of authority), but these stem from the individual, family, and church fulfilling their responsibilities. For example: business flows from the individual and family; education and schools flow from the family, primarily, but from the church, secondarily. A summary of the purpose and responsibilities of individuals and the divine institutions follows.[1]

Purpose and Responsibilities of Individuals and Divine Institutions

The Individual's Purpose and Responsibilities:

1. Worship – "Love the Lord your God." (Luke 10:27, Deut. 6:5)

* Man's primary purpose is to glorify God and enjoy him forever

    a. Personal prayer, Bible reading/study/meditation
    b. Assemble with other believers
    c. Christian Sabbath observance

2. Charity – "Love your neighbor." (Luke 10:27, Lev. 19:9-18, Mt. 25:35-36)

* The Golden rule: Do unto others as you would have them do unto you

    a. Assist the needy and show mercy
    b. Speak the truth – evangelism, exhortation, edification
    c. Involvement in society/government (conversion of institutions)

3. Work – "as [you love] yourself" (Lk. 10:27; Gen. 1:26-28, Gen. 2:15)

* That man is God's creation and made in God's image is the foundation for self-worth, self-preservation, human dignity, and work. Our calling or work is the means of fulfilling the cultural mandate of being fruitful and subduing the earth.

    a. Provide for self and family – individuals will start businesses and create wealth

    b. Bless the nations – occurs as individuals provide needed goods and services

The Family's Purpose and Responsibilities:

A family is simply a man, woman, children who are related by marriage, blood, or adoption. The ideal marriage has a man and woman who covenant together to fulfill God's desire for them to be fruitful and bless the world. Both parents are to fulfill the purpose and responsibilities. In this context fathers (in general, but not exclusively) lead in society, while mothers raise the next generations. (Gen. 2:18, 22-24; 3:16)

1. Dominion and Procreation (Gen. 1:28, 1 Tim. 5:10,14)

* Be fruitful and multiply, subdue the earth.

    a. Pro-life – sanctity of life (Gen. 9:6)
    b. Children – a blessing (Ps. 127:3-5)

2. Education (Deut. 6:6-7)

* "You shall teach your sons."

    a. Fit children to fulfill their individual purposes and responsibilities (Pr. 22:6)
    b. Build Godly character (Gen. 18:19)
    c. Train in a Biblical worldview (Ps. 78:5)
    d. Discipline as well as instruction (Eph. 6:4)

3. Health and Welfare

* Practice hospitality (Rom. 12:13), especially for those of your own household.

    a. Preventative health care – proper exercise, nutrition, sanitation
We are the temple of God (1 Cor. 3:17; 6:17; 2 Cor. 6:16) and should seek to take care of ourselves and those in our charge. God is concerned with sanitation (Deut. 23:12-13; Num. 19:11-22), with what we eat (1 Cor. 6:12-20; Phil. 3:18-19), and with how we take care of our bodies (1 Tim. 4:7-8 tells us that bodily discipline is of profit, but only for a temporal time, while we are in the body).

b. Taking care of the sick, elderly, orphan, widow (1 Tim. 5:4,8,10,16; Deut. 15:7,8,11; Deut. 14:28-29)

c. Saving and investing for your retirement and your posterity (2 Cor. 12:14, Pr. 19:14, Deut. 21:17)

The Church's Purpose and Responsibilities:

* The church prepares people to govern society (to rule, Ps. 8:6), and to fulfill the redemption and creation commissions.

1. Regular instruction of members in Biblical truth for every sphere of life

a. Sunday preaching, regular classes, and other educational means (Mt. 28:18-20, 2 Tim. 3:16-17)

b. Includes starting schools and colleges

2. Administer Sacraments and Church Discipline (1 Cor. 5:8-13; 11:23-25; Mt. 18:15-17)

a. Corporate worship and sacrifice (Gen. 4:3-5,26)

b. Baptism and Lord's Supper (communion)

c. Excommunication

3. Discipling, equipping, and organizing believers (Eph. 4:11-12,16; Titus 3:8,14)

a. Equipping the saints for the work of service, enabling them to fulfill their divine occupation or calling.

b. Providing coordination and support for individuals and families to work in voluntary union with others to fulfill their purpose

c. Pastors are to be role models of what the church teaches in their personal conduct and through their involvement in society.

The Civil Government's (State's) Purpose and Responsibilities:

1. Protect the righteous, i.e. law-abiding citizens (Rom. 13:3-4, 1 Pet. 2:13-14)

a. Protection of life, liberty, and property from domestic and foreign lawbreakers. Governments are to secure God-given inalienable rights:

Life	Liberty	Property
Ex. 20:13 – "You shall not murder"	Ex. 21:16 – "He who kidnaps a man...shall be put to death."	Ex. 20:15 – "You shall not steal."
Self-defense Govt protection	Freedom of worship Freedom of speech Freedom of assembly Freedom of the press Freedom of schools Right to petition government	Private property Individual enterprise Acquire necessities of life

    b. Government coordinates civilian police for order and army for defense.

    c. Protection of rights from government abuse as well, via:
- Decentralized government
- Separation of powers
- Election of representatives

2. Punish the evil doer, i.e. criminal (Ex. 20:13; 21:12; 22:2)

    a. Set up constitution with just laws and penalties

    b. Impartial judges and fair trial to establish justice

3. Administer God's justice

    a. Civil leaders are ministers of God for good (Rom. 13:4).

    b. They are to judge for God in matters under their jurisdiction.

*　*　*

God gives the means to each institution to enforce its authority.

In each of these spheres, the Biblical flow of authority is to be from the internal to the external. As God's Word and Spirit are established in individuals, there will be proper functioning of the family, church, and state. However, since man is fallen, his tendency is to act unlawfully. When this occurs, God has given each divine institution a means to enforce its authority:

- Family — rod (Pr. 13:24; Pr. 22:15; Pr. 23:13-14; Pr. 29:15, 17; Heb. 12:7)
- Church — excommunication (Mt. 18:15-18; 1 Tim 1:20; Tit. 3:10; 1 Cor. 5:11)
- State — sword (Rom. 13:4; Gen. 9:6)

If God's law-word is violated, it should be handled by the appropriate jurisdiction and with an appropriate penalty. We should discern (which requires a thorough knowledge of the Bible) if it is the responsibility of the family, church, or state to administer God's justice. In reality, the Bible teaches that God will Himself execute His justice when many of His laws are violated, hence limiting the punitive action of man. A brief summary of the penalties for violating the civil law in the Hebrew Republic follow:

1. Restitution for theft (Ex. 22:1 ff). Work (via servitude) to make restitution for those unable to pay.

2. Corporal punishment and/or fines for minor offenses (Lev. 19:14; Deut. 22:13-21; Num. 5:5-10; Lev. 5:14-16; Lev. 6:1-7)

3. Death for serious offenses against life or incorrigibility (Ex. 21:12-16; Ex. 22:19-27; Lev. 20:10-21; Deut. 21:18-21)

4. City of refuge for accidental death (Num. 35:1-13)

The Bible also gives guidelines for the authority structure for each of the divine institutions. The Biblical forms of government for the family, church, and state are constructed so as to check the tendency of sinful man to abuse power.[2]

Tyranny is the fruit of usurpation of authority.

Leaders throughout history have abused authority in doing what they are supposed to do (i.e., in trying to fulfill their divine purpose). The result is tyranny and bondage. But tyranny and bondage are also the result of leaders who mean well, yet are trying to do something outside their jurisdiction. Modern examples in American include:

1) Education — As the state has gained a monopoly in education, and humanism has become the religion of the state, the quality of education has declined, even while costs have sky-rocketed.

2) Welfare state — In the 1960s we launched a war against poverty, and poverty won, even though we have spent trillions of dollars in this area.

Government has assumed a primary role in both of these areas as individuals, families, and churches have given up their responsibilities.

II. Civil government is a divinely ordained institution with limited powers (Gen. 9:6; Jn. 19:11; Rom. 13:1)

Another teaching of Jesus we must understand in order to disciple the nations is seen in John 19:11. In answer to Pilate, Jesus said, "You would have no authority over Me, unless it had been given you from above." Here

Jesus asserts that civil authority is delegated and controlled by God. Paul states this in Romans 13:1 by saying, "there is no authority except from God, and those which exist are established by God." This also means that God is sovereign in human history and government; He is "the ruler over the kings of the earth" (Rev. 1:5). This idea is important because many Christians today tend to view civil government as something "worldly" and unspiritual and, therefore, it is not necessary for the believer to study about or be involved in government. Spirituality involves more than religious and ecclesiastical topics.

Thus, Jesus instructed us that God ordained the state, as well as the church and family, and given each certain limited powers.

What relationship should there be between church and state, or God and government?

If church and state are to be separated jurisdictionally, then what relation should there be between the church and state in a nation? As institutions, the church, state, and family must be separated, but we should not separate God from government. In fact we cannot separate God from government any more than we can separate God from the family. God created the family (Gen. 2-3) and God created government (Gen. 9:6; Rom. 13:1-4). Since God created and is sovereign over civil government (John 19:11), it is impossible to separate God from government.

All nations are built upon some religion.

While many governments do not acknowledge God, they, nonetheless, have their foundation in religion or the faith of the people. The predominant faith or worldview held by the citizens dictates a basic morality which will be reflected by those who govern the nation and make the laws. So all governments, and laws that flow from them, are built upon some religion or worldview which provides the basis for right and wrong behavior in society.

Who is the source of law in a society?

The source of law in a society is the god of that society. This fundamental concept is not being discussed today in the marketplace of ideas. If the Bible is the source of law, of what is right and wrong behavior— of what is lawful and unlawful — then the God of the Bible is the god of that society; if man is the source of law, where a majority or ruling minority determines what is right and wrong, then man is the god of that society (this is secular humanism).

The source of law and morality in America has been the Christian religion, though this has been changing as Christians have retreated from the war of worldviews. Christianity has produced ideas and principles fundamental to freedom. Things such as not stealing, not committing murder, and honest dealings with others came from the Bible. We do not want to separate such Biblical principles from government. If we do, the result will be anarchy or tyranny.

We, also, do not want to separate the church from teaching such principles. The pastor and church have the duty to teach Christians everything Christ commanded them, including teachings that relate to the family and the state. The church has authority to speak the truth to all institutions in society — the church is "the pillar and foundation of the truth" (1 Tim. 3:15). In terms of speaking the truth, it must not be separate from the family or the state. The church must inform them, for the church builds the people, and the people build the nation.

The Relation of God and Government

How then should God and government relate? Remember that for a nation to be great it needs the Spirit of God and the law–word of God (Deut. 4:5-8). Therefore, a government and its laws should be built upon God's higher law (i.e., it has the law–word of God), and rulers should be Christian and uphold God's law (it has the presence of God). Both of these, of course, are dependent upon the citizens first displaying these characteristics.

1) Government and laws should be built upon God's higher law.

Proverbs says, "Happy is he who keeps the law." This is true of men and nations. Civil rulers, or judges, are to be ministers of God for good (Rom. 13). They are to judge for God. They are to represent God more so than the people. As the civil leader of Israel, Moses made "known the statutes of God and His laws" (Ex. 18:16). This is how he judged in disputes between people. "God filled the civil officers of Israel with His Spirit, to signify that they were prophets of God, called to speak for God in the ministry of justice (Num. 11:16)."[3]

America's form of government and her system of laws were built upon God's higher law. We will look at this more in later chapters, but one example can be seen in the document which was the precursor of the Bill of Rights, the Massachusetts Body of Liberties, written by Rev. Nathaniel

Ward in 1641. The Pentateuch was the basis for its criminal code, and "in case of the defect of a law in any partecular case" the standard was "the word of God."[4]

The Word of God is the law of liberty (Jam. 2:12). God's Word is the standard for law that will make men free.

2) Rulers should be Christian and uphold God's law.

We will examine the qualifications for Biblical leaders in Chapter 13, and see these include knowledge, morality (Christian character), and true faith (fear of God) (Ex. 18:21; Deut. 1:13). There is a prophetic nature to the civil office. "Every reformation in Israel involved in part a return to the prophetic nature of the civil office."[5] True Biblical revival not only involves reformation of the church but also reformation of the state.

The first chief justice of the U.S. Supreme Court, John Jay, said:

> Providence has given to our people the choice of their rulers, and it is the duty, as well as the privilege and interest, of our Christian nation, to select and prefer Christians for their rulers.[6]

Charles Finney, in his *Revivals of Religion*, listed the following as one necessary ingredient for the continuance of the revival that was occurring:

> The Church must take right ground in regard to politics. . . . The time has come that Christians must vote for honest men, and take consistent ground in politics, or the Lord will curse them. . . . God cannot sustain this free and blessed country, which we love and pray for, unless the Church will take right ground. Politics are a part of a religion in such a country as this, and Christians must do their duty to the country as a part of their duty to God. . . . He will bless or curse this nation, according to the course they [Christians] take [in politics].[7]

We need Biblical leaders in government. Such leaders are much more than men who merely go to church or teach Sunday school or vote for prayer in public schools. Biblical leaders are men full of the presence and law–word of God, ministering His justice in the civil realm. We have much to do to raise up such men, and to educate the populace to want to have such men govern.

Other civil teachings of Jesus needed to disciple nations

The Bible presents many other civil teachings of Jesus that are necessary for the discipling of nations. These include: 1. Government is to serve all men equally. 2. Individuals have inherent value. 3. Government is due the taxes and services of its citizens. 4. Social change is to be gradual and democratic, from the internal to the external. 5. The Mosaic law is applicable today. 6. Political and legal means can be used to achieve social justice. 7. Governmental injustice is to be resisted through protest, flight, and force in self-defense. 8. Military strength can be used to maintain peace. These teachings are examined in *America's Providential History* and *Liberating the Nations.*[8]

Education is a key element in discipling the nations. Remember, Jesus said we are to teach the nations **all** He commanded. In Chapter 15 we will examine how Biblical education is a means of bringing God's kingdom on earth. A nation is discipled as God's kingdom (government) comes to individuals and every sphere of life. As seeds of the kingdom are planted in the hearts of men, they will grow from the inside-out and gradually produce the fruit of the kingdom in all aspects of society.

We will also see how present-day state education is the means of bringing man's kingdom on earth. While Biblical education is rooted in the absolutes of God's Word, state education is rooted in relativism, positivism, and humanism. We are seeing the fruit of this religion in the nations today. Therefore, establishing Biblical or Kingdom education is a must if we are to disciple the nations.

As we are filled with the presence and Word of God, and are taught a Biblical worldview, we will know where and how to act to bring about the discipling of our nation. This action will affect all spheres of life. But when we act, there will be a price to pay.

The price we must pay to disciple the nations is great.

The life of the founder of Pennsylvania, William Penn, provides a great example for those seeking to bring about Godly reform in the nations.[9] While imprisoned in the Tower of London in 1668 for expressing his religious views, Penn wrote the book *No Cross, No Crown,* in which he states that "Christ's cross is Christ's way to Christ's crown." What was true for Him, is true for us. We must bear the cross — pay the price — to see the nations discipled.

Just like William Penn, we will encounter many crosses as we seek to disciple the nations, however **if we bear the cross we will obtain the crown**. Penn gladly bore the cross God had for him, and therefore, he also received a crown — for himself and millions more (as seen in his establishing religious and civil liberty in Pennsylvania, which, in turn, affected liberty in America at large).

Satan will offer us a crossless conquest, as he did Jesus. He will tell us: "you don't have to die to yourself or follow the leading of the Holy Spirit. You don't have to fulfill your duties and responsibilities in all those areas of life. You don't have to stand up in the civil arena."

People are prone to accept this offer for few are willing to die. People shrink back from pain and seek an easier way. We'll avoid anything that brings discomfort.

I am thankful that Jesus stayed upon the cross for me and all mankind. He was mocked and tempted to come down:

> If you are the Son of God, come down from the cross. . . . He saved others; He cannot save Himself. He is the King of Israel; let Him now come down from the cross, and we shall believe in Him. (Mt. 27:40,42)

Jesus could have come down, yet, He endured the cross so we might experience the crown.

What duties have you been neglecting that you must began to carry? What is the cross God would have you to bear? I would encourage you to not lay it down, for if so, you shall wear the crown and bring it to many others as well.

As we each embrace the duties and responsibilities we have in common, as well as our own unique special call, we can see the nations come and bow down before Him, giving Him the praise and honor that is due Him.

End Notes

1. The purpose and responsibilities of individuals and divine institutions is taken from *Liberating the Nations* by Stephen McDowell and Mark Beliles, pp. 90-92, and *Watchmen on the Walls* by Bruce Anderson, Mark Beliles, and Stephen McDowell, pp. 28-31, both published by the Providence Foundation.

2. For more on structures of government see *Liberating the Nations*, Chapter 11 (civil government), *America's Providential History*, Chapter 7 (church government).

3. Rousas John Rushdoony, *The Institutes of Biblical Law*, The Presbyterian and Reformed Publishing Co., 1973, p. 612.

4. "Massachusetts Body of Liberties," *Sources of Our Liberties*, Richard L. Perry, editor, New York: American Bar Foundation, 1952, p. 148.

5. Rushdoony, p. 612.

6. William Jay, *The Life of John Jay*. New York: J. & J. Harper, 1833, vol. II, p. 376, to John Murray, Jr. on October 12, 1816.

7. Mark Beliles and Stephen McDowell, *America's Providential History*, Charlottesville, Vir.: Providence Foundation, 1989, p. 267.

8. For more on these see *America's Providential History* and *Liberating the Nations* by Stephen McDowell and Mark Beliles, published by Providence Foundation.

9. See *In God We Trust Tour Guide*, Chapter 3, by Stephen McDowell and Mark Beliles, and the audiotape *No Cross, No Crown*, both produced by the Providence Foundation.

Section II

Lessons from America's Christian History

"[T]he great vital and conservative element in our system is the belief of our people in the pure doctrines and divine truths of the gospel of Jesus Christ."

United States House of Representatives, 1854

"Men, in a word, must necessarily be controlled either by a power within them or by a power without them; either by the Word of God or by the strong arm of man; either by the Bible or by the bayonet."

Robert C. Winthrop, Speaker of the House of Representatives, 1847-1849

Chapter 4

The Bible: Rock of Our Republic
The Influence of the Bible in the History of America

On June 8, 1845, President Andrew Jackson said that "the Bible is the rock on which our Republic rests." Early Americans would almost universally agree that the religious, social, educational, and political life of America was primarily shaped by the Bible.

Our states were colonized by people who desired to freely worship the God of the Bible; our schools were begun so that everyone would be able to read and understand the Bible for themselves; our universities were founded to train ministers who were knowledgeable of the Scriptures; our laws and constitutions were written based on Biblical ideas; and our founding fathers overwhelmingly had a Biblical worldview.

Most Americans today have not been taught this important truth, even though many still recognize it. Even *Newsweek* magazine, on December 26, 1982, acknowledged that: "Now historians are discovering that the Bible, perhaps even more than the Constitution is our Founding document." It used to be common knowledge that America's Biblical foundation produced America's freedom, justice, and prosperity. In recent generations America has been shifting from a Biblical foundation to a humanistic foundation, where the God of the Bible is being replaced by man as god. The result has been the decay of society and loss of liberty. Noah Webster wrote:

> The moral principles and precepts contained in the Scriptures ought to form the basis of all our civil constitutions and laws. All the miseries and evils which men suffer from vice, crime, ambition, injustice, oppression, slavery, and war, proceed from their despising or neglecting the precepts contained in the Bible.[1]

For the good of America we must once again restore the Bible to the central role it played in shaping this nation. To do this we must first understand that role. Following is a brief outline examining the influence of the Bible in our history.

The Bible was the single most important influence in the lives of colonial Americans.

Lawrence A. Cremin writes:

> Above all, the colonists were acquainted with the Bible itself, principally in the Geneva Version but increasingly in the King James Version. The Bible was read and recited, quoted and consulted, early committed to memory and constantly searched for meaning. Deemed universally relevant, it remained throughout the century the single most important cultural influence in the lives of Anglo-Americans. . . . Though the Bible had been richly valued for generations, it was not until the seventeenth century that it was widely read and studied. The message of Protestantism was that men could find in Scripture the means to salvation, the keys to good and evil, the rules by which to live, and the standards against which to measure the conduct of prince and pastor.[2]

New England of the 1700s was described by historian George Bancroft in this way:

> In the settlements which grew up in the interior, on the margin of the greenwood, the plain meeting-house of the congregation for public worship was everywhere the central point; near it stood the public school. The snug farm-houses, owned as freehold, without quit-rents, were dotted along the way. In every hand was the Bible; every home was a house of prayer; all had been taught, many had comprehended, a methodical theory of the divine purpose in creation, and of the destiny of man.[3]

The Aitken Bible

Prior to America's independence almost every house in the colonies possessed and cherished the English Bible, yet, no English Bibles had ever been printed in the colonies (some had been printed in German and native Indian languages). It would have been piracy to do so. Only after independence were English Bibles printed. When the war cut off the supply of English Bibles, the Congress, in September 1777, resolved to import 20,000 Bibles from Scotland, Holland or elsewhere because "the use of the Bible is so universal and its importance so great."[4]

In 1782, Congress acted the role of a Bible society by officially approving the printing and distribution of the "Bible of the Revolution," an American translation prepared by Robert Aitken. The endorsement of Congress in the front of the Aitken Bible read: "Whereupon, Resolved, That the United States in Congress assembled . . . recommend this edition of the Bible to the inhabitants of the United States."

Oath of Office taken on the Bible

At the first Presidential Inauguration George Washington laid his hand on the Bible and took the oath of office as prescribed by the Constitution, adding the words "so help me God," after which he leaned over and reverently kissed the Bible. Washington then went to the Senate and read his inaugural address. After this they all walked to St. Paul's Chapel for prayers and a service.[5] All the presidents have taken the oath of office on the Bible.

The People who settled America were people of the book. *Sola scriptura* was their motto.

A majority of the settlers of America were a product of the Protestant Reformation. The major impetus of this reform was the Bible being translated into the common languages of the people. Throughout Europe the people read the Scriptures and began looking to them as the standard by which they judged not only their own actions but also that of priest and king. The Bible became the source of their ideas and principles. This brought many trials and persecutions and forced many to flee their native countries to America.

Many of those who had paved the way for settlement were inspired by the Scriptures as well. Composed in 1502 after his third voyage, Columbus' *Book of Prophecies* reveals he felt he was fulfilling a divine mission through his voyages. This work contains hundreds of prophetic passages of Scripture that Columbus related to his great enterprise.[6] The man most responsible for the English colonization of America was a minister, Richard Hakluyt. He said he was first inspired by the Scriptures to promote colonization. His chief motive was to extend God's Kingdom throughout the earth.[7]

Some of the early settlers and their Biblical motivation follow.

Pilgrims

They were enlightened by the Word of God and sought to live according to its precepts. Pastor to the Pilgrims, John Robinson, wrote in his farewell letter:

> I charge you, before God and his blessed angels, that you follow me no farther than you have seen me follow the Lord Jesus Christ. The Lord has more truth yet to break forth out of his holy word. I cannot sufficiently bewail the condition of the reformed churches, who are come to a period in religion, and will go at present no farther than the instruments of their reformation. Luther and Calvin were great and shining lights in their times, yet they penetrated not into the whole counsel of God. I beseech you, remember it – 'tis an article of your church covenant – that you be ready to receive whatever truth shall be made known to you from the written word of God.[8]

Puritans

The early settlers of Salem, Massachusetts were typical of the many Puritans who came to America. One reason they came was to "wynne the natives to the Christian faith." During their voyage from England they "constantly served God, morning and evening, by reading and expounding a chapter in the Bible, singing and prayer."[9]

The First Charter of Massachusetts (1629) states the desire that all the inhabitants would "be so religiously, peaceably, and civilly governed, as their good life and orderly conversation may win and incite the natives of country to the knowledge and obedience of the only true God and Savior of mankind, and the Christian faith, which in Our royal intention and the adventurers' free profession, is the principal end of this plantation."[10]

The center of the seal of the colony of Massachusetts Bay shows an Indian speaking the words, "Come Over And Help Us." The work of John Eliot, "Apostle to the Indians," and Daniel Gookin, a civil magistrate and superintendent to the Indians, shows how many of the early settlers desired to bring the gospel to the native Americans – how they did come over to help them. These two men worked for over 40 years to evangelize and civilize the Algonquin Indians of Massachusetts. Eliot constantly traveled to various Indians villages and taught them the gospel. When many began to be converted he set up "Praying Towns" where these Christian Indians could live out their new life in Christ and learn how to separate themselves from their pagan way of life. In these towns, which came to number fourteen, the Indians were self-governed and self-supporting. Twenty-four of these Christian Indians became ministers in order to carry on the work of the gospel among their own people. Hundreds attended schools and some attended Harvard College.

Eliot believed that the Indians needed the Bible in their own language in order to truly grow in the complete liberty of the gospel, both internally and externally, both personally and civilly. Therefore, after learning the native Indian language, he developed a written language for the Algonquin tongue, as none existed. He then worked for twelve years on translating the Bible, while continuing his pastoral duties in the church in Roxbury and regularly traveling to minister to the Indians. He completed the work in 1658. The Algonquin Bible was first published in 1661-1663 with funds primarily contributed by Englishmen. This was the first Bible printed in America.

Scotch-Irish Presbyterians

Many Scotch-Irish Presbyterians settled on the western frontiers of Pennsylvania, Maryland, Virginia, and North Carolina. At every place they "had their pastor, and trained their children in Bible truth, in the catechism, obedience to parents, — a wholesome doctrine practically enforced by all the colonists, — and reverence for the Sabbath and its sacred duties."[11]

Georgia colonists

Some of the earliest settlers to Georgia were German Lutherans who were driven out of their country when they refused to renounce their Protestant faith, and were invited by the Society in England for Propagating the Gospel to emigrate to Savannah. George Bancroft writes: "On the last day of October 1733, 'the evangelical community,' well supplied with Bibles and hymn-books, catechisms and books of devotion. . . — after a discourse and prayer and benedictions, cheerfully, and in the name of God, began their pilgrimage." They arrived at Charleston on March 18, 1734 and were welcomed by Oglethorpe.[12]

The Bible formed the basis of America's civil laws.

Jamestown

Between 1609 and 1612 a set of laws was drawn up for the colony of Virginia. In these *Lawes Divine, Morall and Martiall, etc.* the colonists were required to serve God, to attend divine services, to not speak against God or blaspheme God's holy name, and to not speak or act in any way that would "tend to the derision, or despight [open defiance] of Gods holy word upon paine of death."[13] While this may seem extreme to us today, it none-theless reveals their desire to live according to God's commands.

In 1619 the first Representative Assembly of the new world met in the Church in Jamestown. It was begun by prayer. One of the resolves of this body was to encourage the farmers and plantation owners to open their homes to Indian youth with the purpose of converting them to Christianity and teaching them the precepts of God's Word.

The Laws of the Pilgrims

The Pilgrims believed that God and His word were the supreme source of all authority. Their compilation of laws during the 1600s clearly re-vealed this. Their *Book of General Laws* (1671) begins by stating that "Laws. . . are so far good and wholesome, as by how much they are derived from, and agreeable to the ancient Platform of Gods Law."[14] As one reads through these laws it is obvious they looked to the Bible to assist them in formulating good and wholesome laws. They even gave Scriptural refer-ences to support their capital laws.

Fundamental Orders of Connecticut

This first American constitution was written by Rev. Thomas Hooker in 1638. The oath imposed on the magistrates bound them to "to administer justice according to the laws here established, and for want thereof accord-ing to the rule of the word of God."[15] The oath of the governor (and simi-larly the Magistrate) ended with these words: "I . . . will further the execution of Justice according to the rule of Gods word; so me God, in the name of the Lo: Jesus Christ."[16]

New Haven Colony

Established in 1638 under the guidance of Rev. John Davenport, this colony rested its frame of government upon the idea that "the Scripturs doe holde forth a perfect rule for the direction and government of all men in all duet[ies] . . . in the government of famyles and commonwealths." God's word was established as the only rule in public affairs. Bancroft wrote that "New Haven made the Bible its statute-book."[17]

Massachusetts Body of Liberties

Written in 1641 by Rev. Nathaniel Ward, the Pentateuch (the first five books of the Bible) was the basis for its criminal code, and "in case of the defect of a law in any case" the standard was "the word of God."[18] Article

65 states: "No custome or prescription shall ever prevaile amongst us in any morall cause, our meaneing is maintaine anythinge that can be proved to bee morrallie sinfull by the word of god."[19] The capital laws in the Body of Liberties give numerous scriptures as justification for carrying out the death penalty.[20]

Arbitrary Government Described (1644)

In explaining how the government of Massachusetts was to work, Governor John Winthrop wrote: "By these it appears, that the officers of this body politic have a rule to walk by in all their administrations, which rule is the Word of God, and such conclusions and deductions as are, or shall be, regularly drawn from thence."[21]

Code of the Connecticut General Court, 1650

No man's life, liberty, or property was to be taken except by specific law established and sufficiently published by the General Court (the legislature), "or in case of the defect of a law, in any particular case, by the Word of God."[22]

The Connecticut Code of Law lists several crimes receiving the death penalty. Specific Scriptures are listed as justification for these capital laws. For example:

> 4. If any person shall commit any willful murder, which is manslaughter, committed upon malice, hatred, or cruelty, not in a man's necessary and just defense, nor by mere casualty against his will, he shall be put to death. Ex. 21:12-14; Num. 35:30,31.
> 10. If any man steals a man or mankind, he shall be put to death. Ex. 21:16[23]

The Code also states that "the open contempt of God's Word, and messengers thereof, is the desolating sin of civil states and churches."[24]

Many other early constitutions, compacts, charters, and laws could be examined that reveal the central role of the Bible in shaping America's civil documents, such as the Charter of Rhode Island, the Frame of Government of Pennsylvania, the Declaration of Independence, various state constitutions, and the U.S. Constitution and Bill of Rights.

Education was rooted in the Bible.

The first schools were Christian

The first schools in America were started by the church to teach people to be able to read the Bible (for example, the Boston Latin School in 1636).

Massachusetts School laws of 1642 and 1647

In 1642 the General Court enacted legislation requiring each town to see that children were taught, especially "to read and understand the principles of religion and the capital laws of this country"[25]

The laws of 1647 begin: "It being one chief project of that old deluder, Satan, to keep men from the knowledge of the Scriptures." The General Court went on to order any town with 50 families to hire a teacher, and those that increased to 100 families to set up a school to prepare youth for the university.[26]

Grammar School at Dorchester, Massachusetts

Rules adopted by town meeting in 1645 required the schoolmaster "to commend his scholars and his labors amongst them unto God by prayer morning and evening, taking care that his scholars do reverently attend during the same." The schoolmaster examined each student at noon on Monday to see what he had learned from the Sabbath sermon. On Friday afternoon at 2:00, he was to catechize them "in the principles of Christian religion."[27]

Connecticut School Laws, 1650

The laws of 1650 required localities to provide for the education of the youth. They began like that of Massachusetts: "It being one chief project of that old deluder, Satan, to keep men from the knowledge of the Scriptures."[28]

A 1690 law declared: "This [legislature] observing that. . . there are many persons unable to read the English tongue and thereby incapable to read the holy Word of God or the good laws of this colony. . . it is ordered that all parents and masters shall cause their respective children and servants, as they are capable, to be taught to read distinctly the English tongue."[29]

Colleges started to train ministers in knowledge of Scriptures

Harvard College (1636)

Started in 1636 by the New England Puritans to train Godly ministers, they thought the greatest curse that could come upon the land would be an impotent, ignorant clergy. Even while struggling to survive as a colony they undertook this task.

> Rules, and precepts that are observed in the college:
>
> 2. Let every student be plainly instructed, and earnestly pressed to consider well, the main end of his life and studies is, to know God and Jesus Christ which is eternal life, John 17:3, and therefore to lay Christ in the bottom, as the only foundation of all sound knowledge and learning.
>
> And seeing the Lord only giveth wisdom, let every one seriously set himself by prayer in secret to seek it of him Prov. 2:3.
>
> 3. Every one shall so exercise himself in reading the Scriptures twice a day, that he shall be ready to give such an account of his proficiency therein, both in theoretical observations of the language, and logic, and in practical and spiritual truths, as his tutor shall require, according to his ability; seeing the entrance of the word giveth light, it giveth understanding to the simple, Psalm 119:130.[30]

Regulations at Yale College, 1745

One of the original rules at Yale College shows the central place the Bible had:

> 1. All scholars shall live religious, godly, and blameless lives according to the rules of God's Word, diligently reading the Holy Scriptures, the fountain of light and truth; and constantly attend upon all the duties of religion, both in public and secret.[31]

We could examine scores of others colleges and see the Biblical foundations. In fact 106 of the first 108 colleges were founded on the Christian faith.

Bookstores in early America had many Bibles and religious works

De Tocqueville observed that bookseller shops in the United States contained "an enormous quantity of religious works, Bibles, sermons, edifying anecdotes, controversial divinity, and reports of charitable societies."[32] They were providing what the American people wanted to read.

Textbooks were Christian

Bible was central text

In 1690, John Locke said that children learned to read by following "the ordinary road of Hornbook, Primer, Psalter, Testament and Bible."[33]

The New Haven Code of 1655 required that children be made "able duly to read the Scriptures . . . and in some competent measure to understand the main grounds and principles of Christian Religion necessary to salvation."[34]

Catechisms and Hornbooks

There were over 500 different catechisms used in colonial times. The most commonly used one was *The Foundation of Christian Religion gathered into sixe Principles*. Later, the Westminster Catechism became the most prominent one.

Hornbooks, which had been used since 1400 in Europe, were made of a flat piece of wood with a handle, upon which a sheet of printed paper was attached and covered with transparent animal horn to protect it. A typical colonial hornbook had the alphabet, the vowels, a list of syllables, the invocation of the Trinity, and the Lord's Prayer.

New England Primer

The New England Primer (first published in 1690) was the most widely used text for 100 years. It taught the alphabet with Biblical examples:

A: In Adam's fall, we sinned all. B: Heaven to find the Bible mind. C: Christ for sinners dy'd. D: The Deluge drown'd the earth around. . . .[35]

Webster's Blue-backed Speller

The Elementary Spelling Book by Noah Webster sold over 100 million copies in the 19th century. It contained many Biblical statements such as:

God will forgive those who repent of their sins, and live a holy life.

Examine the Scriptures daily and carefully, and set an example of good works.

Those who enjoy the light of the gospel, and neglect to observe its precepts, are more criminal than the heathen.[36]

Webster's 1828 Dictionary

In the first exhaustive dictionary in history, Noah Webster used thousands of Scriptural references and gave Biblical definitions, in contrast to humanistic definitions in modern dictionaries.

Most of the other textbooks used in the nineteenth century reflected a Biblical worldview, including McGuffey's Readers, Murray's Reader, Young's Civil Government, and Butler's history.

The Founders acknowledged the centrality of the Bible.

Following are quotes from a few of America's Founding Fathers that show the importance of the Bible in their lives and thinking.

John Adams

"Suppose a nation in some distant Region, should take the Bible for their only law Book, and every member should regulate his conduct by the precepts there exhibited. . . . What a Eutopia what a Paradise would this region be."[37]

Benjamin Rush, Signer of the Declaration

"The great enemy of the salvation of man, in my opinion, never invented a more effectual means of extirpating Christianity from the world than by persuading mankind that it was improper to read the Bible at schools." [38]

"In contemplating the political institutions of the United States, I lament that we waste so much time and money in punishing crimes and take so little pains to prevent them. We profess to be republicans, and yet we neglect the only means of establishing and perpetuating our republican forms of government, that is, the universal education of our youth in the principles of christianity by the means of the bible. For this Divine book, above all others, favors that equality among mankind, that respect for just laws, and those sober and frugal virtues, which constitute the soul of republicanism."[39]

Fisher Ames

"[T]he Bible [should] regain the place it once held as a school book[.] Its morals are pure, its examples captivating and noble. The reverence for the sacred book that is thus early impressed lasts long; and probably, if not impressed in infancy, never takes firm hold of the mind. One consideration more is important. In no book is there so good English, so pure and so elegant; and by teaching all the same book, they will speak alike, and the Bible will justly remain the standard of language as well as of faith."[40]

Samuel Adams

To our founders, the Bible was more than a good book with good principles. It contains the message and words of life. Samuel Adams wrote to his daughter Hannah on Aug. 17, 1780:

"[Y] cannot gratify me so much, as by seeking most earnestly, the Favor of Him who made & supports you – who will supply you with whatever his infinite Wisdom sees best for you in this World, and above all, who has given us his Son to purchase for us the Reward of Eternal Life – Adieu, and believe that I have."[41]

Patrick Henry

"The Bible is worth all the books that ever were printed, and it has been my misfortune that I have never found time to read it with the proper attention and feeling till lately. I trust in the mercy of heaven that it is not yet too late."[42]

Noah Webster

"The brief exposition of the constitution of the United States, will unfold to young persons the principles of republican government; and it is the sincere desire of the writer that our citizens should early understand that the genuine source of correct republican principles is the Bible, particularly the New Testament or the Christian religion."[43]

"The Bible must be considered as the great source of all the truths by which men are to be guided in government, as well as in all social transactions. . . . [T]he Bible [is] the instrument of all reformation in morals and religion."[44]

John Jay, First Chief-Justice of the U.S. Supreme Court

"The Bible is the best of all books, for it is the word of God and teaches us the way to be happy in this world and in the next. Continue therefore to read it and to regulate your life by its precepts."[45]

John Quincy Adams

"[S]o great is my veneration for the Bible, and so strong my belief, that when duly read and meditated on, it is of all books in the world, that which contributes most to make men good, wise, and happy. . . .

"I advise you, my son, in whatever you read, and most of all in reading the Bible, to remember that it is for the purpose of making you wiser and more virtuous. I have myself, for many years, made it a practice to read through the Bible once every year. . . .

"My custom is, to read four or five chapters every morning, immediately after rising from my bed. It employs about an hour of my time, and seems to me the most suitable manner of beginning the day. . .

"It is essential, my son, in order that you may go through life with comfort to yourself, and usefulness to your fellow-creatures, that you should form and adopt certain rules or principles, for the government of your own conduct and temper. . . .

"It is in the Bible, you must learn them, and from the Bible how to practice them. Those duties are to God, to your fellow-creatures, and to yourself. 'Thou shalt love the Lord thy God, with all thy heart, and with all thy soul, and with all thy mind, and all thy strength, and thy neighbor as thyself'. . . .They [our duties] are all to be learned in equal perfection by our searching the Scriptures.

"Let us, then, search the Scriptures;. . . The Bible contains the revelation of the will of God. It contains the history of the creation of the world, and of mankind."[46]

Thomas Jefferson

"The Bible is the cornerstone of liberty. A student's perusal of the sacred volume will make him a better citizen, a better father, a better husband."[47]

Benjamin Franklin

When members of the Constitutional Convention were discussing property qualifications for federal officials, Franklin used the Scriptures to speak against any such qualification. Madison records how Franklin said: "We should remember the character which the Scripture requires in Rulers, that they should be men hating covetousness."[48] When Franklin was presented at the Court of Versailles he tells us that a scripture verse, that his father used to quote to him when he was a boy, passed through his mind. That verse was: "Seest thou a man diligent in his business? He shall stand before kings."[49]

William Samuel Johnson, Signer of the Constitution

As President of Columbia College in New York, William Johnson gave a commencement speech where he reminded the graduates that the purpose of their education was "to qualify you the better to serve your Creator and your country. . . . Your first great duties, you are sensible, are those you owe to Heaven, to your Creator and Redeemer. . . . Remember, too, that you are the redeemed of the Lord, that you are bought with a price, even the inestimable price of the precious blood of the Son of God. . . . Love, fear, and serve Him as your Creator, Redeemer, and Sanctifier. Acquaint yourselves with Him in His Word and holy ordinances. Make Him your friend and protector and your felicity is secured both here and hereafter."[50]

James McHenry, Signer of the Constitution

"The Holy Scriptures . . . can alone secure to society, order and peace, and to our courts of justice and constitutions of government, purity, stability, and usefulness. In vain, without the Bible, we increase penal laws and draw entrenchments around our institutions."[51]

Robert C. Winthrop, Speaker of the House of Representatives, 1847-1849

"Men, in a word, must necessarily be controlled either by a power within them or by a power without them; either by the Word of God or by the strong arm of man; either by the Bible or by the bayonet."[52]

The Founders started numerous Bible societies

Following our independence scores of local societies were started to circulate the Bible. Many of our founding fathers were greatly involved in these. Some of these include:
- John Marshall (Supreme Court Chief Justice), Vice-president of American Bible Society
- James McHenry (Signer of Constitution), President of the Baltimore Bible Society
- John Langdon (Signer of Constitution), VP of the American Bible Society
- Rufus King (signer of Constitution). Member of NY Bible Society
- John Quincy Adams, VP of the American Bible Society

- Elias Boudinot (President of the Continental Congress), Founder and first President of the American Bible Society, President of the NJ Bible Society
- James Burrill, Jr. (Chief-Justice of Rhode Island Supreme Court; US Senator), President of the Providence Auxiliary Bible Society
- Dewitt Clinton (Gov. NY; US Senator), Manager and VP of the American Bible Society
- Caleb Strong (Constitutional Convention), VP of the American Bible Society
- John Hamilton (Major-General in the Revolution, US Congress), Member of the NJ Bible Society
- John Jay (Original Chief-Justice of the US Supreme Court), President of the American Bible Society
- Charles Cotesworth Pinckney (Signer of Constitution), President of the Charleston Bible Society, VP of American Bible Society
- Rufus Putnam (General in American Revolution, Federal Judge), President of the Ohio Bible Society
- Benjamin Rush (Signer of Declaration), Founder and manager of the Philadelphia Bible Society
- John Cotton Smith (Gov of Conn.; US Congressman), First President of the Connecticut Bible Society
- Daniel Tompkins (Gov NY, VP of the United States), VP of the American Bible Society
- Bushrod Washington (US Supreme Court Justice), VP of the American Bible Society

In 1816 sixty delegates representing 35 of these local societies gathered in New York City and formed the American Bible Society. During the first year 85 local societies joined with it. Elias Boudinot became the first President. Boudinot had been a member of the Continental Congress, chosen as President in 1782 and in that capacity a signer of the Treaty of Peace officially ending the war, a member of the first House of Representatives (1789-1796), and the Director of the National Mint (1796-1805).

In accepting the office of President of the American Bible Society, Boudinot wrote: "I am not ashamed to confess that I accept the appointment of President of the American Bible Society as the greatest honor that could have been conferred on me this side of the grave."[53] He continued as president of the society until his death in 1821.

The first Supreme Court Chief Justice, John Jay, served as President of American Bible Society as well. General Rufus Putnam founded the first Bible society west of the Alleghenies.

The Bible was the primary source of the Founders worldview.

Source of political ideas

Dr. Donald Lutz conducted an exhaustive ten-year research of about 15,000 political documents of the Founders' Era (1760-1805), and recorded every reference our founders made to other sources. This list of 3154 citations reveals those writings and men that most shaped the political ideas of our founders. By far, the most quoted source of their political ideas was the Bible, 34% of citations. The next most quoted sources were from men who largely derived their ideas from the Bible (Montesquieu, 8.3%, Blackstone, 7.9%, and Locke, 2.9%). In fact 80% or more of all the citations were from the Bible or Biblical thinkers.[54]

Source of ideas for American Independence

Churches and ministers were a great support in the cause of American liberty. The Bible provided the major source of ammunition for the clergy. Ministers had for years preached political sermons. Many of these were printed and read by the people. George Bancroft writes how the pastors were heard "with reverence by their congregations in their meeting-houses on every Lord's day, and on special occasions of fasts, thanksgivings, lectures, and military musters. Elijah's mantle being caught up was a happy token that the Lord would be with this generation, as he had been with their fathers. Their exhaustless armory was the Bible, whose scriptures furnished sharp words to point their appeals, apt examples of resistance, prophetic denunciations of the enemies of God's people, and promises of the divine blessing on the defenders of his law."[55]

Ideas were presented in:
- Election Sermons
- Thanksgiving Day Sermons
- Fast Day Sermons
- Anniversary Sermons
- Execution Sermons

The Bible shaped their social ideas

One social evil that confronted America's founders was slavery. Most of the founders opposed slavery because it was inconsistent with the Bible. They saw it as a social evil that needed to be eradicated (see Chapter 12).

Benjamin Rush said:

Domestic slavery is repugnant to the principles of Christianity. . . . It is rebellion against the authority of a common Father. It is a practical denial of the extent and efficacy of the death of a common Savior. It is an usurpation of the prerogative of the great Sovereign of the universe who has solemnly claimed an exclusive property in the souls of men.[56]

In 1773, Patrick Henry wrote:

Is it not amazing that, at a time when the rights of humanity are defined and understood with precision, in a country above all others fond of liberty, in such an age, we find men professing a religion the most humane, mild, meek, gentle, and generous, adopting a principle as repugnant to humanity as it is inconsistent with the Bible and destructive to liberty?. . . . I believe a time will come when an opportunity will be offered to abolish this lamentable evil; everything we can do is to improve it, if it happens in our day; if not, let us transmit to our descendants, together with our slaves, a pity for their unhappy lot and an abhorrence of slavery. We owe to the purity of our religion to show that it is at variance with that law which warrants slavery.[57]

In the mid-1800s the leader of the Underground Railroad, Levi Coffin, was motivated by the precepts of the Bible to aid fugitive slaves to escape to Canada. After listening to friends warn him of dangers to his life and property, Coffin responded: "I told them that I felt no condemnation for anything that I had ever done for the fugitive slaves. If by doing my duty and endeavoring to fulfill the injunctions of the Bible, I injured my business, then let my business go. As to my safety, my life was in the hands of my Divine Master, and I felt that I had his approval."[58]

The Biblical faith of many slaves in America caused them to look to God for their deliverance: "[T]he slaves of the South . . . longed for liberty, but they looked for it through the intervention of others [rather than through violent insurrections]; they drew their hopes from the case of the Israelites led from Egypt by the hand of Moses; they trusted God would come to their aid in a similar way — raise up for them a Moses; and in this trust in Providence their faith was marvelous. The gospel of forgiveness had been preached to them by preachers both of the white race and their own, and the truths of the Bible, thus orally presented, had a wonderful influence in preparing them for the events about to follow."[59]

Christians in the North and the South led the anti-slavery movement of the mid-nineteenth century.

Numerous Bibles were available in early America

The first book printed in America was the Bible. As mentioned earlier this was in the Algonquin language and was the work of John Eliot (1604-1690) who began evangelizing the Massachusetts Indians in the 1640s. Eliot organized the Indians who became Christians into communities. He wrote: "The Bible, and the Catechism drawn out of the Bible . . . are the ground-work of Community amongst all our Indian-Churches and Christians."[60]

There were hundreds of different Bibles in numerous languages in use in colonial America. The Evans micro-print collection has over 500 different Bibles listed.

Sabbath Observance

The Christian Sabbath has been observed and recognized by law from the beginning of America. Sabbath laws could be found in all the early colonies and states.

Alexis de Tocqueville described the Sabbath observance of the 1830s in *Democracy in America:*

> In the United States, on the seventh day of every week, the trading and working life of the nation seems suspended; all noises cease; a deep tranquillity, say rather the solemn calm of meditation, succeeds the turmoil of the week, and the soul resumes possession and contemplation of itself. Upon this day the marts of traffic are deserted; every member of the community, accompanied by his children, goes to church, where he listens to strange language which would seem unsuited to his ear. He is told of the countless evils caused by pride and covetousness: he is reminded of the necessity of checking his desires, of the finer pleasures which belong to virtue alone, and of the true happiness which attends it. On his return home, he does not turn to the ledgers of his calling, but he opens the book of Holy Scripture; there he meets with sublime or affecting descriptions of the greatness and goodness of the Creator, of the infinite magnificence of the handiwork of God, of the lofty destinies of man, of his duties, and of his immortal privileges. Thus it is that the American at times steals an hour from himself; and laying aside for a while the petty passions which agitate his life, and the ephemeral interests which engross it, he strays at once into an ideal world, where all is great, eternal, and pure.[61]

Pioneers and the Bible

As early Americans went west to settle new lands they carried the Bible and its truths with them. De Tocqueville wrote of the contrast of the physical homes of western pioneers and their personal characteristics: "Everything about him is primitive and unformed, but he is himself the result of the labor and the experience of eighteen centuries. He wears the dress, and he speaks the language of cities; he is acquainted with the past, curious of the future, and ready for argument upon the present; he is, in short, a highly civilized being, who consents, for a time, to inhabit the backwoods, and who penetrates into the wilds of the New World with the Bible, an axe, and a file of newspapers."[62] The Bible was the great civilizing and educational influence for these pioneers. De Tocqueville wrote of visiting log cabins in the wilderness that had a Bible if no other book.[63]

Revivals impact the nation

The Bible spurred numerous awakenings and revivals which had great effect in America's history. It also inspired much missionary work to the American Indians in the west. The states of Washington and Oregon were founded by missionaries, Marcus and Narcissa Whitman and Jason Lee. Johnny Appleseed not only planted orchards throughout the frontier, but he also planted the Word of God, carrying a Bible and sowing its truth wherever he went. One of the first explorers of the west, Jedidiah Smith, always packed his Bible.

* * *

We have just touched on the great impact that the Bible has had on America. We could examine much more, including the records of the U.S. Congress, the words and laws of the state legislatures, and federal and state court rulings. The more you look, the more convinced you will become that there would be no America, the land of liberty, without God and the Bible.

As the Bible and its principles have been removed from our schools, missing from our leaders ideas and actions, extirpated from the marketplace of ideas, and not adhered to by enough of our citizens, America has declined and will continue to decline.

America must once again restore the Bible to its place of influence. We must consider the Bible, in the words of Noah Webster, "as the great source of all the truths by which men are to be guided in government, as well as in all social transactions. . . . The Bible [is] the instrument of all reformation in morals and religion."[64]

End Notes

1. Noah Webster, *History of the United States,* New Haven: Durrie & Peck, 1832, p. 309.

2. Lawrence A. Cremin, *American Education, the Colonial Experience 1607-1683,* Harper and Row, Publishers, 1970, p. 40.

3. George Bancroft, *History of the United States,* Vol. 2, p. 402, in *CD Sourcebook of American History,* produced by Infobases, 1995.

4. Robert Dearden & Douglas Watson, *The Bible and the Revolution,* in Rosalie J. Slater, *Teaching and Learning America's Christian History,* San Francisco: Foundation for American Christian Education, 1980, p. 142.

5. *Historical Almanac of the U.S. Senate,* p. 30, in CD Sourcebook of American History.

6. *Christopher Columbus's Book of Prophecies,* Reproduction of the Original Manuscript with English Translation, by Kay Brigham, Fort Lauderdale: TSELF, Inc., 1992.

7. Stephen McDowell, "Richard Hakluyt and the Providential Colonization of America," *Providential Perspective,* Vol. 12, no. 1, Feb. 1997, published by the Providence Foundation.

8. Bancroft, Vol. 1, p. 205.

9. Bancroft, Vol. 1, p. 226-227.

10. *Annals of America,* Vol. 1, Chicago: Encyclopedia Britannica, Inc., 1976, p. 103

11. William J. Jackman, *History of the American Nation,* Vol. 2, p. 390, in CD Sourcebook of American History.

12. Bancroft, vol. 2, p. 284-285

13. *For the Colony in Virginea Britannia, Lawes Divine, Morall and Martiall, etc.,* compiled by William Strachey, Edited by David H. Flaherty, The University Press of Virginia, Charlottesville, 1969, pp. 10-11.

14. *The Laws of the Pilgrims,* A facsimile edition of *The Book of the General Laws of the Inhabitants of the Jurisdiction of New Plimouth. 1672 & 1685.* Michael Glazier, Inc. and Pilgrim Society, 1977.

15. *Sources of Our Liberties,* edited by Richard Perry, American Bar Foundation, 1959, p. 120.

16. *American Historical Documents,* The Harvard Classics, Danbury, CT: Grolier Enterprises, 1987, p. 65.

17. Bancroft, Vol. 1, p. 271-272.

18. *Sources of Our Liberties, p. 148.*

19. *Sources of Our Liberties, p. 155.*

20. *See Sources of Our Liberties, pp. 158-159.*

21. *American Historical Documents,* p. 90

22. *The Annals of America,* Vol. 1, p. 199.

23. Ibid. p. 200.

24. Ibid., p. 201.

25. *Significant Documents in US History,* Vol. 1, Richard B. Morris, editor, New York: Van Nostrand Reinhold Co., 1969, p. 19.

26. Ibid., p. 20.

27. *The Pageant of America,* Ralph Henry Gabriel, editor, New Haven: Yale University Press, Vol. 10, 1928, p. 258.

28. *Annals of America,* Vol. 1, p. 203.

29. Edward Kendall, *Kendall's Travels,* New York: I. Riley, 1809, Vol. 1, p. 299-305.

30. "New England's First Fruits in Respect to the Progress of Learning in the College at Cambridge, in Massachusetts Bay," America, Vol. 2, pp. 155-156.

31. *Annals of America,* Vol. 1, p. 464.

32. Alexis DeTocqueville, *Democracy in America,* Vol. 2, p. 58, in CD Sourcebook of American History.

33. *The Pageant of America,* 10:258.

34. Ibid.

35. *The New England Primer,* facsimile of 1777 edition, published by WallBuilders, 1991.

36. Noah Webster, *The Elementary Spelling Book,* New York: D. Appleton & Co., 1880.

37. *The Earliest Diary of John Adams*, ed. L.H. Butterfield, Cambridge, MA: The Belknap Press of Harvard Univ. Press, 1966, 1:9.

38. Benjamin Rush, *Letters of Benjamin Rush*, L.H. Butterfield, ed., Princeton, New Jersey: American Philosophical Society, 1951, Vol. 1, p. 521.

39. Benjamin Rush, *Essays, Literary, Moral and Philosophical*, Philadelphia: printed by Thomas and William Bradford, 1806, p. 113.

40. *Works of Fisher Ames*, as published by Seth Ames (1854), edited and enlarged by W.B. Allen, Vol. 1, Indianapolis: Liberty Classics, 1983, p. 12.

41. *Writings of Samuel Adams*, edited by Henry Alonzo Cushing, Vol. 4, New York, 1908. In *The Christian History of the American Revolution,* Verna M. Hall, compiler, San Francisco: Foundation for American Christian Education, 1976, p.82.

42. William Wirt, *Sketches of the Life and Character of Patrick Henry,* Philadelphia: James Webster, publisher, 1818, p. 402.

43. Noah Webster, *History of the United States*, New Haven: Durrie & Peck, 1833, p. v.

44. Noah Webster, *Value of the Bible and Excellence of the Christian Religion*, 1834. Republished by Foundation for American Christian Education, 1988, p. 78.

45. John Jay, *John Jay: The Winning of the Peace.* Unpublished Papers 1780-1784, Richard B. Morris, editor, New York: Harper & Row Publishers, 1980, Vol. 2, p. 709.

46. *Letters of John Quincy Adams to His Son on the Bible and Its Teachings* (Auburn: James M. Alden, 1850), pp. 9-21.

47. Cited in *A Christian History of the American Republic* by Walker Whitman, 1939.

48. James Madison, *Notes of Debates in the Federal Convention of 1787*, New York: W.W. Norton & Co., 1987, p. 426.

49. Jackman, Vol. 9, pp. 2690-2691.

50. Edward Beardsley, *Life and Times of William Samuel Johnson,* Boston: Houghton, Mifflin and Company, 1886, pp. 141-142.

51. Bernard C. Steiner, *One Hundred and Ten Years of Bible Society Work in Maryland*, Baltimore: Maryland Bible Society, 1921, p. 14.

52. *Addresses and Speeches on Various Occasions*, Boston: Little, Brown & Co., 1852, p. 172.

53. *American Eloquence: A Collection of Speeches and Addresses, by the Most Eminent Orators of America*, Frank Moore, editor, New York: D. Appleton and Co., 1858, Vol. 2, p. 263.

54. Donald Lutz, "The Relative Influence of European Writers on Late 18th Century American Political Thought," *American Political Science Review*, LXXVIII (1984), p. 189-197.

55. Bancroft, Vol. 4, p.95.

56. Benjamin Rush, *Minutes of the Proceedings of a Convention of Delegates from the Abolition Societies Established in Different Parts of the United States Assembled at Philadelphia* (Philadelphia: Zachariah Poulson, 1794), p. 24.

57. Bancroft, Vol. 3, p. 412-413.

58. "The Underground Railroad," Levi Coffin, *America*, Vol. 7, p. 157, in CD Sourcebook of American History.

59. Jackman, Vol.4, p. 1097-1098.

60. "Eliot's Brief Narrative (1670)", *American Historical Documents*, p. 141.

61. DeTocqueville, Vol.2, p. 152.

62. DeTocqueville, Vol.1, p. 322.

63. DeTocqueville, Vol. 2, p. 374.

64. Noah Webster, *Value of the Bible and Excellence of the Christian Religion*, 1834. Republished by Foundation for American Christian Education, San Francisco, 1988, p. 78.

Chapter 5

Pastors and American Independence

"To the pulpit, the Puritan pulpit, we owe the moral force which won our independence."[1] Thus wrote J. Wingate Thorton summarizing the role of the clergy in the birth of our nation. Such a significant role did not begin at the time of the American Revolution, but it was one that the church and her ministers had played from the beginning of the colonies. In fact, pastors were involved in colonizing our states, writing our laws and constitutions, starting our schools and colleges, and serving as leaders in all areas of civil government.[2]

As the primary educators of the colonial period, the clergy had a tremendous impact upon the character and thinking of the people. Professor Harry S. Stout of Yale University writes: "The average weekly churchgoer in New England (and there were far more churchgoers than church members) listened to something like seven thousand sermons in a lifetime, totaling somewhere around fifteen thousand hours of concentrated listening." These statistics become even more significant when one considers there were essentially no "competing public speakers offering alternative messages. For all intents and purposes, the sermon was the only regular voice of authority."[3]

Ministers were the primary educators not only at churches but also at schools, academies, and colleges. Many of the Founding Fathers were tutored by ministers, including Thomas Jefferson, James Madison, George Mason, Patrick Henry, and Noah Webster. Those who attended college would have been trained by ministers as well.

These and others factors led Alice Baldwin to write that "the Constitutional Convention and the written Constitution were the children of the pulpit."[4] Pastors in early America provided leadership in all areas — they prayed, taught, led, and fought. They literally discipled this nation.

Pastors Prayed

One of the first acts of the First Continental Congress that met in Philadelphia on September 5, 1774, was to call for the session to be opened in prayer. Rev. Jacob Duché of Christ Church was asked to conduct the opening service, which he did on the morning of September 7. John Adams recorded the historic event in a letter to his wife:

> Next morning he appeared with his clerk and having on his pontificals, and read several prayers in the established form, and then read the Psalter for the seventh day of September, which was the thirty-fifth Psalm. You must remember that this was the next morning after we had heard of the horrible cannonade of Boston [the account proved to be an error]. It seemed as if heaven had ordered that Psalm to be read on that morning. After this, Mr. Duché, unexpectedly to everybody, struck out into extemporary prayer, which filled the bosom of every man present. I must confess, I never heard a better prayer, or one so well pronounced.[5]

The prayer was in part:

> Be thou present, O God of wisdom! And direct the councils of this honorable assembly, enable them to settle things on the best and surest foundation, that the scene of blood may be effectually restored, and truth and justice, religion and piety, prevail and flourish amongst Thy people.[6]

Jacob Duché was later arrested by the British for serving as chaplain to Congress.

Pastors throughout the colonies prayed similarly throughout the war. They prayed when the states and Congress declared Days of Fasting and Prayer and Thanksgiving. They prayed in their churches and in their homes. And they prayed with the troops on the battlefield.

Presbyterian pastor and chaplain of the Pennsylvania militia, George Duffield, was frequently in camp, where "his visits were always welcome, for the soldiers loved the eloquent, earnest, fearless patriot." Duffield had become a chaplain after closing one Sunday sermon with the words: "There are too many men in this congregation. . . . Next Sunday there'll be one less!"

Historian J.T. Headley gives the following incident of the courageous Duffield:

> When the enemy occupied Staten Island, and the American forces were across the river on the Jersey shore, he repaired to camp to spend the Sabbath. Assembling a portion of the troops in an orchard, he climbed into the forks of a tree and commenced religious exercises. He gave out a

hymn. . . . The British on the island heard the sound of the singing, and immediately directed some cannon to play on the orchard, from whence it proceeded. Soon the heavy shot came crashing through the branches, and went singing overhead, arresting for a moment the voices that were lifted in worship. Mr. Duffield . . . proposed that they should adjourn behind an adjacent hillock. They did so, and continued their worship, while the iron storm hurled harmlessly overhead.[7]

Pastors Taught

Through their Biblical teaching, pastors guided the America people through their struggle for independence and freedom.

Rev. George Duffield was pastor of Pine Street Presbyterian Church from 1772 to 1790. He served as chaplain of the Continental Congress and of the Pennsylvania militia during the war. Duffield delivered many fiery, patriotic sermons to the many prominent men who attended his church. He inspired many to action, including John Adams, who was a member of his congregation while in Philadelphia.

In May 1776 John Adams listened to a sermon of Rev. Duffield that likened the way King George III treated the Americans to the way Pharaoh had treated the Israelites. Duffield concluded that God intended for the Americans to be liberated just as He intended the Israelites to be liberated. On May 17 Adams wrote to his wife:

> Is it not a saying of Moses, Who am I that I should go in and out before this great people? When I consider the great events which are passed, and those greater which are rapidly advancing, and that I may have been instrumental in touching some springs, and turning some small wheels, which have had and will have such effects, I feel an awe upon my mind, which is not easily described. Great Britain has at last driven America to the last step, complete separation from her; a total, absolute independence.[8]

J.T. Headley writes of the influence of Rev. Duffield:

> The patriots of the first Congress flocked to his church, and John Adams and his compeers were often his hearers. . . . In a discourse delivered before several companies of the Pennsylvania militia and members of Congress, four months before the Declaration of Independence, he took bold and decided ground in favor of that step, and pleaded his cause with sublime eloquence, which afterwards made him so obnoxious to the British that they placed a reward of fifty pounds for his capture.[9]

Later on in that sermon, Duffield delivered a prophetic word we must heed today:

> Whilst sun and moon endure, America shall remain a city of refuge for the whole earth, until she herself shall play the tyrant, forget her destiny, disgrace her freedom, and provoke her God.[10]

Pastors Led

Ministers led the fight for both religious and civil liberty from America's earliest years. Rev. Roger Williams and Rev. Thomas Hooker were champions of the idea of liberty of conscience. Williams was one of the first men to maintain

> that the civil magistrate has no compulsive jurisdiction in the concerns of religion; that the punishment of any person on account of his opinions was an encroachment on conscience and an act of persecution. . . . It is worthy of note, that the sentiments respecting toleration which he first proclaimed, and for which he was severely persecuted . . . are now the unanimous opinions of this great nation.[11]

Another leader in the struggle for religious freedom was Francis Makemie. In 1680 Colonel William Stevens and a number of Presbyterians in Maryland asked the Presbytery of Laggan in Ireland to send a Godly minister to help them form a church. In response Francis Makemie was sent and under his leadership the first Presbyterian Church in America was organized and was called Rehoboth Church. (It was named after Stevens' plantation which was begun in 1665. He had chosen the name from Genesis 26:22.) For many years Makemie traveled and preached and organized churches. Though he had a certificate from the court to preach in Maryland, he still faced many trying times. His greatest trial, though, occurred in New York.

His arrest and subsequent trial in 1707 link him as a leader in the struggle for religious liberty. After preaching in the city of New York a warrant was issued for his arrest. The charge, signed by Lord Cornbury, said that he had taken upon himself "to Preach in a Private House, without having obtained My Licence for so doing, which is directly contrary to the known Laws of England."[12]

When brought before Lord Cornbury, Makemie said: "We have Liberty from an Act of Parliament, made the first year of the Reign of King William and Queen Mary, which gave us Liberty, with which Law we have complied." But Lord Cornbury replied: "No one shall Preach in my Government without my Licence. . . . That Law does not extend to the American Plantations, but only to England. . . . I know, for I was at Making thereof. . . . That Act of Parliament was made against Strowling Preachers, and you are such, and shall not Preach in my Government."[13] Makemie refused to pay bail and to agree to preach no more, so he was imprisoned. He defended himself at the trial and was found "not guilty," but was forced to pay all court costs. It cost Makemie more than 80 pounds (a tremendous sum) when all expenses were totaled for the trial.

The great burden of the arrest and trial hastened his death a few months later. But he had not suffered in vain, for his struggles for religious liberty were to bear much fruit in the years to come. It was another dissenting minister, John Leland of Virginia, who played an important role in the proposal and approval of the Virginia Statute for Religious Freedom (1786), which was a culminating event in the development of religious freedom.

James Caldwell

Rev. James Caldwell was pastor of the First Presbyterian Church of Elizabeth Town, New Jersey. Members of his congregation included William Livingston, the Governor of the State, Elias Boudinot, Commissary General of Prisons and President of the Congress, Abraham Clark, one of the signers of the Declaration of Independence, and more than 40 commissioned officers of the Continental Army. In 1776 Caldwell was chosen chaplain of the regiment that was largely composed of members of his church. Later he became Assistant Commissary General.

John T. Faris writes:

> The British called him the *Fighting Chaplain,* and he was cordially hated because of his zeal for the cause of the patriots. His life was always in danger, and when he was able to spend a Sunday with his congregation he would preach with his cavalry pistols on the pulpit, while sentinels were stationed at the doors to give warning.[14]

Caldwell sought to defend himself from his enemies because he felt he was engaged in "the cause of God and that cause he did not consider would be advanced by yielding himself unresistingly into the hands of a skulking Tory to be dragged to the scaffold."[15]

> The enmity of the British led to the burning of the chaplain's church, and the murder, a few months later, of Mrs. Caldwell. While she was sitting in a rear room at the house at Connecticutt Farms, where she had been sent for safety, surrounded by her children, a soldier thrust his musket through the window and fired at her.[16]

Mrs. Caldwell was killed. Soldiers then set the house on fire. Neighbors rescued the Caldwell's nine children and the body of Mrs. Caldwell. Upon hearing of this tragedy, Rev. Caldwell returned from camp to bury his wife. He then made arrangements for the care of his children and returned to the battlefield.

A few weeks later the following incident occurred:

> The British under General Knyphausen, determined to drive Washington and his men from the New Jersey hills and to destroy his supplies, marched from Elizabeth Town on June 23, 1780. There were five thousand men, with fifteen or twenty pieces of artillery, in the expedition. A few miles away, near Springfield, was a small company of patriots, poorly equipped but ready to die in the defence of their country.
>
> Warning of the approach of the enemy was given to the Continentals by the firing of the eighteen-pounder signal gun on Prospect Hill; twelve Continentals stationed at the Cross Roads, after firing on the enemy, had hurried to the hill. After firing the gun they lighted the tar barrel on the signal pole.
>
> Instantly the members of the militia dropped their scythes, seized their muskets, and hurried to quarters. "There were no feathers in their caps, no gilt buttons on their home-spun coats, nor flashing bayonets on their old fowling pieces . . . but there was in their hearts the resolute purpose to defend their homes and their liberty at the price of their lives."
>
> The sturdy farmers joined forces with the regular soldiers. For a time the battle was fierce. The enemy were soon compelled to retreat, but not before they had burned the village. . . . Chaplain James Caldwell was in the hottest of the fight. "Seeing the fire of one of the companies slacking for want of wadding, he galloped to the Presbyterian meeting house nearby, and rushing in, ran from pew to pew, filling his arms with hymn books," wrote Headley, in *Chaplains and Clergy of the Revolution.* "Hastening back with them into the battle, he scattered them about in every direction, saying as he pitched one here and another there, 'Now put Watts into them, boys.' With a laugh and a cheer they pulled out the leaves, and ramming home the charge did give the British Watts with a will."[17]
>
> Mr. Caldwell survived the war, in spite of the efforts of the British to capture him, only to be murdered on November 24, 1781, by a Continental soldier who was thought to have been bribed by those whose enmity the chaplain had earned during the conflict.[18]

During the Revolution the people of Horseneck (now Caldwell), New Jersey began organizing a new church. Since James Caldwell provided them much support in their initial endeavors, they renamed their church, Caldwell, in his honor after his death. The first pastor of this church was

Rev. Stephen Grover, who served in this capacity for 46 years. His successor was Rev. Richard F. Cleveland. Rev. Cleveland's son, who was born in the church manse in 1837, was named after the first pastor at Caldwell Presbyterian Church. Stephen Grover Cleveland would later serve two terms as President of the United States (1885-1889, 1893-1897).

Samuel Davies

Rev. Samuel Davies was a bold ambassador for Christ. In his desire to see the Kingdom of God come *on earth as it is in heaven* he served not only as a pastor but also as a lawyer, an ambassador to England, and President of Princeton College. E.L. Magoon writes that

> he had made himself a thorough master of English law, civil and ecclesiastical, and always chose to meet every persecuting indictment in the highest courts with his own plea. . . . [H]e went to England and obtained the explicit sanction of the highest authority with respect to the extension of the Toleration law to Virginia. It was during this mission that . . . George II and many of his court were in the congregation of this American Dissenter. His majesty, struck with admiration, or forgetting the proprieties of the occasion, spoke several times to those around him and smiled. Davies paused a moment, and then looking sternly at the king, exclaimed, "When the lion roars, the beasts of the forest all tremble; and when King Jesus speaks, the princes of earth should keep silence."[19]

Davies, one of the greatest orators in colonial America, served as the mentor for the man Jefferson called "the greatest orator that ever lived" — Patrick Henry. When Patrick was around 12 years old his mother joined the church where Samuel Davies preached. Mrs. Henry would attend regularly and always take Patrick, who from the first showed a high appreciation for the preacher. Each Sunday as they rode home in their buggy, Mrs. Henry and Patrick would review the sermon. This greatly influenced Patrick and the development of his oratorical skills. Patrick ever declared that Davies was "the greatest orator he ever heard."[20] But Patrick Henry also learned from Davies a sound Biblical theology, one which has produced some of the leading men in all history. William Wirt Henry writes: "His early example of eloquence . . . was Mr. Davies, and the effect of his teaching upon his after life may be plainly traced."[21] Pastors today should be mentors for our youth, inspiring and equipping them to lead in all areas of life.

Many other ministers provided leadership in significant ways. Rev. Jonas Clark of Lexington, Massachusetts, prepared his congregation to pay whatever price was necessary for liberty. Some of his church members were the first to give their lives for the cause of American independence on the morning of April 19, 1775. Rev. John Witherspoon not only signed the Declaration of Independence, but as President of the College of New Jersey (now Princeton) he trained one fifth of the men who gave us the Constitution, including its chief architect, James Madison.

Pastors Fought

Peter Muhlenberg

So many ministers participated in the war for independence that they were called "the Black Regiment," in reference to their pulpit gowns, by the opposition. One member of the "Black Regiment," Peter Muhlenberg, is honored by a statue in the United States Capitol Building. Benson J. Lossing writes of his beginning involvement:

> In those days politics were preached in the pulpits and men were led to action on the side of freedom by faithful pastors. The eminent General Muhlenberg was one of this stamp. When the war for independence was kindling, he was a clergymen in Virginia, and at the close of 1775, he concluded a sermon with the words of Scripture: "There is a time for all things—a time to preach and a time to pray;" but those times, he said, had passed away; and then, in a voice that sounded like a trumpet-blast through the church, he exclaimed: "There is a time to fight, and that time has now come." Then laying aside his sacerdotal gown, he stood before his flock in the full uniform of a Virginia colonel. He ordered the drums to be beaten at the church door for recruits; and almost the entire male audience, capable of bearing arms, joined his standard. Nearly three hundred men enlisted his banner on that day.[22]

Rev. Peter Muhlenberg became one of Washington's primary Brigadier Generals in the Continental Army. As a minister, his brother, Frederick, first opposed his involvement in civil affairs. Headley writes:

> It is but just to the memory of this unflinching patriot to let him be heard in his own defence for his course in abandoning the pulpit for the army. In a letter to his brother Frederick, a clergyman also, who had written to another brother condemning his (Peter's) course for laying aside the ministerial profession for that of arms, he says: "Thus far I had written when I received brother Henry's letter from you to him, wherein you make observations on my conduct in the present alarming crisis. You say, as a clergyman nothing can excuse my conduct. I am a clergyman, it is true, but I am a member of society as well as the poorest layman, and my liberty is

as dear to me as to any man. Shall I then sit still, and enjoy myself at home, when the best blood of the continent is spilling? Heaven forbid it! . . .

But even if you was on the opposite side of the question, you must allow that in this last step I have acted for the best. You know that from the beginning of these troubles I have been compelled to have a hand in public affairs. I h ave b een c hairman t o the c ommittee o f d elegates from t his county from the first. *Do you think, if America should be conquered, I should be safe?* Far from it. *And would you not sooner fight like a man than die like a dog?* I am called by my country to its defence. The cause is just and noble. Were I a bishop, even a Lutheran one, I should obey without hesitation, and so far am I from thinking that I am wrong, I am convinced it is my duty so to do, a duty I owe to my God and to my country."

This same Frederick, notwithstanding his condemnation of his brother, two or three years later, under the pressure of the Revolution, left the church for the state, and entered Congress under the Federal Constitution.[23]

Frederick A.C. Muhlenberg was elected the first speaker of the House of Representatives in 1789.

Naphtali Dagget

Another minister, even though growing old in age, readily took up arms to defend the cause of liberty. J.T. Headley records the story of Rev. Dagget.

NAPHTHALI DAGGET, D.D., professor of divinity, and for a time President of Yale College, was another distinguished clergyman, who was as illustrious for his patriotism as for his theological learning. He instructed the students in the duty of resistance to Great Britain as earnestly as he did in that of obedience to God; indeed, he regarded them as one and the same duty.

In 1779, the college had recovered from the panic that had scattered the students into various towns in the interior, and was in a prosperous condition. But, in the midst of its tranquillity, a rumor reached New Haven that General Tryon was preparing to make a descent upon it. The place was immediately thrown into great alarm, and a meeting was called to deliberate on w hat was to be done. Counsels were various as to the best course to pursue, but Dr. Dagget declared that whatever else was determined upon, one thing was clear, *the citizens must fight.*

At length the dreaded calamity came, and swift riders galloped into town, bringing the startling news that the British, twenty-five hundred strong, had landed about five miles distant at West Haven. At once all was confusion and terror. The college was hurriedly broken up, and, as all regarded it useless to attempt to resist so large a body of regular troops, it was determined that early in the morning the inhabitants and students should take their flight into the interior, and leave the place to the mercy of the marauders. To give the former as much time as possible to remove their goods, a volunteer company of a hundred young men was formed, to retard the march of the British, by beating back their advance guards. Accordingly they assembled on the green, with such arms as they could lay their hands on, and paraded in front of the deserted college. The streets were filled with the terrified fugitives, as in wagons, on horseback, and on foot, they streamed towards the country. It was a scene of wild confusion, and contrasted strangely with that courageous little detachment preparing to go forth against such an overwhelming force.

At length every thing being ready, drum and fife struck up a lively strain, and taking up its line of march, the band passed out of the city. It had not proceeded far, when the clatter of horse's hoofs was heard along the road, and the next moment the reverend professor of divinity galloped up on his old black mare, with a long fowling-piece in his hand. He had not contented himself with giving good patriotic advice, but had resolved to set an example. To their surprise, however, he did not stop to join them, but pushed straight on towards the enemy. The little band gave him a loud cheer as he passed, but the old man never turned to the right or left, but dashed resolutely onward, and, ascending a hill, halted in a grove, and commenced reconnoitering the enemy.

The detachment, turning a little to the south, swept round the base of the hill, and kept on till they came in sight of the advance guard of the British; when, throwing themselves behind a fence, they poured in a destructive volley. The guard halted, and returned the fire. But as volley succeeded volley, each more deadly than the last, they turned and fled. The young volunteers then broke cover, and leaping the fence, pursed them, firing and shouting as they went. Driving them from fence to fence, and across field after field, they kept courageously on, till they suddenly found themselves face to face with the whole hostile army. As for as the eye could reach on either side, the green fields were red with scarlet uniforms — the extended wings ready, at the word of command, to enfold them, and cut off every avenue of escape. Suddenly halting, and taking in the full extent of their danger, they without waiting for orders, turned, and ran for their lives.

As they fled along the base of the hill, on the top of which Dr. Dagget had taken his station, they saw the venerable man quietly watching the advancing enemy. As the noise and confusion of the flying detachment reached his ears he turned a quiet glance below, then leveling his fowling-piece at the foe, blazed away. As the British pressed after the fugitives, they were surprised at the solitary report of a gun every few minutes from the grove of trees on that hill. At first they paid but little attention to it, but the bullets finding their way steadily into the ranks, they were compelled to notice it, and an officer sent a detachment up to see what it meant. The professor saw them coming, but never moved from his position. His black mare stood near him, and he could any moment have mounted and fled, but this seemed never to have entered his head. He was thinking only of the enemy, and loaded and fired as fast as he could.

When the detachment reached the spot where he stood, the commanding officer, to his surprise, saw only a venerable man in black before him, quietly loading his gun to have another shot. Pausing a moment at the extraordinary spectacle of a single man thus coolly fighting a whole army, he explained, "What are you doing there, you old fool, firing on His Majesty's troops?" The staunch old patriot looked up in the most unconcerned manner, and replied, "*Exercising the rights of war.*" The whole affair seemed to strike the officer comically; and, rather amused than offended at the audacity of the proceeding, he said, "If I let you go this time, you old rascal, will you ever fire again on the troops of His Majesty?" "*Nothing more likely,*" was the imperturbable reply. This was too much for the good temper of the Briton, and he ordered his men to seize him. They did so; and dragged him roughly down the hill to the head of the column.

The Americans, in their retreat, had torn down the bridge over the river, after crossing it, thus compelling the British to march two miles farther north to another bridge. The latter immediately placed Dr. Dagget, on foot, at the head of the column as a guide, and pressed rapidly forward.

It was the 5th of July, and one of the hottest days of the year. Under the burning rays of the noonday sun, and the driving pace they were kept at, even the hardened soldiers wilted; while Dr. Dagget, unused to such exposure, soon became completely exhausted. But the moment he showed signs of faltering, the soldiers pricked him on with their bayonets, at the same time showering curses and insults upon his head. Before the five miles' march was completed, the brave old man was ready to sink to the earth. But every time he paused and reeled as if about to fall, they caught him on the points of their bayonets, and forced him to rally, while the blood flowed in streams down his dress. As they entered the streets of the town, they commenced shooting down the peaceable citizens who had remained behind, and Dr. Dagget expected every moment to share their fate. At length they reached the green, when a tory, who had come out to welcome the enemy, recognised Dr. Dagget, as he lay covered with blood and dust, and requested the officer to release him. He did so, and the wounded patriot was carried into a house near by, more dead than alive.

His utter exhaustion and brutal wounds combined brought him to the very gates of death, and his life for some time was despaired of. He however rallied, and was able a part of the next year to preach in the chapel, but his constitution had received a shock from which it could not fully re-cover, and in sixteen months he was borne to the grave, one more added to the list of noble souls who felt that the offer of their lives to their country was a small sacrifice.[24]

Pastors took the lead in the battle for American independence. They prayed, preached, taught, and fought. John Adams wrote to his wife from Philadelphia on July 7, 1775, telling her to make sure their minister was preaching patriotically: "Tell him [their pastor, Rev. Wibird] the clergy here, of every denomination, thunder and lighten every Sabbath. They pray for Boston and the Massachusetts. They thank God explicitly and fervently for our remarkable successes. They pray for the American army. They seem to feel as if they were among you."[25]

America needs faithful pastors — those who will pray, who will preach liberty, and who will lead men to action on the side of freedom.

END NOTES

1. J. Wingate Thorton, *The Pulpit of the American Revolution*, 1860, p. XXXVII.

2. For more on this see *America's Providential History* by Mark Beliles and Stephen McDowell, published by the Providence Foundation.

3. Quoted in *Three Churches, One Nation* by Charles Hull Wolfe.

4. Alice Baldwin, *The New England Clergy and the American Revolution*, 1928.

5. John T. Faris, *Historic Shrines of America*, New York: George H. Doran Co., 1918, pp. 150-151.

6. Faris, p. 151.

7. Faris, p. 161.

8. Quoted in Faris, p. 160.

9. Quoted in Faris, p. 160-161.

10. Faris, p. 161.

11. E. L. Magoon, *Orators of the American Revolution*, New York: C. Scribner, 1857, pp. 201-202.

12. Faris, p. 213.

13. Faris, p. 214.

14. Faris, p. 120-121.

15. J.T. Headley, in Faris, p. 121.

16. Faris, p. 121.

17. Faris, pp. 138-140.

18. Faris, p. 121.

19. Magoon, pp. 207-208.

20. William Wirt Henry, *Patrick Henry, Life, Correspondence and Speeches*, Vol. 1, 1891, p. 15.

21. Ibid., p. 16.

22. Quoted in *Teaching and Learning America's Christian History*, Rosalie Slater, p. 248.

23. J.T. Headley, *The Chaplains and Clergy of the Revolution*, (New York: Charles Scribner, 1864).

24. Ibid.

25. Magoon, p. 220.

Chapter 6

The American Christian Revolution
Religion and Morality: Foundation of America's Liberty and Independence

On July 8th, 1776, the Liberty Bell rang out from the State House in Philadelphia, calling together the assembly of the citizens to hear the first public reading of the *Declaration of Independence*, which had been approved four days before. Its ringing led the celebration that followed.

A scripture was engraved on that bell, Leviticus 25:10 — "Proclaim Liberty throughout all the land, unto all the inhabitants thereof. Lev. XXV, X". This verse was very appropriate because it speaks of the jubilee year of liberty, where debts were forgiven, land was returned to the original owners, and enslaved Israelites were set free. With the birth of America, a new era of liberty was beginning in the world. As Rev. Jonas Clark stated concerning events initiating the independence of America, "From this day will be dated the liberty of the world!"[1]

God's liberty could be proclaimed, and eventually secured, because the people had been prepared from within to support freedom. A foundation of religion, morality, and Biblical truth had been established in their lives.

George Washington said in his *Farewell Address* in 1796: "Of all the dispositions and habits which lead to political prosperity, religion and morality are indispensable supports."[2] In 1797 Washington wrote: "Religion and Morality are the essential pillars of Civil society."[3]

External liberty comes from internal liberty.

Our external liberty is a product of the internal liberty in the heart of the American people, which is reflected in the leaders in early America. An example in the life of George Washington illustrates this well.

As the Revolutionary War was coming to a close, a number of officers and soldiers began to grumble due to the many problems that existed in the new nation, including their lack of pay. As a solution to the problems that Congress seemed unable to resolve, many officers wanted to set up a monarchy making George Washington king. (This was not unusual, for most of the world was ruled by kings or monarchs, and most civil wars ended with a new monarch replacing the old.) Col. Lewis Nicola proposed the idea to him in a letter in the Spring of 1782. Washington could have possibly become king, for the army and the people would have supported him. Washington's response reveals well the heart of this great man. In a letter to Colonel Lewis Nicola dated May 22, 1782, he wrote:

> Sir, With a mixture of great surprise and astonishment, I have read with attention the sentiments you have submitted to my perusal. Be assured, Sir, no occurrence in the course of the war has given me more painful sensations, than your information of their being such ideas existing in the army, as you have expressed, and I must view with abhorrence and reprehend with severity. . . .
>
> I am much at a loss to conceive what part of my conduct could have given encouragement to an address, which to me seems big with the greatest mischiefs, that can befall my country. If I am not deceived in the knowledge of my self, you could not have found a person to whom your schemes are more disagreeable.[4]

Washington's response to the proposition of his being declared king was, first, to rebuke the officer who suggested the idea, and then to look within himself to see if his heart or actions were in anyway in agreement with the idea, because he said as far as he knew, he was more against the idea than anyone.

Our external liberty is a product of the internal ideas and character of the citizens and leaders of our nation. Had Washington been like many of our leaders today we might have established a monarchy, and certainly we would have less freedom. It was men like Washington, who gave us this land of liberty. He was a reflection of the American people, for our leaders are a reflection of the character and thinking of our citizens. This was true then, and is still true today.

Our founders gave birth to the most free nation in history. We have the great task of restoring liberty to the land — of planting the seeds of liberty.

Christianity is the source of liberty, both personal and civil.

Historian of the American Revolution, David Ramsay, said: "There can be no political happiness, without liberty; there can be no liberty without morality; and there can be no morality, without religion."[5]

When our founders spoke of religion, they meant Christianity, for Christianity was true religion to them. Noah Webster wrote in his *History of the United States*, 1832:

> Almost all the civil liberty now enjoyed in the world owes its origin to the principles of the Christian religion. . . The religion which has introduced civil liberty, is the religion of Christ and his apostles, which enjoins humility, piety, and benevolence; which acknowledges in every person a brother, or a sister, and a citizen with equal rights. This is genuine Christianity, and to this we owe our free constitutions of government.[6]

Signer of the Declaration Benjamin Rush wrote in 1806:

> Christianity is the only true and perfect religion, and that in proportion as mankind adopt its principles and obeys its precepts, they will be wise and happy.[7]

The United States House of Representatives declared in 1854:

> [T]he great vital and conservative element in our system is the belief of our people in the pure doctrines and divine truths of the gospel of Jesus Christ.[8]

Our founders knew that the Bible and history teach that the most free nations have been those that have best applied the principles of Christianity in every sphere of society. They agreed with Thomas Jefferson's pastor, Rev. Charles Clay, as he said in an Artillery Sermon, c. 1777, that "the sacred cause of liberty [is] the cause of God."[9]

Jesus and Liberty

Jesus came to set us free, both internally and externally. Galatians 5:1 states: "It was for freedom that Christ set us free." He gave us internal freedom from the bondage of sin as well as external freedom from the fruit of sin in the earth. He came to give us both personal and civil freedom. He came to not only bring internal personal salvation, but also external political freedom.

In what could be called Jesus' inaugural address (Luke 4:18-19), He tells us that He was sent to proclaim release to the captives and to set at liberty those who are oppressed. Jesus manifested the kingdom of God by liberating man, physically, mentally, and spiritually, and casting out Satan and his cohorts, who seek only to destroy and bring man into bondage.

In Acts 1:6 Jesus' disciples asked Him when the Kingdom of God would be restored? They were thinking of an external kingdom. They thought the messiah would set up such a kingdom and deliver them from external bondage. How did Jesus respond to this question? He did not deny that the Kingdom would be manifested externally on the earth. He said that times and epochs would follow that would contribute to bringing God's rule and reign on the earth (see Acts 1:7-8). We can look back over the centuries and see those times and epochs. Since the time of Christ there has been no end to the increase of His government or Kingdom in the earth — it has grown steadily. But Jesus did correct their wrong understanding of how the Kingdom would come. He said it would first be birthed within man's heart (the Kingdom of God is within you) which would then flow out from him and affect every sphere of life.

God's plan is to bring liberty to man, both internal and external, spiritual and physical, personal and civil. God is the author of liberty — all liberty. "Where the Spirit of the Lord is, there is liberty" (2 Cor. 3:17).

America and Liberty

The story of America's independence reveals there would be no liberty without Christianity. Though this story starts centuries before, we will began in the year 1765 and look briefly at some of the events that resulted in our becoming a nation — and in so doing see the central role that Christianity played.

To pay for the debt of the French and Indian War, England imposed a tax upon the colonists through the Stamp Act. The colonists were not opposed to paying for their defense, but they were opposed to the idea of the Parliament being able to tax them without their consent, or the consent of their representatives, for this violated the principle of property. One man who led the opposition to the Stamp Act was Patrick Henry in Virginia.

In May, 1765, Patrick Henry was elected to the House of Burgesses from Louisa County. The topic of foremost concern for the Virginia legislature was the newly passed Stamp Act. Though Henry was a novice at the assembly, when he found no one willing to oppose the tax he felt compelled to take action, so he wrote down some resolutions on his own. He would later write of the events:

> Upon offering them to the house, violent debates ensued. Many threats were uttered, and much abuse cast on me, by the party for submission. Af-

ter a long and warm contest, the resolutions passed by a very small major-ity, perhaps of one or two only. The alarm spread throughout America with astonishing quickness, and the ministerial party were overwhelmed. The great point of resistance to British taxation was universally estab-lished in the colonies. This brought on the war, which finally separated the two countries, and gave independence to ours. Whether this will prove a blessing or a curse, will depend upon the use our people make of the bless-ings which a gracious God hath bestowed on us. If they are wise, they will be great and happy. If they are of a contrary character, they will be misera-ble. — Righteousness alone can exalt them as a nation. Reader! whoever thou art, remember this; and in thy sphere, practice virtue thyself, and en-courage it in others.[10]

During the debates on his resolutions, Patrick Henry spoke out boldly against the Stamp Act saying that only the legislatures of the colonies had the right to tax the American people. On the floor of the House of Bur-gesses he went on to say:

"Caesar had his Brutus; Charles the First, his Cromwell; and George the Third . . ."
"Treason! Treason!" shouted the Speaker of the House.
"Treason! Treason!" echoed from every part of the room.
Without faltering for an instant, and fixing on the Speaker an eye that flashed fire, the orator added—
". . . may profit by their example. If this be treason, make the most of it."[11]

In his autobiography, Jefferson said of Henry's speech:

I attended the debate at the door of the lobby of the House of Bur-gesses, and heard the splendid display of Mr. Henry's talents as a popular orator. They were great indeed; such as I have never heard from any other man. He appeared to me to speak as Homer wrote.[12]

Patrick Henry wrote on his copies of the resolutions that "they formed the first opposition to the stamp act, and the scheme of taxing America by the British parliament."[13]

Numerous leaders in America attributed to Henry the leading role in the great revolution. William Wirt Henry writes:

America was filled with Mr. Henry's fame, and he was recognized on both sides of the Atlantic as the man who rang the alarm bell which had aroused the continent. His wonderful powers of oratory engaged the atten-tion and excited the admiration of men, and the more so as they were not considered the result of laborious training, but as the direct gift of Heaven.

Long before the British poet applied the description to him, he was recognized as—*the forest-born Demosthenes, Whose thunder shook the Philip of the seas.*[14]

Patrick Henry "was hailed as the leader raised up by Providence for the occasion."[15]

Patrick Henry reflected the faith of most of our founders. In his last will and testament, bearing the date of November 20, 1798, and written throughout, as he says, "with my own hand," he chose to insert a touching affirmation of his own deep faith in Christianity. After distributing his estate among his descendants, he thus concludes: "This is all the inheritance I can give to my dear family. The religion of Christ can give them one which will make them rich indeed."[16]

The Boston Tea Party

The Stamp Act was repealed, but the belief of the English government to tax the colonies without their consent continued with the Townsend Act in 1767 and the Tea Act in 1773. With a tax on tea, the colonists refused to buy English tea and so it began to pile up in warehouses in England. Merchants petitioned the Parliament to do something about this. Parliament's response was to vote to subsidize the tea and make it cheap, thinking the colonists would then buy it. Benjamin Franklin said:

> They have no idea that any people can act from any other principle but that of interest; and they believe that three pence on a pound of tea, of which one does not perhaps drink ten pounds in a year, is sufficient to overcome all the patriotism of an American.[17]

Unfortunately, this may be enough to overcome the patriotism of many Americans today, though thankfully not then. Our founders were men of principle. They reasoned and acted from principles that were rooted in the Bible.

It was not money but principles that motivated the colonists. The attempt of England to tax them without their consent violated the principle of property. The Americans refused to buy the tea even though it was cheap.

When the King decided to send the tea and make the colonists purchase it, patriots in the major shipping ports held town meetings to decide what to do when the tea arrived. When the ships arrived in Boston, the patriots put a guard at the docks to prevent the tea from being unloaded. Almost 7000 people gathered at the Old South Meeting House to hear from Mr. Rotch, the owner of the ships. He explained that if he attempted to sail from Boston without unloading the tea, his life and business would be in danger, for the British said they would confiscate his ships unless the tea was un-loaded by a certain date. The colonists decided, therefore, that in order to protect Mr. Rotch, they must accept the tea, but they wouldn't have to drink it! By accepting the shipment they were agreeing to pay for it, but they would make a radical sacrifice in order to protest this injustice before the eyes of the world. Thus ensued the "Boston Tea Party." To protect the individuals involved, the men disguised themselves as Indians.

Richard Frothingham records the incident:

> The party in disguise ... whooping like Indians, went on board the vessels, and, warning their officers and those of the customhouse to keep out of the way, unlaid the hatches, hoisted the chests of tea on deck, cut them open, and hove the tea overboard. They proved quiet and systematic workers. No one interfered with them. No other property was injured; no person was harmed; no tea was allowed to be carried away; and the silence of the crowd on shore was such that the breaking of the chests was distinctly heard by them. "The whole," Hutchinson wrote, "was done with very little tumult."[18]

Boston Port Bill

When the King got word of what the colonists had done, you might say he was "tead off." The English government responded by passing the Boston Port Bill, which closed the port of Boston and was intended to shut down all commerce on June 1st and starve the townspeople into submission. Committees of Correspondence spread the news by letter through all the colonies. The colonies began to respond. Massachusetts, Connecticut and Virginia called for days of fasting and prayer. Thomas Jefferson penned the resolve in Virginia "to invoke the divine interposition to give to the American people one heart and one mind to oppose by all just means every injury to American rights."[19]

Frothingham writes of the day the Port Act went into effect:

> The day was widely observed as a day of fasting and prayer. The manifestations of sympathy were general. Business was suspended. Bells were muffled, and tolled from morning to night; flags were kept at halfmast; streets were dressed in mourning; public buildings and shops were draped in black; large congregations filled the churches.
>
> In Virginia the members of the House of Burgesses assembled at their place of meeting; went in procession, with the speaker at their head, to the church and listened to a discourse. "Never," a lady wrote, "since my residence in Virginia have I seen so large a congregation as was this day assembled to hear divine service." The preacher selected for his text the

words: "be strong and of good courage, fear not, nor be afraid of them; for
the Lord thy God, He it is that doth go with thee. He will not fail thee not
forsake thee." "The people," Jefferson says, "met generally, with anxiety
and alarm in their countenances; and the effect of the day, through the
whole colony, was like a shock of electricity, arousing every man and
placing him erect and solidly on his centre." These words describe the effect of the Port Act throughout the thirteen colonies.[20]

The colonies responded with material support as well, obtained, not by
governmental decree but, more significantly, by individual action. A grass-
roots movement of zealous workers went door to door to gather patriotic
offerings. These gifts were sent to Boston accompanied with letters of support. Out of the diversity of the colonies, a deep Christian unity was being
revealed on a national level. John Adams spoke of the miraculous nature of
this union: "Thirteen clocks were made to strike together, a perfection of
mechanism which no artist had ever before effected."[21]

Here we see an excellent historical example of the principle of Christian union. The external union of the colonies came about due to an internal
unity of ideas and principles that had been sown in the hearts of the American people by the families and churches. Our national motto reflects this
Christian union: *E Pluribus Unum* (*one from the many*).

The First Continental Congress

Further evidence of our national unity and union was found in the con-
vening of the first Continental Congress in September, 1774. One of the
first acts of the Congress that met in Carpenters Hall in Philadelphia was to
pass the following resolution:

> Resolved, That the reverend Mr. Duché be desired to open the Con-
> gress tomorrow morning with prayers, at the Carpenter's Hall at nine
> o'clock.

The Journal of the Proceeding of Congress records for September 7,
1774:

> Agreeable to the resolve of yesterday, the meeting was opened with
> prayers by the reverend Mr. Duché. Voted, That the thanks of the Con-
> gress be given to Mr. Duché, by Mr. Cushing and Mr. Ward, for perform-
> ing divine service, and for the excellent prayer, which he composed and
> delivered on the occasion.[22]

John Adams wrote to his wife, Abigail, of Rev. Duché's prayer at Congress:

[N]ext Morning he appeared ... and read several Prayers, in the established Form; and then read the Collect for the seventh day of September, which was the Thirty fifth Psalm.—You must remember this was the next Morning after we heard the horrible Rumour, of the Cannonade of Boston.—I never saw a greater Effect upon an Audience. It seemed as if Heaven had ordained that Psalm to be read on that Morning.

After this Mr. Duché, unexpected to every Body struck out into an extemporary Prayer, which filled the Bosom of every Man present. I must confess I never heard a better Prayer or one, so well pronounced. Episcopalian as he is, Dr. Cooper himself never prayed with such fervour, such Ardor, such Earnestness and Pathos, and in Language so elegant and sublime —for America, for the Congress, for The Province of Massachusetts Bay, and especially the Town of Boston, It has had an excellent Effect upon every Body here.[23]

Silas Deane wrote that "Mr. Duché . . . prayed without book about ten minutes so pertinently, with such fervency, purity, and sublimity of style and sentiment . . . that even Quakers shed tears."[24]

The Battle of Lexington

About seven months after the first Continental Congress met in Philadelphia, Paul Revere set out on his famous ride to warn the colonists, and in particular two leaders of the "rebellion," Samuel Adams and John Hancock (who were at Rev. Jonas Clark's home in Lexington), that the British were coming. The shot that was heard around the world took place on the morning of April 19, 1775. Rev. Jonas Clark (upon whose Church lawn fighting began and whose parishioners took part) declared: "From this day will be dated the liberty of the world!"[25]

About one month before the Battle of Lexington, the Governor of Connecticut had called upon the colony to observe a:

Day of public Fasting and Prayer...that God would graciously pour out his Holy Spirit on us, to bring us to a thorough repentance and effectual reformation; . . . That He would restore, preserve and secure the liberties of this, and all the other American Colonies, and make this land a mountain of Holiness and habitation of Righteousness forever. . . . That God would preserve and confirm the Union of the Colonies in the pursuit and practice of that Religion and virtue which will honour Him.[26]

What day had Governor Jonathan Trumbull selected for them to be praying? "Wednesday, the nineteenth Day of April."[27] — the very day fighting had begun!

In response to the battle at Lexington and Concord, England declared Massachusetts would be put under martial law. The response of the Continental Congress was to proclaim the first Colony-wide day of Fasting and Prayer to be observed on July 20, 1775, the day martial law was to go into effect. In the proclamation they appealed to "the Great Governor of the World" who "frequently influences the minds of men to serve the wise and gracious purposes of His providential government." They "recommended to Christians of all denominations to assemble for public . . . Humiliation, Fasting and Prayer."[28] It is estimated that two of the three million inhabitants of America observed this day of fasting and prayer.

The Price the Signers Paid

Fighting had begun, but it would be 14 months before the colonists declared their independence. They still considered themselves Britains and sought all means possible to end the conflict without a total break from England. By July 1776 all the delegates to the Congress had come to agree it was time to declare independence.

The men who signed the *Declaration of Independence* were not thinking *we will be famous,* but rather, as Benjamin Rush later wrote John Adams, that they were signing their "own death warrants."[29] After signing the document with unusually large writing, the President of the Continental Congress, John Hancock, declared: "His majesty can now read my name without glasses. And he can also double the price on my head." Then he went on to say at this tense moment, "we must be unanimous; there must be no pulling different ways; we must all hang together."[30] Benjamin Franklin responded in his characteristic wit, "Yes, we must indeed all hang together, or most assuredly we shall all hang separately!"[31]

Death was a very real possibility, and so the fifty-six men who signed the Declaration did so only after much thought and consideration. After all, they had more to lose than anyone in the colonies. They were the brightest minds, had the greatest talents, many were wealthy with large estates, and most had families they loved dearly. In signing that document they were not considering it as a avenue for fame, glory, or future advancement. They all knew they would be identified above all others by the British as the leaders of the "rebellion", and, consequently, those most likely to suffer retribution. They knew that "history was strewn with the bones and blood of freedom fighters."[32] And they were up against the greatest military power on earth, and so faced a very real chance of losing everything.

They all suffered in some way. Virtually all the men had greater wealth before taking up the cause of liberty than afterwards.

> Nine Signers died of wounds or hardships during the Revolutionary War. Five were captured or imprisoned, in some cases with brutal treatment. The wives, sons, and daughters of others were killed, jailed, mistreated, persecuted, or left penniless. One was driven from his wife's deathbed and lost all his children. The houses of twelve Signers were burned to the ground. Seventeen lost everything they owned. Every Signer was proscribed as a traitor; every one was hunted. Most were driven into flight; most were at one time or another barred from their families or homes. Most were offered immunity, freedom, rewards, their property, or the lives and release of loved ones to break their pledged word or to take the King's protection. Their fortunes were forfeit, but their honor was not. No Signer defected, or changed his stand, throughout the darkest hours. Their honor, like the nation, remained intact.[33]

These men have died and most have been forgotten by Americans today. It is sad that we have forgotten these founders of America, but it is tragic that we have forgotten the high price they paid for liberty—that liberty which we possess today, but may lose if we forget its great cost.

Since our liberty and happiness is a result of faith and morality, we must cry out to God, seek to obey Him, and imitate His Son.

John Adams wrote that the day of Independence

> will be the most memorable epocha in the history of America.—I am apt to believe that it will be celebrated, by succeeding generations...as the day of deliverance, by solemn acts of devotion to God Almighty,... from one end of this continent to the other, from this time forward forever more.[34]

We as a nation have forgotten how our founders said the Fourth of July should be celebrated, for we have forgotten the source of and the price paid for our liberty. Each July 4th should be celebrated with "acts of devotion to God Almighty," and this holiday should also remind us to remember that God is the giver of life and liberty, for if we forget Him we shall surely lose our liberty.

End Notes

1. Franklin Cole, ed., *They Preached Liberty*, Indianapolis, p. 39.

2. George Washington's Farewell Address, September 17, 1796, *A Compilation of the Messages and Papers of the Presidents*, by James D. Richardson, Washington: Bureau of National Literature and Art, 1910, 1:205-216.

3. Letter to the Clergy of Different Denominations Residing in and near the City of Philadelphia, March 3, 1797.

4. Letter to Colonel Lewis Nicola, Newburg, 22 May 1782, *The Writings of George Washington,* Vol. 8, Jared Sparks, Ed., Boston, 1835.

5. *Maxims of Washington*, compiled by John Frederick Schroeder, New York: D. Appleton & Co., 1854, p. 352.

6. Noah Webster, *History of the United States*, New Haven: Durrie & Peck, 1833, pp. 273-274.

7. Benjamin Rush, *Essays, Literary, Moral and Philosophical*, Philadelphia: printed by Thomas and William Bradford, 1806, p. 93.

8. B.F. Morris, *Christian Life and Character of the Civil Institutions of the United States*, Philadelphia: George W. Childs, 1864, p. 328.

9. Charles Clay, Sermon on *The Governor Among the Nations*, contained in the Clay Family Papers (Mss 1c5795a), Virginia Historical Society, Richmond, Virginia.

10. William Wirt, *Sketches of the Life and Character of Patrick Henry*, Philadelphia: James Webster, publisher, 1818, p. 58.

11. Francis Simkins et al, *Virginia: History, Government, Geography,* New York: Charles Scribner's Sons, 1964, p. 231.

12. William Wirt Henry, *Patrick Henry, Life, Correspondence and Speeches*, Vol. 1, 1891, p. 83.

13. Wirt, p. 58.

14. W.W. Henry, p. 101.

15. W.W. Henry, p. 94.

16. Patrick Henry's Will. From a photocopy in our possession.

17. Verna Hall, *The Christian History of the Constitution of the United States of America*, San Francisco: Foundation of American Christian Education, 1980, p. 328.

18. Mark Beliles and Stephen McDowell, *America's Providential History*, Charlottesville, VA: Providence Foundation, 1989, p. 131.

19. Ibid., p. 131.

20. Ibid, p. 131-132.

21. *The Patriots*, Virginius Dabney, editor, New York: Atheneum, 1975, p. 7.

22. *Journal of the Proceedings of the Congress Held at Philadelphia September 5, 1774,* A Facsimile of the Official Edition Printed in 1774, Philadelphia: printed for the Library Company of Philadelphia, 1974, pp. 214-215.

23. *The Book of Abigail and John, Selected Letters of the Adams Family, 1762-1784*, Cambridge, MA.: Harvard University Press, 1975, p. 76.

24. Quoted in David Barton, *Original Intent*, Aledo, TX: WallBuilder Press, 1996, p. 93.

25. Beliles and McDowell, p. 141.

26. Ibid.

27. Ibid.

28. Ibid., p. 142.

29. Letter of Benjamin Rush to John Adams, July 20, 1811, quoted in *Our Sacred Honor*, edited by William J. Bennett, New York: Simon & Schuster, 1997, pp. 29-30.

30. Beliles and McDowell, p. 148.

31. Ibid.

32. T.R. Fehrenbach, *Greatness to Spare,* Princeton, NJ: D. Van Nostrand Company, Inc., 1968, p. 23.

33. Ibid., p. 247.

34. Letter of John Adams to Abigail, July 3d. 1776, *The Book of Abigail and John*, p. 142.

Chapter 7

The Influence of the Bible on the Development of American Constitutionalism

Noah Webster, God' s Law, and the United States Constitution

American constitutionalism has been a keystone in the establishment of civil liberty in recent history. It has been said that next to the Holy Bible, America's Constitution is the most important document ever written for the benefit of mankind. Such a statement seems justified when you consider that since the United States Constitution went into effect about two hundred years ago, over 175 nations have adopted constitutions, most modeled on that of America. To the extent these nations have applied, both internally and externally, the governmental principles in that document is the extent to which they have experienced liberty, justice, and prosperity. The civil liberty the world has experienced in the past two centuries is largely due to the gradual expansion of American constitutionalism.

Christianity is the source of civil liberty and American constitutionalism.

Where did American constitutionalism and ideas of liberty and individual rights originate? Their development can be traced to the origins of British law, but are ultimately rooted in the Christian religion. The foundation of American constitutionalism was an understanding by the American people of the Gospel and Biblical law. The founding father of American education, Noah Webster, understood the importance of imparting this truth to American youth. In the *Preface* to his *History of the United States* (first published in 1832) he wrote:

The brief exposition of the constitution of the United States, will unfold to young persons the principles of republican government; and it is
the sincere desire of the writer that our citizens should early understand
that the genuine source of correct republican principles is the Bible, particularly the New Testament or the Christian religion.[1]

The source of true liberty is the Christian religion. Webster expressed
this idea before and after his conversion in 1808. In 1802 in "An Oration on
the Anniversary of the Declaration of Independence" Webster said:

If there is a possibility of founding a perfectly free government, and
giving it permanent duration, it must be raised upon the pure maxims, and
supported by the undecaying practice, of that religion, which breathes
"peace on earth, and good will to men." That religion [Christianity] is
perfectly republican . . . . it is calculated to humble the pride and allay the
discontents of men. . . . It restrains the magistrate from oppression, and
the subject from revolt . . . . it secures a perfect equality of rights, by en-
joining a discharge of all social duties, and a strict subordination to law.
The universal prevalence of that religion, in its true spirit, would banish
tyranny from the earth.[2]

The primary reason civil liberty could be developed in America was
because the people understood Biblical law and lived according to the
principles set forth in the law and the gospel. Their internal
self-government and Christian character, and their understanding of important Biblical concepts such as covenant and rule of law, allowed them
to be able to develop external civil liberty and constitutionalism. Alexis De
Tocqueville observed in *Democracy in America* that "in America, religion
is the road to knowledge, and the observance of the divine laws leads man
to civil freedom."[3]

The governmental philosophy of a nation is the product of the educational philosophy of a nation. Webster knew that in order for America to be
free and prosper, the youth and adults of America must be educated in governmental principles of liberty, which could only be found in the Christian
religion. In 1829 he wrote to James Madison

that the christian religion, in its purity, is the basis or rather the source of
all genuine freedom in government. . . . I am persuaded that no civil government of a republican form can exist & be durable, in which the principles of that religion have not a controlling influence.[4]

In addition to an understanding of the Christian religion, Webster believed citizens should also be taught fundamental governmental principles
and a knowledge of how free governments are structured and operate.

Webster provided the first instruction for Americans in our federal constitutional form of government in his *American Spelling Book* of 1794, which contained a Federal catechism. This was America's first civics book.

American constitutionalism was not a product of human reason. Webster wrote how the American people rejected the ideas of the French Revolution because the Americans "believe the opinion, that man can be governed by his reason improved, without the usual aids of religion and law, to be not merely a chimera, but a dangerous doctrine, calculated to undermine the foundation of morals and all social confidence and security."[5]

American constitutionalism was rooted in the absolutes of God's law. True law is in accord with God's law. William Blackstone, whose *Commentaries of the Laws of England* (1765) was a primary resource for those studying law in America until the 20th century, said that "no human laws are of any validity, if contrary to [the] law of nature [which is] dictated by God himself . . . [or to] the law of revelation [which is] to be found only in the holy Scriptures."[6] Early American commentators on law, such as Joseph Story and James Kent, agreed with Blackstone on the Christian source of true law.[7]

De Tocqueville wrote in 1835 that "there is no country in the whole world in which the Christian religion retains a greater influence over the souls of men than in America."[8] This influence affected every sphere of life, including law and government.

Attack against Christian foundation of law in America

In his *Spirit of the Common Law*, Roscoe Pound, who was President of Harvard Law School in the 1920s, revealed the nature of the changing view of law in America. Pound, who was not a Christian, did not directly attack the Christian foundation of law in the United States. In fact, he said that the old Christian legal foundation was good and produced many good results; but, he went on to say that this foundation was not good enough to bring us into the modern era. According to him, we needed a new law system, one founded on a different premise. Pound and others claimed that law was rooted in the best that society had to offer—in the consensus of the society and what they deemed best for mankind—and as society grew and became better, the law would change with it. Evolving law and the sovereignty of the state replaced the absolutes of God's law. Pound said "the state takes the place of Jehovah."[9] He sought to implement change through the law professors. Many in the judicial system began to embrace this evolving view of law. In the words of Charles Evans Hughes, Supreme Court Chief

Justice from 1930 to 1941: "We are under a Constitution, but the Constitution is what the judges say it is."[10]

The idea of evolutionary law, rooted in the will of man, has grown rapidly in recent decades. Many people today in America, and throughout the world, claim to be lovers of liberty and democratic government, yet through their attempts to remove every vestige of the Christian religion from our education, government, media, economy, and law are undermining the foundation of our liberty. "Strange, indeed," Webster proclaimed, "that the zealous advocates of a republican government, should wage an inveterate war against the only system of religious principles, compatible with rational freedom, and calculated to maintain a republican constitution!"[11]

Historical Development of Constitutionalism

Civil liberty is a product of the Bible in the hands of the people. The Bible is the law of liberty—personal, religious, and civil. Modern civil liberty has its roots in the Law of God given to Moses by God around 3500 years ago. Jesus Christ affirmed the law of God and especially emphasized the internal aspect of the law. Webster said that the Gospel contains "the genuine principles of civil life—the only principles which can perfect the work of civilization."[12]

Civil documents of liberty in history have been a product, directly or indirectly, of Biblical ideas. When one examines the history of the civil documents, as well as the ideas contained in them, their Biblical and Christian foundations are apparent. These especially took root and grew in Britain. This was due to the unique impact that Christianity had in the history of that nation.

Our civil liberties have been secured by some fundamental principles. One is the rule of law, where all men, including the rulers, are subject to the law of the land. Men are not a law unto themselves. Over the centuries written documents have emerged putting forth and developing this idea. Written law is important, but the source of that law is also important in securing liberty. As mentioned, the source of laws of liberty have been the law of God, revealed both in the laws of nature and in the Scriptures, His revealed will to mankind.

British Roots of Constitutionalism

American constitutionalism has its roots in British law. British law has its roots in Christianity. Christianity was introduced in Britain in the first century. As the Celts were converted they established decentralized churches, unlike those that developed in the Roman and Byzantine Empires. This was due in part to their being located on the outer edge of the Roman Empire where little power existed to control them.

Patrick's Liber Ex Lege Moisi

By A.D. 150 the pastors of the Celtic Churches preached in the common language from interlinear Bible translations called *glosses*. The greatest of the pastors was Patrick who left England and went to evangelize Ireland in the first part of the fifth century. King Loeghaire was converted and made Patrick his counselor, in which capacity he worked to introduce Biblical law into the civil realm. Patrick wrote *Liber Ex Lege Moisi (Book of the Law of Moses)* which was applied by local chieftains or kings throughout Ireland. *Liber* was a compilation of laws from the Scriptures dealing with civil matters. It emphasized the rule of law and local self government.[13]

Alfred's Code of Laws

Alfred the Great was the first king to unite all of England. He ruled from 871 to 899. Alfred instituted Christian reforms in many areas including establishing a government that served the people. Alfred was taught how to read by a Celtic Christian scholar known as Asser. He studied Patrick's *Liber* and established the Ten Commandments as the basis of law and adopted many other patterns of government from the Hebrew Republic. The people in the nation organized themselves into units of tens, fifties, hundreds and thousands and had an elected assembly known as the "Witen." These representatives were called a tithingman (over ten families), a vilman (over 50), a hundredman, and an earl. The earl's territory which he oversaw was called a "shire," and his assistant called the "shire-reef," where we get our word "Sheriff" today. The Witen also had an unelected House made up of the noblemen, but the king was elected; he was not a hereditary king. Their laws were established by their consent. Alfred's uniform code of Laws (890) recognized "common law" and had provisions for individual rights, such as trial by jury and habeas corpus. Alfred's code was derived from Mosaic law and Jesus' golden rule. Noah

Webster said "Alfred's code is formed from the laws of Moses, and from those of his own predecessors. It begins with the Ten Commandments."[14]

Magna Charta (1215)

Anglo-Saxon law reached its height under King Alfred. It was in decline when William the Conqueror and the Normans invaded England in 1066. The Norman system of government removed the rights of the people. The kings abused the people, barons as well as commoners. Things worsened to the point under King John that the English barons drew up a contract that addressed the abuses and guaranteed the barons certain rights and privileges as contained in Biblical law. King John, needing the help of the barons to raise money, reluctantly signed the Magna Charta in 1215. A Catholic clergyman, Stephen Langton, is likely the chief architect of the document. The Pope said it was illegal but the English Catholic Church, due to its Celtic origins, ignored the Pope and preserved the document and expounded it.

A foundation of American constitutionalism is having an established and known set of laws. "Magna Carta announced the rule of law."[15] It asserted the principle that rulers were subject to the law as well as the common people. Throughout history most people have lived under "rulers' law" where the rulers, in many ways, were the law. There is no security for the liberty and rights of man in such a system. Magna Carta was a great step forward in changing this. It proclaimed the power of the king was limited.

Initially, Magna Carta had little practical effect, especially for the commoners for it applied only to "freemen", but over time the principles asserted in that document began to take root and grow and were extended to all subjects. A process had begun that would eventually remove the power from the crown and place it in the hands of the people at large. Many Englishmen, including American colonists, appealed to the Magna Carta as a written source of their rights and liberties. "The American colonists . . . viewed Magna Carta as a written constitution limiting the power of government and securing to the individual the rights of trial by jury, the protection of the writ of habeas corpus, and the guarantee that no person could be deprived of life, liberty, or property without due process of law."[16]

Some provisions in the Magna Carta that contributed to the advancement of individual rights and civil liberty include:

- Rule of law — the entire document reflects the idea that the rulers are subject to the fundamental law. Article 61 says that anything done contrary to the charter should be considered invalid, and a provision was even given for a committee to use armed force against the king if he attempted to violate the charter (this was never used and this provision was omitted from later reissues of the charter).

- Due process of law — "No free man shall be taken or imprisoned or dispossessed, or outlawed, or banished, or in any way destroyed . . . except by the legal judgment of his peers or by the law of the land." Article 39. (This idea is seen in Amendment 5 of the U.S. Constitution.)
- Trial by jury of peers —(see article 39)
- No taxation without representation — "No scutage or aid shall be imposed in our kingdom except by the common council of our kingdom." Article 12. (John Adams and other Americans cited Magna Carta to support this principle.)
- Religious liberty — "[T]he English church shall be free, and shall hold its rights entire and its liberties uninjured." Article 1. (This applied to the church rather than the individual.)

In the years that followed there were numerous reissues and confirmations of Magna Carta that helped to establish it as the fundamental law of the land. In addition, there were other documents issued over the centuries that built upon Magna Carta. This document came to be seen as a "higher law" similar to a constitution, which had greater force than ordinary laws.

Confirmatio Cartarum (1297)

Confirmatio Cartarum is one of the documents that confirmed the Magna Carta as a "higher law" by declaring any judgments contrary to Magna Carta were void. Confirmatio Cartarum recognized law as a sacred thing, in that the charters were sent to the churches to be kept and to be read twice a year to the people.[17] This followed the Biblical example where the Law of Moses was to be read to all the people every year. (Similarly, in 1776, the government of Massachusetts ordered that a copy of the Declaration of Independence be sent "to the Ministers of each parish, of every denomination, within this state" and "that they severally be required to read the same to their respective congregations, as soon as divine Service is ended.")[18] Those who violated the charters were to be excommunicated.[19]

In addition to helping to establish the Magna Carta as the fundamental law of the land, Confirmatio Cartarum "established Parliament [which had been put into place in 1295] as a truly representative organ of government by providing in section 6 that the taxes must be raised by the common assent of the realm."[20]

English Petition of Rights (1628)

The Petition of Right was "the first of those great constitutional documents since Magna Carta, which safeguard the liberties of the people by securing the supremacy of the law."[21] Abuses of power by King James I (1603-25) and King Charles I (1625-49) helped motivate Sir Edward Coke to lead the battle for individual liberties in the House of Commons. Charles agreed to the Petition of Rights in 1628, which strengthened many concepts of personal liberty, though it did little to stop Charles from governing in an arbitrary fashion. Ideas in this document include: principles of due process and trial by jury upheld; Habeas corpus strengthened; stopped quartering troops in private homes; no imprisonment without show of cause; restriction of the King's power to levy taxes without the consent of Parliament.

The Abolition of the Star Chamber in 1641 by the English Parliament was an important step in protecting the rights of individuals by advancing the ideas of due process of law, writ of habeas corpus, and privilege against self-incrimination (which is embodied in the fifth amendment of the U.S. Constitution). This act helped establish in England "a system of justice administered by the courts instead of by the administrative agencies of the executive branch of the government."[22]

English Bill of Rights (1689)

The English Bill of Rights reasserted and reenforced ideas that had been expressed before. It contained previously existing rights of the Parliament and people that had been violated by Charles II and James II, and which the newly proclaimed King William was required to observe.

Lord Macaulay summarized the general significance of the document as follows:

> The Declaration of Right, though it made nothing law which had not been law before, contained the germ of the law which gave religious freedom to the Dissenter, of the law which secured the independence of the Judges, of the law which limited the duration of Parliaments, of the law which placed the liberty of the press under the protection of juries, of the law which prohibited the slave trade, of the law which abolished the sacramental test, of the law which relieved the Roman Catholics from civil disabilities, of the law which reformed the representative system, of every law which has been passed during more than a century and a half, of every good law which may hereafter, in the course of ages, be found necessary to promote the public weal, and to satisfy the demands of public opinion.[23]

The American Colonies were already applying these ideas better than England (see next section), but the Bill of Rights reenforced these principles and gave the colonists another document to appeal to when they resisted England during the revolution. In addition to those mentioned above, other ideas in the English Bill of Rights that came to be expressed in the early U.S. and state constitutions include: the right to bear arms, control of the army by the legislative branch, the prohibition of cruel and unusual punishments, the prohibition of excessive bail, freedom of elections, the right to petition the government, and the prohibition of suspension of laws without the consent of the representatives of the people.

Development of Constitutionalism in America

English law was brought to America by the early settlers; but Americans added to and modified English law such that they took a great forward step in the development of civil liberty. There were at least 86 constitution-like documents written in colonial America from the time of colonization until 1722, and there were 42 others written in England during America's first century.[24] These documents were laying foundational ideas upon which American constitutionalism was being built. They contain general principles, such as covenant, self-government, virtue, and the Biblical purpose of government, and also show the direct Biblical foundation of American law, for example, acknowledging God, quoting Scripture in capital laws, and presenting Biblical penalties for violation of the law (such as restitution and repeat offenders put to death).

The spreading of Christianity was a primary motive for many of the early explorers and settlers of America—from Leif Erikson, who was sent by King Olaf around the year 1000 to proclaim Christianity to Greenland and Vinland,[25] and Columbus, who believed the Lord inspired him to set sail,[26] to the Pilgrims, Quakers, and Scotch-Irish Presbyterians. Twelve of the original 13 charters, upon which the original 13 colonies were established, specifically mention the propagation of the Gospel as a primary reason for their establishment. These charters also contain numerous rights and liberties. We will examine some of these charters and other important American documents that are sources of our liberties.

First Charter of Virginia (1606)

The First Charter of Virginia assured that the rights of Englishmen traveled with the colonists to North America. This view was unique to the English colonies of America, for other countries viewed their colonists as outside the legal system of the home country. The Virginia Charter of 1606 was the first of many colonial documents that stated the American settlers had the rights of English citizens.[27] Patrick Henry mentioned this charter when he spoke of colonists' right to have representatives levy taxes in his famous 1765 speech in the Virginia House of Burgesses.

The third paragraph of the charter speaks of their desire to propagate the "Christian Religion to such People, as yet live in Darkness and miserable Ignorance of the true Knowledge and Worship of God, and in time bring the Infidels and Savages, living in those parts, to human Civility, and to a settled and quiet Government."[28]

The first Virginia settlers brought English law with them, but it was not established all at once, nor in total. Joseph Story wrote:

> The common law of England is not to be taken, in all respects, to be that of America. Our ancestors brought with them its general principles, and claimed it as their birthright; but they brought with them and adopted only that portion which was applicable to their situations.[29]

The first written laws in America came out of a provision in the Second Virginia Charter for "Laws Divine, Morall, and Martiall, etc." They were written between 1609 and 1612 by Sir Thomas Gates, Sir Thomas West (Lord Delaware), and Sir Thomas Dale. These laws "represented the first written manifestations of the common law in America."[30] The authors of these laws sought to honor God, with requirements for all to worship, for no ungodly speech, for no blasphemy of God's name, for no words or acts against God's holy word, to name only a few. Strict discipline was required for the survival of the colony, and consequently, freedoms were restricted. Many of these laws seem harsh today, but were in keeping with the laws then in effect in England.

Ordinances for Virginia (1618)

The Jamestown Colony was governed, in essence, by martial law for its early years. In 1618 the London Company appointed Sir George Yeardley as governor. Under the new charter or Ordinances for Virginia, he abolished various cruel laws and put into effect new laws, which among other things, called for a legislative assembly. Elections were held in the summer of 1619 and on July 30 the first legislative assembly in the American continent met in the church in Jamestown. The proceedings were opened in prayer by Rev. Richard Buck.[31] The rights of suffrage in Virginia were broader than in England, with even indentured servants possibly being able to vote for the legislators, called burgesses.

The Virginia Charter was revoked in 1624 but the colonists held onto the right and desire to govern themselves. In the following years several assemblies convened to deal with various special matters, even though they had no authorization. In 1639 and 1641 the King gave royal consent to Governors Wyatt and Berkeley for a regular assembly of the people. Thus the right of the colonists to elect representatives for governing affairs in their colony became well established. Virginia served as a precedent for many other colonies, though some of them were taking their own steps to assure self-government.

Mayflower Compact (1620)

The Mayflower Compact is one of the most significant of the founding political documents in America. It was written by a small group of English separatists seeking religious and civil freedom, who were undertaking the planting of a colony "for the Glory of God, and Advancement of the Christian Faith."[32]   The Compact contains principles of self-government and covenant, which are foundational to American constitutionalism. Andrew McLaughlin writes that "[b]ehind the compact lie the Puritan beliefs in the word of God as a higher law, the establishment of the higher law in written documents, and the formation of government by the consent of individuals."[33]

The covenantal nature of American constitutionalism can be traced to these settlers, who on November 11, 1620, still on board the Mayflower, "Do . . . solemnly and mutually, in the Presence of God and one another, covenant and combine ourselves together in to a civil Body Politick."[34]

This political document had its origin in the church covenant the Pilgrims had drawn up years earlier—their political philosophy was derived from their Puritan theology.

> This theology found in the Scriptures the right of men to associate and covenant to form a church and civil government and to choose their own officers to administer both religious and civil affairs. Each member of the congregation had a vote in the election of officers, and each congregation was considered as independent and autonomous of every other and not subject to the authority of any centralized church hierarchy.[35]

In 1623 the Pilgrims instituted trial by jury and private property rights. In 1636 they compiled "the first comprehensive body of law in North America,"[36] which served as a model for future American codes of laws. These laws were based upon Scripture and English precedent. The Laws of the Pilgrims were later revised in 1658, 1671, and 1685, but they all were based upon the idea that the only true law was the law of God as revealed in the Bible. The preface to the 1671 *Book of Laws* states that "Laws . . . are so far good and wholesome, as by how much they are derived from, and agreeable to the ancient Platform of Gods Law."[37] The specific statutes reflected their Biblical philosophy of life. They even quoted Scriptures to support many of their Capital Laws.

A great Puritan exodus from England began about 10 years after the Pilgrims first settled in America. The Puritans came not just for religious freedom but to set up a Bible commonwealth.[38] This was certainly reflected in their laws and constitutions. The magistrates relied on the Old Testament law, but to make civil laws more plain, Rev. Ward drafted the Massachusetts Body of Liberties in 1641. This combined Biblical law and English common law (which was itself rooted in Biblical truth).[39] The early Puritan civil documents firmly established the basic premise of American civil society, that of the rule of established law, rather than the rule of capricious men.

Charter of Massachusetts Bay (1629)

The men who formed a company to settle in Massachusetts Bay had a goal "to found a state based upon the principles of the Bible and governed by the laws of God."[40] Before emigrating, they obtained an agreement that amounted to the transfer of governmental power from England to the colony. Charters for some of the later colonies followed this example and permitted the colonial governments to reside in the colonies.

The Charter of Massachusetts Bay provided the colonists power to elect officers to govern themselves (representative government) and power to make their own laws that were not inconsistent with the laws of England (a degree of self-government). Under the provisions of the Charter, the General Court of Massachusetts would later (in 1646) assert that their colonial government was not subordinate to Parliament. Thus, the charter "provided at an early date the basis for the idea, often voiced by the colonial patriots at the time of the American Revolution, that the statutes of England were limited in their application to England and did not reach beyond the seas."[41]

The charter reveals the Christian mission as the central motive of those behind colonization. In the charter, provisions were made for establishing laws, electing representatives, punishing offences, etc. "whereby our said People, Inhabitants there, may be soe religiously, peaceablie, and civilly governed, as their good Life and orderlie Conversacon, maie wynn and incite the Natives of Country, to the Knowledg and Obedience of the onlie true God and Sauior of Mankinde, and the Christian Fayth, which in our Royall Intencon, and the Adventurers free Profession, is the principall Ende of this Plantacion."[42]

The Charter of Maryland (1632)

The Charter of Maryland revealed the motive of Catholic proprietor Cecil Calvert, Lord Baltimore, in establishing the colony of Maryland — "being animated with a laudable, and pious Zeal for extending the Christian religion."[43] Lord Baltimore established a policy of religious toleration in 1634, which furnished a strong motive for many of the early settlers (both Protestant and Catholic), without which the colony would probably not have been planted. The right of religious freedom was established by law in the Act Concerning Religion (or the Toleration Act) of 1649. During its first century, Maryland was the scene of continued struggle over application of English laws in the colony. By 1732 it was firmly established that the English statutes of liberty did apply to the colonists in Maryland.

Fundamental Orders of Connecticut (1639)

In 1636 Rev. Thomas Hooker led about 100 members from his church in New Town, Massachusetts, to settle along the Connecticut River. Not long after this, two other congregations from Massachusetts went to settle in Connecticut. Thus, covenant church communities adhering to the principle of self-government under God comprised the foundation of the Connecticut Colony. Religious and political differences with the Massachusetts leaders motivated them to emigrate. They were especially concerned with the almost unlimited power of the magistrates. Hooker wrote Winthrop that "the judges must have some rule to judge by or government would degenerate into tyranny and confusion."[44] Their experiences helped shape the writing in 1639 of the Fundamental Orders of Connecticut, the first written constitution in history that led to the formation of a new commonwealth.

The content of the Fundamental Orders was greatly influenced by a sermon Hooker preached before the General Court on May 31, 1638, in which he maintained that "the foundation of authority is laid in the free consent of the people," "that the choice of public magistrates belongs unto the people by God's own allowance," and that "they who have power to appoint officers and magistrates have the right also to set the bounds and limitations of the power and place unto which they call them."[45] This constitution, which contained many Biblical rights and ideas expressed politically, would have a great influence on American constitutionalism. Historian John Fiske wrote that "the government of the United States today is in lineal descent more nearly related to that of Connecticut than to that of any of the other thirteen colonies."[46]

Adopted January 14, 1639, the Fundamental Orders began with the inhabitants covenanting together under God "to maintain and preserve the liberty and purity of the gospel of our Lord Jesus which we now profess."[47] It gave the governor and magistrates "power to administer justice according to the Laws here established, and for want thereof according to the rule of the word of God."[48] The required oath of office ended with the elected official saying: "I . . . will further the execution of Justice according to the rule of Gods word; so helpe me God, in the name of the Lo: Jesus Christ."[49] Some of the principles in the document include the rule of law, poplar elections, representative government, freedom of speech, local self-government, and taxes levied only by representatives.

Noah Webster used Connecticut's Constitution as a model for a new federal constitution in his *Sketches of American Policy*. He said it was "the most perfect on earth" and provided a great example of the balance of power between local and state governments.[50]

Connecticut's code of laws (1642 and following, see *Blue Laws* below) were a model for many other colonies. In 1662 Connecticut was granted a charter by Charles II which allowed much freedom in local matters, even up until the time of the revolution.

Massachusetts Body of Liberties (1641)

The Massachusetts Body of Liberties was probably the first real bill of rights and expresses the colonists' claims to individual liberties. It was a precursor of the U.S. Bill of Rights and was a great step forward in civil liberty. The mixture of Puritan theology with English law shows the distinct trends of American constitutionalism. Here are contained the important American ideas that the fundamental law of the land should be written down and consented to by the citizens, that such a constitution expresses the limits on civil government, and that individual liberties should be written as a bill of rights. The election of representatives was also affirmed.

Some of the rights and liberties contained in this document include: trial by jury, freedom of speech and assembly, religious freedom, no double jeopardy, and no self-incrimination. In addition, monopolies were forbidden, except for a short time in the case of inventions; cruel and inhuman punishment was forbidden; and cattle and goods were not to be taken without reasonable compensation.

The Biblical worldview of the colonists was evident in this document. The Scriptures were the source of the penal laws, civil liberties, and other ideas in the Body of Liberties. Section 1 states that no man's life or property can be taken except by some express law that has been sufficiently published, "or in case of the defect of a law in any parteculer case by the word of god."[51] In section 94 where the capital laws are listed, specific scripture verses are given to support such laws. Section 95 is "A Declaration of the Liberties the Lord Jesus hath given to the Churches." Many other ideas in the document come directly from the Scriptures, such as section 47: "No man shall be put to death without the testimony of two or three witnesses or that which is equivalent thereunto."[52]

Other colonies would later follow the example of what Massachusetts did in the Body of Liberties. These would eventually have a great effect on the Bill of Rights of the U.S. Constitution.

Charter of Rhode Island (1663)

Religious liberty was part of the fundamental law of the colony of Rhode Island—the first such constitutional provision. (This was more than a legislative enactment, like in the Maryland Toleration Act.) Religious liberty up until this time was more religious toleration. Establishment of true religious liberty was distinctly an American idea, and first became part of the fundamental law in Rhode Island.

Roger Williams founded Rhode Island in 1636 when he was forced to flee Massachusetts due to conflicts with the Puritans. His extreme views concerning religious practices brought disfavor with the Puritan authorities in Massachusetts Bay and with the Pilgrims in the Plymouth Colony. After establishing Providence with some other individuals who for various reasons were out of favor with the Massachusetts authorities, they drew up a written covenant in 1636 that, among other things, said the authority of civil government should not extend to religious matters. The idea was that legislative powers should extend only to actions and not opinions.

Over the years other like-minded settlers came to Rhode Island. In 1644 Williams obtained a patent for Rhode Island from the Long Parliament. In 1663, after the restoration of the English monarchy, the leaders in Rhode Island obtained a charter from King Charles II. Since this charter recognized the rights and form of self-government already in place, it remained in force through American independence, up until 1842 when a formal constitution replaced it.

In addition to the guarantee of religious liberty, the Charter of Rhode Island contained provisions for the colony to make their own laws, provided that they were conformable to the laws of England, and to set up their own forms of government. The American ideas of self-government and religious liberty were further extended. Other colonies, such as Carolina and New Jersey, would copy the provision of religious liberty found in Rhode Island.

The charter mentioned their intentions of "godlie edifieing themselves, and one another, in the holie Christian ffaith and worshipp" and their desire for the "conversione of the poore ignorant Indian natives."[53] Their plan for conversion was to be through their examplary lifestyle, both personally and civilly—that the inhabitants "may be soe religiously, peaceably and civilly governed, as that, by theire good life and orderlie conversatione, they may win and invite the native Indians of the countrie to the knowledge and obedience of the onlie true God, and Saviour of mankinde."[54]

"Blue Laws" of New Haven Colony (1656)

In 1655 Governor Eaton, as an "able, judicious and godly man,"[55] was appointed to form a code of laws for the New Haven colony based upon the laws of the colony that had been developed over the years, aided by the laws of the colony of Massachusetts and other writings. The past laws had been passed on verbally and through hand-made copies. Five hundred copies of the new compilation were printed in England in 1656. These came to be known as "blue laws" because these first printed laws were enveloped in blue colored paper. The name "Blue Laws" was later applied to laws in many other colonies, and, after independence, various states, even in use up until recent times.

Governor Eaton made "the sacred volume his guide, and has cited scripture in all cases upon which his laws were founded."[56] Upon reading these laws, it is obvious that the Bible was the central source for what constituted lawful and unlawful behavior. Scripture is quoted for capital offences, and in cases of theft the Biblical idea of restitution was applied. The incorrigible criminal was also addressed.[57]

The Blue Laws acknowledged "that the supreme power of making laws, and of repealing them, belong to God only, and that by him, this power is given to Jesus Christ, as Mediator, Math. 28:19. Joh. 5:22. And that the Laws for holinesse, and Righteousness, are already made, and given us in the scriptures."[58] This code of law formed the foundation of the civil government of the state and influenced laws throughout the United States.

Frame of Government of Pennsylvania (1682)

Pennsylvania was established in 1681 when Quaker William Penn was given a tract of land between New York and Maryland by the King of England in payment for a debt the Crown owed to William's father, Admiral William Penn. Having experienced much persecution for his Christian beliefs, Penn asked for the land desiring to plant a colony "which should open its doors to every kindred" and be a refuge for men of all creeds. He wanted it to be a model state — "a holy experiment" — in which his ideals could be realized; an example of toleration and liberty on a grand scale. After Penn received the charter for Pennsylvania he wrote that "my God that has given it me through many difficultys, will, I believe bless and make it the seed of a nation."[59]

Penn worked more than a year on formulating a constitution or Frame of Government for Pennsylvania, which was adopted in England on April 25, 1682. The Christian nature of this document is readily evident. The Preamble begins:

> When the great and wise God had made the world, of all his creatures, it pleased him to chuse man his Deputy to rule it: and to fit him for so great a charge and trust, he did not only qualify him with skill and power, but with integrity to use them justly.[60]

Penn then summarizes the purpose of law by quoting the Apostle Paul from Romans 13 and other of his epistles. He then writes of the divine nature of civil government:

> This settles the divine right of government beyond exception, and that for two ends: first, to terrify e vil doers: secondly, to cherish those that do well. . . . So that government seems to me a part of religion itself, a thing sacred in its institution and end. For, . . . it crushes the effects of evil, and is as such,. . . an emanation of the same Divine Power, that is both author and object of pure religion.[61]

The Frame of Government recognized the Lord's Day (the Sabbath), Biblical standards for marriage — "all marriages (not forbidden by the law of God, as to nearness of blood and affinity by marriage) shall be encouraged,"— and Biblical qualifications for civil officials — "all . . . shall be such as possess faith in Jesus Christ."[62] All offenses against God were to be discouraged and punished, and many were listed. Religious freedom was granted to all persons "who confess and acknowledge the one Almighty and eternal God, to be the Creator, Upholder and Ruler of the world."[63]

Besides direct recognition of Christianity, there were many civil rights and governmental ideas that were derived from the Bible. These included the rule of law, representative government, freedom of the individual, no arbitrary taxation, free and fair elections, trial by jury of peers, need for true witnesses, punishment of perjury, and restitution to the wronged party. Private property rights were also protected and ownership of land by all people was made easy. Ownership of land was a requirement to vote or hold office, but it was easy for anyone to acquire land, including indentured servants. Freemen were to own 100 acres of land and have 10 acres cultivated, but they could purchase the land at one penny an acre. Those who came as indentured servants, and had paid off their debt, were to own 50 acres, with 20 cultivated, to be able to vote and hold office. Inhabitants could even become freemen by paying "scot and lot" (a contribution paid by the subject according to his ability) to the government.[64] Some people today have depicted the founders as non-egalitarians by restricting freemen to property owners, but they fail to point out how easy it was to acquire property in many of the colonies, such as in Pennsylvania.

Many of these ideas existed in various degrees in other colonies but were greatly strengthened by William Penn. His preface states the importance of these for liberty and communicates his spirit in ideas of constitutionalism, which would be seen later in the U.S. Constitution and the Bill of Rights.[65]

Pennsylvania Charter of Privileges (1701)

Penn's original Frame of Government was replaced in 1701 by the Charter of Privileges. This document has been described as "the most famous of all colonial constitutions,"[66] and is a further assertion of constitutionalism where the liberties contained therein cannot be usurped by capricious legislation of a majority. This document required six-sevenths of the Assembly to change it. It contains many important rights and ideas such as: liberty of conscience (which Penn considered so important that he declared in section eight that it should remain inviolable forever), religious liberty, representative government, and due process. Section one contains qualifications of officers where "all Persons who also profess to believe in Jesus Christ, the Saviour of the World, shall be capable (notwithstanding their other Persuasions and Practices in Point of Conscience and Religion) to serve this Government in any Capacity, both legislatively and executively."[67]

Resolutions of the Stamp Act Congress (1765)

Nine of the colonies were represented at this Congress which met to deal with the Stamp Act and the unjust attempt by Britain to impose taxes on the colonists without their consent. The Americans began to assert their rights as Englishmen and stand upon the various liberties that had become a part of English and American law. These were men of principle acting upon constitutional rights and duties.

In resisting the Stamp Act, the colonists not only argued that it violated their rights as Englishmen, but it violated the higher laws of nature and of nature's God. Samuel Adams said of the Stamp Act that it "is utterly void, and of no binding force upon us; for it is against our Rights as Men and our Privileges as Englishmen. An act made in defiance of the first principles of Justice. . . . There are certain Principles fixed unalterably in Nature."[68]

Declaration and Resolves of the First Continental Congress (1774)

In September 1774 delegates from all of the colonies, except Georgia, met in Philadelphia to address the oppressive actions of England. For nearly a decade prior to this, the colonists had resisted various acts of Parliament which asserted the belief that England had the right to full powers of sovereignty in colonial matters. The colonists' resistance was met by acts of retaliation. These conflicts helped to solidify colonial ideas of individual liberty. Many of these ideas are well expressed in the Declaration and Resolves of the First Continental Congress.

Before taking up the important issues before them, the First Continental Congress passed a resolve asking the Rev. Mr. Duché to open the Congress in prayer, revealing their Christian character. The Journal of the Proceedings of Congress record the vote of thanks of Congress given to Mr. Duché "for performing divine service, and for the excellent prayer." John Adams wrote to his wife Abigail of the great effect Rev. Duché's prayer had upon the Congress.[69]

The Declaration and Resolves of the First Continental Congress was an important forerunner of the Declaration of Independence and the declarations of rights found in various state constitutions. It based the rights of the colonists on "the immutable laws of nature, the principles of the English constitutions, and the several charters or compacts."[70] The laws of nature were thus adopted as one of the foundations of the rights of the colonists, and would be appealed to again in the other documents. James Otis, in his famous pamphlet "The Rights of the British Colonies Asserted and

Proved," had some years earlier shown the colonists' understanding of the laws of nature:

> To say the Parliament is absolute and arbitrary is a contradiction. The Parliament cannot make 2 and 2, 5: Omnipotency cannot do it. The supreme power in a state . . . strictly speaking, belongs alone to God. Parliaments are in all cases to declare what is for the good of the whole; but it is not the declaration of Parliament that makes it so: There must be in every instance a higher authority, viz. God. Should an Act of Parliament be against any of His natural laws, which are immutably true, their declaration would be contrary to eternal truth, equity, and justice, and consequently void.[71]

This was certainly not a new idea. As we have seen, the colonists often appealed to God's higher law as the source of their rights and liberties. Locke, Blackstone, and others also wrote of the laws of nature being the will of God as revealed in His creation and in the conscience of man, and the laws of nature's God as being the will of God revealed in the Scriptures. (For more on this see Chapter 11.)

Rights exerted in this document include: no taxation without representation, no standing armies or the quartering of troops without the consent of the colonial legislatures, no suspension of colonial legislatures or representative bodies, trial by jury, and right of petition.

Declaration of the Causes and Necessity of Taking up Arms (July 6, 1775)

Though fighting had already begun (on April 19, 1775 at Lexington), the Second Continental Congress expressed hope for reconciliation with Great Britain in the Declaration of the Causes and Necessity of Taking up Arms, but at the same time approved and justified the use of force against the British. This document lists various reasons why force was now necessary to defend themselves. It states numerous violations of their rights by British policy including being deprived of trial by jury, suspension of various legislatures, imposition of taxes without representation, and quartering soldiers in the colonists' homes in times of peace. It lists one statute of parliament as a summary of all the abuses — that parliament can "of right make laws to bind us in all cases whatsoever."[72]

This document was to be proclaimed by General George Washington when he assumed command of the Continental Army in Boston. They wanted the world to see that, "Our cause is just." They gratefully acknowledged God's Providence and his "Divine favour," and declared they would exert the utmost energy of "those powers, which our beneficent Creator hath graciously bestowed upon us. . . ; being with one mind resolved to die freemen rather than to live slaves." They ended the Declaration:

> With an humble confidence in the mercies of the supreme and impartial Judge and Ruler of the Universe, we most devoutly implore his divine goodness to protect us happily through this great conflict, to dispose our adversaries to reconciliation on reasonable terms, and thereby to relieve the empire from the calamities of civil war.[73]

Declaration of Independence (July 4, 1776)

Most Americans were hesitant to declare independence, even after fighting had begun. It was only after a series of events over many months that public opinion solidified in favor of such action. These events included: England sending troops to fight against the colonists; King George issuing a proclamation on August 23, 1775, declaring that the colonists were all traitors in rebellion; and the Parliament suspending trade with all of the colonies on December 22, 1775. After these events, no other action except independence seemed possible for the Americans to secure their liberties.

In accordance with the instructions from the Virginia Convention of May 1776, Richard Henry Lee introduced in Congress on June 7 three resolutions which included a proposal for a declaration of independence. A committee of five was appointed on June 11 to prepare such a document, and included Thomas Jefferson who wrote the initial draft. After a few changes by the committee and Congress at large, the Declaration was approved. The first paragraph states its purpose and appeals to "the laws of nature and of nature's God" as the source of the authority for their action. As stated earlier, this phrase meant the will of God as revealed in nature and in the Holy Scriptures.

The second paragraph sets forth their political philosophy. This did not contain anything new, but merely built upon the ideas that had developed over the centuries, especially since the beginning of the American colonies. They acknowledged the Creator as the source of unalienable rights — not men nor government. They then present a Biblical view of the purpose of civil government and the appropriate manner to go about correcting governments that are not fulfilling their Biblical responsibilities. The listing of numerous grievances shows the principled response of the Americans in establishing the justice of their cause before a "candid world." They concluded by "appealing to the Supreme Judge of the world" and "with a firm reliance on the protection of Divine Providence." The addition of these two phrases by the entire Congress to Jefferson's original draft makes them even more significant, as it appears the Congress wanted to make plain to the world their Christian convictions.

State Constitutions

Even before independence, Virginia had approved a Bill of Rights (on June 12) and a constitution (on June 29). Both of these were a model for many other state constitutions and bills of rights that began to be passed after approval of the Declaration of Independence. The Virginia Bill of Rights, largely written by George Mason, was "one of the most important forerunners of the first ten amendments to the Constitution of the United States."[74] These various bills of rights reflected the Founders' view that individual liberties should be embodied in the fundamental law of the land.

The Virginia Bill of Rights (as those of other states) contained fundamental principles that were rooted in Biblical truth and Christian civilization and had developed over centuries. It stated

> that no free government, or the blessings of liberty, can be preserved to any people, but by a firm adherence to justice, moderation, temperance, frugality, and virtue, and by a frequent recurrence to fundamental principles.[75]

One of these fundamental principles was freedom of religion — "that religion, or the duty which we owe to our Creator, and the manner of discharging it, can be directed only by reason and conviction, not by force or violence." The Bill of Rights concludes by stating "that it is the mutual duty of all to practise Christian forbearance, love, and charity towards each other."[76]

Within a few years of independence all the states except Connecticut and Rhode Island had adopted constitutions. Connecticut and Rhode Island were already operating under charters that allowed much self-government and so only slight modifications were necessary to reflect their independent status. All of the new constitutions of the states recognized certain fundamental rights of citizens. The Pennsylvania Declaration of Rights was similar to Virginia's and acknowledged many inalienable rights including: frequent and free elections, trial by jury, right to confront accusers and present evidence of defense, privilege not to be compelled to testify against oneself, freedom of the press, liberty of conscience, freedom of speech and worship. The Constitution of Pennsylvania (August 16, 1776) recognized the Biblical purpose of government to protect "the community . . . and to enable the individuals who compose it to enjoy their natural rights, and the other blessings which the Author of existence has bestowed upon man." It acknowledges "the goodness of the great Governor of the universe (who alone knows to what degree of earthly happiness mankind may attain, by perfecting the arts of government)."[77]

Delaware's Constitution and Declaration of Rights (1776) was similar in protecting individual liberties, but like many other states restricted the guarantee of civil liberties to Christians. Section 3 of the Declaration of Rights states "that all persons professing the Christian religion ought forever to enjoy equal rights and privileges in this state."[78] Since nearly every American at this time identified themselves with the Christian religion this was not as restrictive as some may suppose today. Eight of the original 13 states favored one denomination above others and four had required general affirmations of faith in Protestant Christianity. The establishment of particular denominations would end by the 1830s, but the requirement of officials to adhere to Christian convictions would remain for some time. It could well be argued that even today the U.S. Constitution (as well as various state constitutions) only allows Christians in public office, for, among other reasons, elected officials must take an oath of office. Upon examination, this oath was clearly a Christian oath.[79]

All of the State Constitutions acknowledged God and protected numerous God-given rights. The Constitution of Maryland (1776) states: "it is the duty of every man to worship God in such manner as he thinks most acceptable to him; all persons, professing the Christian religion, are equally entitled to protection in their religious liberty." The oath of office included "a declaration of a belief in the Christian religion."[80]

The Constitution of Massachusetts (1780) acknowledged "the goodness of the great Legislator of the universe . . . His providence. . . . and devoutly imploring His direction." It declared: "It is the right as well as the duty of all men in society, publicly, and at stated seasons, to worship the SUPREME BEING, the great Creator and Preserver of the universe." It also recognized that "the happiness of a people, and the good order and preservation of civil government, essentially depend upon piety, religion, and morality."[81]

The unalienable right to worship God according to the dictates of conscience is contained in the Constitution of New Hampshire (1784). It also recognizes "morality and piety, rightly grounded on evangelical principles" as the "best and greatest security to government."[82]

Northwest Ordinance (1787)

Initially passed by Congress on July 13, 1787 (and re-ratified under the U.S. Constitution of 1789), the Northwest Ordinance provided government for the territory northwest of the Ohio River and set requirements for the admission of new states into the union. It established the policy that the settlers of the territories should enjoy the same liberties as citizens of the states, thus extending individual rights to new states. This was similar to the way that the Virginia Charter of 1606 extended English rights to the settlers. During the 180 years separating the two documents, many new unalienable rights and liberties had become firmly established in American society. In keeping with what had become a familiar feature of American law, the Northwest Ordinance contained a written bill of rights, the first such list by the federal government. This assured extension of the individual rights guaranteed in the states, and listed in the various bills of rights of the states, to new territories and states.

The Ordinance required officials to take an oath of fidelity and of office, and promoted "extending the fundamental principles of civil and religious liberty, which form the basis whereon these republics, their laws and constitutions, are erected." Article I provides for religious liberty, and Article II lists various individual rights including habeas corpus, trial by jury, proportionate representation, no cruel or unusual punishment, judgment of peers, and private property rights. Article III acknowledges the religious foundation of schools and government when it states: "Religion, morality, and knowledge being necessary to good government and the happiness of mankind, schools and the means of education shall forever be encouraged." Article VI prohibited slavery in the new territory and in any states that would be formed.[83]

United States Constitution (1789)

After independence, the states entered into a "league of friendship" with each other under the Articles of Confederation (agreed to by Congress in 1777 and approved by all the states in 1781). The weaknesses under the Articles were such that no permanent union of the states was likely. A lack of power for the central government, no executive, and no taxing powers limited the Congress from adequately handling problems faced during the war and in the early years after the Treaty of Peace (1783) with Britain. Most people recognized the weaknesses of the confederation, but many thought revising the Articles was sufficient. Others such as James Madison and Noah Webster knew more needed to be done.

Webster's Contribution to American Constitutionalism

In the decade following America's independence, Noah Webster sought to produce a strong union among the newly independent American states. He saw that education was a key means of accomplishing this and wrote three textbooks — *Speller* (1783), *Grammar* (1784), and *Reader* (1785) — that provided a content that was uniquely American, and also principles that were necessary to support the nation. His textbooks and educational reforms were intended to strengthen the unity among the American people, which would strengthen their external union. Webster saw his work to bring a standardization to the American English language as a means to unify the American people because he felt the union would be strong as the people spoke the same language.

In his *Sketches of American Policy* (1785) he was one of the first (if not the first) to put in print a plan for a new national government. Webster believed his plan contained "the first distinct proposal, made through the medium of the press, for a new constitution of the United States."[84] Webster promoted his ideas as he traveled throughout the colonies. He visited George Washington and left a copy of his booklet with him, who in turn showed it to James Madison. These men carried Webster's ideas for a new form of national government with them when they participated in forming the United States Constitution during the summer of 1787.

Webster had seen the weakness of the national government under the Articles of Confederation when he attempted to secure copyright legislation to protect his textbooks. Though agreeing with Webster's policy, the Congress was unable to enact copyright legislation under the provisions of the Articles and so Webster had to travel to all the states to promote copyright legislation laws.

Copyright legislation was just one of many of Webster's ideas that were incorporated into the United States Constitution. Not only had Washington and Madison read his *Sketches*, but virtually every man who participated in the convention read it as well. Most of the principles Webster presented for creating a new government were put into the Constitution by the framers. His provisions included a surrender of a degree of state sovereignty to a stronger Congress, "a supreme power at the head of the union," "all power is vested in the people," equal representation of the states in Congress, and congressional power to regulate and impose duties on interstate commerce.[85] Webster also proposed the abolition of slavery.[86]

Most of his ideas were not original. He was simply drawing from the best available sources and included many of the documents examined

above, including the Declaration of Independence and various state constitutions (especially Connecticut's). Washington, Hamilton and others had
presented various ideas for a new government, yet Webster was the first to
give an overall framework. Madison and others acknowledged Webster's
key role. New York State Chief Justice James Kent said Webster was "the
first man who proposed the present government" of the United States.[87]

The document that was approved by the Constitutional Convention in
September 1787 and sent to the states for ratification had both a Christian
power and form— a Christian power because the source of the Founders'
ideas primarily came from the Bible. The brief summary of the development of ideas of liberty given above reveals this to be the case, plus this is
affirmed by a direct examination of the source of their political ideas. A
study was published in *The American Political Science Review* that listed
the citations from about 15,000 political documents written by the
Founders between 1760 and 1805. By far the most quoted source in these
political documents was the Bible—34% of all citations. The great majority of the remaining sources were from writers with Biblical ideas.[88] In addition, almost ever one of the Founders were Christians who had a Biblical
worldview. Even the 2 or 3 non-professing Christians at the Convention
had a Biblical view of life. (Franklin is the most famous of these. His call
for prayer at the Constitutional Convention reveals his belief in God's active involvement in His creation.[89])

The form of the Constitution is Christian as well; that is, the framework
of the document reflects a Christian view of man and government. These
general ideas include representative government, the separation of powers,
the rule of law, and the unique concept of federalism.[90] The Preamble to the
Constitution contains a good summary of the Biblical purpose of civil government. The document directly acknowledges God in the requirement of
an oath of office (Article 6), in recognizing the Christian Sabbath (Article
1, section 7, paragraph 2), and in dating itself "in the year of our Lord" (Article 7).[91] The first ten amendments to the Constitution were ratified in
1791. The individual liberties secured in this Bill of Rights were developed
out of Christian civilization and were derived from the Bible and a Biblical
understanding of unalienable rights. These ideas were not new, but, as we
have seen, were developed over many centuries. To our Founders, the primary purpose of civil government is to protect the citizens' God-given
rights. Lack of a listing of these rights in the original Constitution caused
many to oppose ratifying it. Many of those who voted to ratify it in various
states did so only after being assured a Bill of Rights would be added.

During the summer of the Constitutional Convention Webster was living in Philadelphia and he had numerous discussions with many of the delegates. Near the close of the convention, Webster was asked by one of the delegates to write a paper in support of the new constitution as a means of encouraging ratification by the states. His 55 page essay — *An Examination into the Leading Principles of the Federal Constitution Proposed by the Late Convention Held at Philadelphia*[92] — was completed in about a month, and then was printed and distributed widely. It played an important part in assuring the ratification of the new constitution.

In *Examination* Webster compares the Constitution to "the promulgation of the Jewish laws at Mount Sinai."[93] He wrote that

> the origin of the AMERICAN REPUBLIC is distinguished by peculiar circumstances. Other nations have been driven together by fear and necessity. . . . In the formation of our constitution the wisdom of all ages is collected—the legislators of antiquity are consulted, as well as the opinions and interests of the millions who are concerned. In short, it is an empire of reason.[94]

As we have examined the development of ideas of liberty and constitutional principles, we have seen that the greatest "wisdom of the ages" affecting civil documents of liberty has arisen from the Christian religion and the precepts of the Bible. This is the primary source of American constitutionalism, and consequently, civil liberty throughout the world. Such an understanding must be transferred to all Americans in this and future generations if liberty is to be maintained.

Noah Webster had a vision for educating all Americans, and posterity, in principles of liberty. His entire life was devoted to fulfilling this end. His *Speller* of 1794 had a Federal catechism and was the first text to educate Americans in the form of our government. His *History of the United States* taught fundamental governmental principles. His textbooks also contained writings of the best of American literature which he intended to inspire youth with "a love of virtue, patriotism, and religion."[95] His *An American Dictionary of the English Language* (1828) gave American Christian constitutional definitions.[96]

Webster not only sought to educate Americans in the source of our liberties, in constitutional principles, and in a knowledge of how our form of government works, but he, most importantly, sought to infuse into Americans the power or spirit necessary to support liberty. Both the power and form of free nations is rooted in Christianity. Webster wrote: "Men may devise and adopt new forms of government; they may amend old forms, repair breaches, and punish violators of the constitution; but there is, there can be, no effectual remedy, but obedience to the divine law."[97] As we obey God's law and act upon the principles of Christianity, we shall see mankind advance, for, according to Webster, the gospel of the Savior contains "the genuine principles of civil life—the only principles which can perfect the work of civilization."[98]

End Notes

1. Noah Webster, *History of the United States*, New Haven: Durrie & Peck, 1833, p. v.

2. Noah Webster, "An Oration on the Anniversary of the Declaration of Independence," New Haven, 1802, in *American Political Writing during the Founding Era, 1760-1805*, vol, 2, Charles S. Hyneman and Donald S. Lutz, editors, Indianapolis: Liberty Press, 1983, p. 1227.

3. Alexis de Tocqueville, *Democracy in America*, edited by Richard D. Heffner, New York: The New American Library, 1956, p. 47.

4. Webster to James Madison, 16 October 1829, *Madison Papers*, Series 2, Library of Congress. Quoted in *Defining Noah Webster, Mind and Morals in the Early Republic*, by K. Alan Snyder, New York: University Press of America, 1990, p. 253.

5. Webster, *Ten Letters to Dr. Joseph Priestly* (New Haven: Read and Morse, 1800), p. 8. Quoted in Snyder, p. 191.

6. William Blackstone, *Commentaries on the Laws of England* (4 Vols. 1765-1769), St. George Tucker's American Edition, pp. 41-42.

7. See *Commentaries on the Constitution of the United States* (1833) by Joseph Story and *Commentaries on American Law* (1826-1830) by James Kent.

8. Herbert W. Titus, *God, Man, and Law: The Biblical Principles*, Oak Brook, Il: Institute in Basic Life Principles, p. 19.

9. Roscoe Pound, *The Spirit of the Common Law*, New York: The Legal Classics Library.

10. Quoted in David Barton, *Original Intent*, Aledo, Tex: WallBuilder Press, 1996, p. 172.

11. Noah Webster, "An Oration on the Anniversary of the Declaration of Independence," New Haven, 1802, in *American Political Writing during the Founding Era, 1760-1805*, vol, 2, p. 1227.

12. Noah Webster, Letter IX, *Letters to a Young Gentleman Commencing His Education*, New Haven: Howe & Spalding, 1823, p. 149.

13. For more on the Celtic Church and Patrick's *Liber* see, Leslie Hardinge, *The Celtic Church in Britain*, London: Church Historical Society, 1973.

14. Noah Webster, Letter IX, *Letters to a Young Gentleman Commencing His Education*, p. 144.

15. *Sources of Our Liberties*, Richard L. Perry, editor, New York: American Bar Foundation, 1952, p. 1.

16. *Ibid.*, p. 5.

17. See clause 3 of Confirmatio Cartarum, November 5, 1297, in *Sources of Our Liberties*, p. 30.

18. See *America's Providential History* by Mark Beliles and Stephen McDowell, Charlottesville, Va.: Providence Foundation, 1989, pp. 145-146.

19. See clause 4 of Confirmatio Cartarum, in *Sources of Our Liberties*, p. 30.

20. *Sources of Our Liberties*, p. 25, 31.

21. *Ibid.*, p. 62.

22. *Ibid.*, p. 132.

23. *Ibid.*, p. 244.

24. See Donald S. Lutz, "From Covenant to Constitution in American Political Thought," *Publius*, Fall 1980, pp. 101-133.

25. See Edward Channing, *A History of the United States*, vol. 1, New York: The MacMillan Company, 1919, pp. 1 ff.

26. See *Christopher Columbus's Book of Prophecies*, reproduction of the original manuscript with English translation by Kay Brigham, quincentenary edition, Barcelona, Spain: CLIE Publishers.

27. See The First Charter of Virginia, paragraph 15, in *Sources of Our Liberties*, p. 44.

28. Ibid., p. 40.

29. *Sources of Our Liberties*, p. 36.

30. Introduction, *For the Colony in Virginea Britannia, Lawes Divine, Morall and Martiall, etc.*, compiled by William Strachey, edited by David H. Flaherty, the University Press of Virginia, Charlottesville, 1969, pp. ix.

31. See *In God We Trust Tour Guide*, by Stephen McDowell and Mark Beliles, Charlottesville, Va.: Providence Foundation, 1998, p. 124.

32. The Mayflower Compact, in *Sources of Our Liberties*, p. 60.

33. *Sources of Our Liberties*, p. 57.

34. The Mayflower Compact, in *Sources of Our Liberties*, p. 60.

35. *Sources of Our Liberties*, p. 57.

36. *The Laws of the Pilgrims*, A Facsimile Edition of *The Book of the General Laws of the Inhabitants of the Jurisdiction of New , 1672 & 1685*, Wilmington, Del.: Pilgrim Society, 1977, p. xiv.

37. *Ibid.*, p. 1.

38. See *Builders of the Republic*, vol. 8 of *The Pageant of America,* New Haven: Yale University Press, 1927, p. 8.

39. For the origins of common law see, Gary Amos, *Defending the Declaration*, Charlottesville, Va.: Providence Foundation, 1994.

40. *Sources of Our Liberties*, p. 77.

41. *Ibid.*, p. 80.

42. Charter of Massachusetts Bay, in *Sources of Our Liberties*, p. 94.

43. The Charter of Maryland, June 20, 1632, in *Sources of Our Liberties*, p. 105.

44. *Sources of Our Liberties*, footnote 4, p. 105.

45. John Fiske, *The Beginnings of New England*, New York: Houghton, Mifflin and Co., 1898, p. 136.

46. *Ibid.*, pp. 137, 140.

47. Fundamental Orders of Connecticut (spelling is modernized), in *Sources of Our Liberties*, p. 120.

48. *Ibid.*

49. *Ibid.*, p. 123.

50. Harlow Giles Unger, *Noah Webster, The Life and Times of an American Patriot*, New York: John Wiley & Sons, Inc, 1998, p.88.

51. Massachusetts Body of Liberties, in *Sources of Our Liberties*, p. 148.

52. *Ibid.*, p. 153.

53. Charter of Rhode Island, in *Sources of Our Liberties*, p. 169.

54. *Ibid.*, p. 173.

55. *The Blue Laws of New Haven Colony, usually called Blue Laws of Connecticut . . .*, By An Antiquarian, Hartford: printed by Case, Tiffany & Co., 1838, p. iii.

56. *Ibid.*, p. v.

57. *Ibid.*, see pp. 157 ff and 155-156.

58. *Ibid.*, p. 145.

59. *Remember William Penn,* compiled by the William Penn Tercentenary Committee, Harrisburg, PA: Commonwealth of Pennsylvania, 1945, p. 74.

60. Frame of Government of Pennsylvania, in *Sources of Our Liberties*, p. 209.

61. *Ibid.*, p. 210.

62. *Ibid.*, pp. 216, 218, 220.

63. *Ibid.*, p. 220.

64. *Ibid.*, p. 217.

65. *Sources of Our Liberties*, p. xviii.

66. Ibid., p. 66.

67. Pennsylvania Charter of Privileges, in *Sources of Our Liberties*, p. 256.

68. *Sources of Our Liberties*, p. 28. See also *The Rights of the Colonists* by Samuel Adams, in *Christian History of the Constitution*, by Verna Hall, Foundation for American Christian Education, 1980, pp. 365-370.

69. See *Journal of the Proceedings of Congress, 1774*, a facsimile edition, Philadelphia: Library Company of Philadelphia, 1974, pp. 24-25; and *The Book of Abigail and John, Selected Letters of the Adams Family, 1762-1784*, Cambridge, Ma.: Harvard University Press, 1975, p. 76.

70. Declaration and Resolves of the First Continental Congress, 1774, in *Sources of Our Liberties*, p. 287.

71. *Sources of Our Liberties*, pp. 264-265.

72. Declaration of the Causes and Necessity of Taking up Arms, in *Sources of Our Liberties*, p. 296.

73. Ibid., p. 299.

74. *Sources of Our Liberties*, p. 309.

75. Sec. 15, Bill of Rights, Constitution of Virginia, in *Sources of Our Liberties*, p. 312.

76. *Ibid.*

77. Constitution of Pennsylvania, *Sources of Our Liberties*, p. 328.

78. *Sources of Our Liberties*, p. 338.

79. For more on state established religion see Daniel Dreisbach, *Real Threat and Mere Shadow*, Westchester, Ill.: Crossway Books, 1987. The oath in American law was clearly rooted in a Biblical context. For example: An Agreement of the Settlers at Exeter in New Hampshire, July 5, 1639, contained a rulers oath which stated: "You shall swear by the great and dreadful Name of the High God, Maker and Governor of Heaven and earth and by the Lord Jesus Christ, the Prince of the Kings and rulers of the earth, that in his Name and fear you will rule and govern his people according to the righteous will of God. . . ." [*Colonial Origins of the American Constitution*, Donald Lutz, ed., Liberty Fund, p. 4.] The Laws of Virginia of March 1659 contain a section on "The Oath," which states: "You and every of you shall swear upon the holy Evangelist and in the sight of God to deliver your opinions faithfully." [*A Collection of all the Laws of Virginia*, by William Waller Hening, New York: R.&W.&G. Bartow, 1823, vol. 1, p. 508.] *The Tennessee Justice's Manual and Civil Officer's Guide* of 1834 shows how Tennessee, which was typical of the early states, required "the party to be sworn, to lay his hand upon the holy evangelists of Almighty God, in token of his engagement to speak the truth, as he hopes to be saved in the way and method of salvation pointed out in that blessed volume; and in further token, that if he should swerve from the truth, he may be justly deprived of all the blessings of the gospels, and be made liable to that vengeance which he has imprecated on his own head; and after repeating the words, 'So help me God,' shall kiss the holy gospels as a seal of confirmation to said engagement." [by Judge James Coffield Mitchell, Nashville: Mitchell and Norvell, 1834, pp. 457-458.]

80. *Sources of Our Liberties*, pp. 349, 350.

81. *Sources of Our Liberties*, pp. 373, 374.

82. *Sources of Our Liberties*, p. 382.

83. Northwest Ordinance, *Sources of Our Liberties*, pp. 395-396.

84. Letter of Webster, quoted in Harlow Giles Unger, *Noah Webster, The Life and Times of an American Patriot*, New York: John Wiley & Sons, Inc., 1998, p. 83.

85. "Sketches of American Policy", in *Noah Webster: On Being American, Selected Writings, 1783-1828*, Homer d. Babbidge, Jr., editor, New York: Frederick A. Praeger, 1967, p. 31.

86. Unger, p. 89.

87. Unger, p. 84.

88. Donald S. Lutz, "The Relative Influence of European Writers on Late Eighteenth-Century American Political Thought," *The American Political Science Review*, Vol. 78, 1983, pp. 189-197.

89. See James Madison, *Notes of the Debates in the Federal Convention of 1787*, New York: W.W. Norton & Co., 1987, pp. 209-210; and *America's Providential History*, pp. 170-173.

90. For more see *In God We Trust Tour Guide*, by Stephen McDowell and Mark Beliles, Charlottesville, Va.: Providence Foundation, 1998, pp. 37-48; and *America's Providential History*, pp. 185-192.

91. See *America's Providential History*, pp. 179-180.

92. See *Noah Webster: On Being American, Selected Writings, 1783-1828*, p. 48.

93. *Ibid.*, p. 50.

94. *Ibid.*, pp. 50-51.

95. Unger, p. 60.

96. For more on Webster's influence on early America see "Reforming America by Propagating a Christian Philosophy of Education and Government, An Example from the Life of Noah Webster," Stephen McDowell, *The Journal of the Foundation for American Christian Education, Vol. 5*, 1993, pp. 166-181.

97. Noah Webster, *Value of the Bible and Excellence of the Christian Religion*, 1834, republished by the Foundation for American Christian Education, p. 78.

98. Noah Webster, *Letters to a Young Gentleman Commencing His Education*, New Haven: Howe & Spalding, 1823, p. 149.

Chapter 8

Separation of Church and State?

Christianity is increasingly coming under attack in America today from judges, elected officials, media, academia, and various activist groups. These people claim that our Constitution mandates a separation of church and state, which to them means that Christianity can have nothing to do with public life; that God must be separate from government. In their thinking God is unconstitutional.

The men who gave us the Constitution certainly believed there should be a jurisdictional separation of church and state, where these two divine institutions did not usurp authority from one another. This was primarily to keep the state out of the affairs of the church. But this did not mean that God should be completely removed from government or that godly principles should not shape civil life and law.

When you compare the action and reasoning of these modern separationists with that of America's Founding Fathers, it is readily apparent that these people are merely interpreting the Constitution according to their own view of life and not that of the Founders. Their interpretation of the Constitution is much different than the Founders' original intent. Modern jurists have embraced an evolutionary view of law that is rooted in the will of the people. The Founders believed in absolute law that was based upon the will of God. They believed mankind receives a general revelation of His will in creation—"the laws of nature"—and a specific revelation of His will in the Bible—"the laws of nature's God." We saw in the last chapter how Harvard Law School President Roscoe Pound worked to replace the Christian view of law, held by almost all Americans, with a humanistic view of law. His vision of our law being rooted in the consensus of man has become a reality, such that the state has taken "the place of Jehovah."[1]

Comparing the Founders and the Modern View of the Relationship of Christianity and Public Life

Government Proclamations

A few years ago, a bill was introduced in Congress recommending—not requiring— Americans to observe a national day of prayer and fasting in response to various violent acts in America, such as the shooting in Littleton, Colorado. It was voted on under special rules for non-controversial bills and thus needed a two-thirds majority to pass. It fell two votes short, 275 to 140. One opponent, Rep. Chet Edwards (D–Texas), harshly attacked the bill as unconstitutional and morally wrong. He said that Congress has no business telling Americans when to pray.

While Rep. Edwards claimed this was unconstitutional, he certainly did not obtain this view from the founders for they were continually declaring days of prayer. From the landing of the Jamestown settlers at Cape Henry in 1607 to the Pilgrims at Plymouth and the New England Puritans through the establishment of Georgia as the thirteenth colony, governments at all levels proclaimed numerous Days of Prayer and Fasting and Thanksgiving.

One example of this occurred in October 1746 when France sent a fleet to attack Boston. Governor Shirley proclaimed a Fast Day and people everywhere thronged to the churches to pray for deliverance. God miraculously answered their prayers by sending a storm and pestilence to wipe out the French fleet. Everyone gave thanks to God.[2]

This not only occurred before independence, but throughout the Revolution and up to the present. During the Revolutionary War the Continental Congress issued at least six different prayer and fast day proclamations and seven different thanksgiving proclamations. These were issued after events such as the surrender of British General Burgoyne at Saratoga, the discovery of the treason of Benedict Arnold, and the surrender of Cornwallis at Yorktown. In the proclamation from the fall of 1777, they recommended for everyone to confess their sins and humbly ask God, "through the merits of Jesus Christ, mercifully to forgive and blot them out of remembrance" and thus He would be able to pour out His blessings upon every aspect of the nation.[3]

The individual states proclaimed numerous such days as well. The Virginia House of Burgesses set apart June 1, 1774, as a day of fasting and prayer in response to England closing the port of Boston. On the day British troops fired upon the minutemen at Lexington (April 19, 1775) the colony of Connecticut was observing a "Day of publick Fasting and Prayer" as proclaimed by Governor Trumbull a month before. Massachusetts set aside August 1, 1776, as a "day of solemn humiliation, fasting, and prayer" where they called upon the people "to humble themselves under the righteous hand of God; penitently to acknowledge their many heinous and aggravated sins" and asking Him to "pour out of his Spirit upon this people. . . and that he would spread the peaceful Kingdom of the Divine Redeemer over the face of the whole habitable world." New York set aside August 27, 1776, "as a day of Fasting, Humiliation, and Prayer to Almighty God, for the imploring of His Divine assistance in the organization and establishment of a form of Government for the security and perpetuation of the Civil and Religious Rights and Liberties of Mankind."[4]

The modern separationists often look to Thomas Jefferson to justify their beliefs, saying he gave us separation of church and state. But Jefferson was no strict separationist, as many of his public actions reveal. He penned the resolve for Virginia's day of fasting and prayer on June 1, 1774. While Governor in 1779, he issued a proclamation "appointing Thursday the 9th day of December next, a day of publick and solemn thanksgiving and prayer to Almighty God, earnestly recommending to all the good people of this commonwealth, to set apart the said day for those purposes."[5]

If in session, Congress and the state assemblies would even go to church together as a body to observe these days. In 1787 a committee of representatives of all the states, gratefully looking back over all the preceding years, set apart October 19, 1787, "as a day of public prayer and thanksgiving" to their "all-bountiful Creator" who had conducted them "through the perils and dangers of the war" and established them as a free nation, and gave "them a name and a place among the princes and nations of the earth."[6]

The first President, George Washington, issued days of thanksgiving and days of prayer as recommended by Congress. Most Presidents up until today have followed this example, with about 200 such proclamations being issued by national government leaders.[7] The 140 congressmen who voted against the recent bill appointing a day of prayer and fasting were separating themselves from the precedent of American history.

Christianity and Public Education

Until recently, a school district in Texas had a program where they invited local clergy members to visit the schools once or twice a year to discuss topics such as violence, peer pressure, and drugs. The clergy were told not to wear religious clothing, lead students in prayer, or reveal their religious affiliation. Someone challenged this in court and Judge Jacques Wiener of the 5th Circuit Court of Appeals ruled in *Doe vs. Beaumont Independent School District* that this was unconstitutional because this program endorsed religion and coerced children to participate, since they might be "traumatized" if they opted out of the voluntary sessions.

In another ruling, U.S. District Judge Ira DeMent restricted the right of students to pray and lead prayers in public schools in DeKalb County, Alabama. His order prohibited students from reading their Bibles during study hall, praying with other students, and even praying before lunch. The order did allow students to "quietly engage in religious activity during noninstructional times, so long as it does not unduly call attention thereto." (What a benevolent gesture from this activist judge.) To implement this, the court appointed monitors to visit schools and report on student prayer activities.[8]

These judges were certainly not looking at the history of education in America to direct their opinions. The Bible and Christianity have been central to education from the beginning. The first schools were started by the church to teach people how to read the Bible. The first common or public schools were started in the 1640s in Massachusetts for the same reason—to enable children "to read and understand the principles of religion and the capital laws of this country."[9]

America's Founders considered teaching Christianity in the schools as foundational for freedom. In the Northwest Ordinance of 1787 and 1789 they said: "Religion, morality, and knowledge, being necessary to good government and the happiness of mankind, schools and the means of education shall forever be encouraged." Signer of the Constitution, Gouverneur Morris, said "education should teach the precepts of religion, and the duties of man towards God."[10] Many other founders expressed similar ideas.

In early America, ministers were the primary teachers in communities. Other teachers who were trained at American colleges and universities received a Biblical education. One hundred and six of the first 108 colleges were started on the Christian faith. By the close of 1860 there were 246 colleges in America. Seventeen of these were state institutions; almost every other one was founded by Christian denominations or by individuals who avowed a religious purpose.[11] Many of the state colleges were Christian as well.[12]

The textbooks used in schools for centuries were thoroughly Christian—the Bible was the central text. Hornbooks generally contained the Lord's Prayer; Christian Catechisms were used extensively in early American education; the New England Primer was a chief text from 1690 to 1800 and taught the alphabet using Biblical ideas; Webster's Blue Back Speller, used for over a century by tens of millions of Americans, taught "just ideas of religion, morals, and domestic economy;" for his Readers, which sold over 122 million copies, McGuffey looked firstly to the "sacred Scriptures" as a source; and even texts used up until the 1960s readily mentioned God.[13]

While almost all past textbooks acknowledged God, today using this three-letter word in books is grounds for removal, not only from the classrooms but also from the libraries of some schools. Recently, a school library in California removed books from a Christian publisher when the ACLU threatened them with a lawsuit, even though parents and the school board had already approved their use. One reason given for their removal was that the books mentioned that God helped Columbus discover America.

Religious Expression on Public Property

Modern separationists believe there should be no religious expression on public property. Consequently, there have been judicial rulings prohibiting nativity creches on government property, attempts to remove the ten commandments from school and courtroom walls, and rulings requiring the removal of crosses from municipal cemeteries. Not only have religious symbols been prohibited from public property, but prayer has also been restricted. A few years ago a pastor was told he, and the small group with him, could not *quietly* pray in the Capitol Building because it violated the constitutional mandate of a separation of church and state. Such ideas would seem completely foreign to the men who gave us the Constitution.

Consider this question: Where did the largest Protestant church in America meet in 1867? The answer: in the Hall of Representatives in the U.S. Capitol Building—in the very building where people have today been told they cannot pray. But in 1867 about 2000 members of the newly formed First Congregational Church assembled every Sabbath to pray and hear from their pastor Charles Boynton, who was also the chaplain of the House.[14]

This was not unusual for church meetings had been taking place in the Capitol since it opened in 1800. Church meetings were even held in the

Capitol while it was u nder c onstruction in 1796. J ust a few days after
Thomas Jefferson wrote his now famous Danbury Baptist letter containing
the phrase "separation of church and state," he went to the Capitol Building
to a church service that was held in the chamber of the House of Representatives. He regularly attended worship services in the Capitol throughout
his presidency. A senator's wife records stepping on his toes at the conclu-
sion of one service. In 1827 President John Quincy Adams attended a special service in the House where a woman, Harriet Livermore, preached.
The room was so packed that he had to sit on the steps of the stage leading
up to her feet. Church services were conducted in the Supreme court chamber in the Capitol, as well as in many other government buildings in Washington.[15]

Christianity and the Law

To the modern separationist, Christian ideas must be kept out of the
public arena. They have no place in our courts or legal system. Such thinking recently caused an appeals court to overturn a 51-year prison sentence a
Cincinnati judge gave a convicted rapist because during the sentencing the
judge quoted the Bible. Surely the founders did not want Americans to use
some out-dated religious book in the important arena of legal justice.

If this were so, why did our national, state, and local governments require elected officials to take an oath of office on the Bible? Courts of law
also required Christian oaths. Tennessee, which was typical of the early
states, required

> the party to be sworn, to lay his hand upon the holy evangelists of Al-
> mighty God, in token of his engagement to speak the truth, as he hopes to
> be saved in the way and method of salvation pointed out in that blessed
> volume; and in further token, that if he should swerve from the truth, he
> may be justly deprived of all the blessings of the gospels, and be made lia-
> ble to that vengeance which he has imprecated on his own head; and after
> repeating the words, "So help me God," shall kiss the holy gospels as a
> seal of confirmation to said engagement.[16]

To the modern separationist, Christians have no right to impose laws
on the rest of the nation that reflect their narrow Biblical view of life. Never
mind that these same people have no problem imposing their laws upon the
nation—laws that are not rooted in the absolutes of an omniscient, loving
God, but in the ever-changing whelms of a selfish people. In actuality, the
Bible formed the basis of America's civil laws.[17] Without this foundation

America would have never presented to the world an example of a free republic.

Christian Involvement in Government

Today, some people think Christians should not be involved in government. Most of our founders thought that only Christians should serve in civil government. Many of the states had provisions in their early Constitutions only allowing Christians to serve in public office. For example, Delaware's Constitution of 1776 states:

> Everyone appointed to public office must say, "I do profess faith in God the Father, and in the Lord Jesus Christ his only Son, and in the Holy Ghost, one God and blessed forevermore; and I do acknowledge the Holy Scriptures of the Old and New Testaments to be given by divine inspiration."

Over the years the states would eliminate religious tests and state establishments of religion, yet would continue to require Christian oaths and provisions for believers in government. Tennessee's Constitution of 1834 said "[t]hat no religious test shall ever be required as a qualification to any office or public trust within this state," but it also had a provision where "[n]o person who denies the being of a God, or a future state of rewards and punishments, shall hold any office in the civil department of this state." They recognized the jurisdictional separation of church and state, but also realized the complete removal of God and government—of godly principles from public life—is not possible, and in fact would be destructive to the nation.

Many other actions of our Founding Fathers reveal their Christian faith. One of these was the appointment of chaplains and the use of ministers to open their governmental meetings. The First Continental Congress meeting in September, 1774, invited the Rev. Jacob Duché to open them in prayer. After the Congress declared independence, they appointed chaplains on July 8, 1776. The first Congress under the U.S. Constitution appointed chaplains for the House and Senate that were paid by public funds. This tradition has continued up to the present. The armies during the American Revolution had chaplains as well.[18]

Congress also acted as a Bible Society. In 1777 they approved the importation of 20,000 Bibles because their supply from England had been cut off and they recognized "that the use of the Bible is so universal and its importance so great." A few years later, in 1782, Congress officially endorsed the printing of the Aitken Bible, which was the first English language Bible published in North America.[19]

The long tradition of Election Sermons also shows the Founders faith. Begun in Massachusetts in the 1630s, this became an annual event in New England and was practiced throughout the colonies. After elections, a minister was invited to deliver a sermon appropriate for the occasion to the newly elected officials and members of the community. Topics on liberty, godly government, patriotism, and good citizenship were addressed. These were often printed and widely distributed. They became the political textbooks of early America.[20]

To restrict public expression of Christian ideas under the guise of it being unconstitutional, reflects either great ignorance or a subversive attempt to change the philosophical foundation of constitutionalism in America, from that of a Biblical worldview to that a humanistic worldview. Either way, the result will be an erosion of liberty and movement toward centralized authoritarian government.

These two views of the source of law in America are at the foundation of the battle in our society today. Which view prevails will determine the future course of our nation. If the humanistic view prevails, the result will be increased license, leading to the continued growth of the state, which will be necessary to control and regulate individual behavior. With the increase of statism will come a loss of individual liberty and national productivity. If the Biblical view prevails, the result will be liberty, justice, and prosperity. Daniel Webster stated:

> If we and our posterity shall be true to the Christian religion, if we and they shall live always in the fear of God and shall respect His Commandments, . . . we may have the highest hopes of the future fortunes of our country. . . . But if we and our posterity neglect religious instruction and authority, violate the rules of eternal justice, trifle with the injunctions of morality, and recklessly destroy the political constitution which holds us together, no man can tell how sudden a catastrophe may overwhelm us that shall bury all our glory in profound obscurity.[21]

The assault on Christianity in America must stop. If it does not then we will destroy the only source of moral and civil reformation. Noah Webster said that "moral evils constitute or produce most of the miseries of mankind and these may be prevented or avoided. Be it remembered then that disobedience to God's law, or sin is the procuring cause of almost all the sufferings of mankind."[22]

Should we separate church and state in America? Yes, if it means prohibiting state-mandated worship or the establishment of a state church; yes, if it means limiting governmental authority to its Biblical duty of punishing evil men and protecting the righteous. However, if it means extirpating God or Biblical principles from public life, then we should be eternally vigilant to resist such a separation, for this would cause the death of the American Republic—the America that has been the land of liberty and prosperity, and a light to the nations.

End Notes

1. See Chapter 11 for more.

2. Catherine Drinker Bowen, *John Adams and the American Revolution*, New York: Grosset & Dunlap, 1950, p. 10-12.

3. B.F. Morris, *Christian Life and Character of the Civil Institutions of the United States*, Philadelphia: George W. Childs, pp. 530-531.

4. See Mark A. Beliles and Stephen K. McDowell, *America's Providential History*, Charlottesville, VA: Providence Foundation, 1989, p. 141. Peter Force, *American Archives: A Documentary History of the English Colonies in North America, Fourth Series*, Washington: M. St. Clair and Peter Force, 1846, pp. 1278, 1471.

5. *The Virginia Gazette*, Nov. 20, 1779, Number 4, Williamsburg: Printed by Dixon & Nicolson.

6. Morris. See W. DeLoss Love, *The Fast and Thanksgiving Days of New England*, New York: Houghton, Mifflin and Company, 1895. Love lists over 1300 Days of Prayer and Fasting, and Prayer and Thanksgiving declared by governments at all levels from 1620 - 1813.

7. See *A Compilation of the Messages of the Presidents*, James D. Richardson, ed., New York: Bureau of National Literature, 1897.

8. The 11th U.S. Circuit Court of Appeals did overturn key portions of Judge DeMent's ruling, recognizing that such "suppression of . . . religious speech demonstrate not neutrality but hostility toward religion. . . . 'Cleansing' our public schools of all religious expression . . . inevitably results in the 'establishment' of disbelief — atheism — as the State's religion." (The State's religion is actually humanism, where man is god, and America's state schools are propagating this religion.)

9. Richard Morris, ed, *Significant Documents in United States History*, Vol. 1, New York: Van Nostrand Reinhold Co., 1969, p. 19.

10. Jared Sparks, *The Life of Governeur Morris*, vol. 3, 1832, p. 483.

11. The Pageant of America, Ralph Henry Gabriel, ed., New Haven: Yale University Press, vol. 10, 1928, p. 315.

12. See Stephen McDowell, *Reforming America through Restoring America's Christian Education*, Charlottesville, VA: Providence Foundation, 2000.

13. *Ibid.*

14. James H. Hutson, *Religion and the Founding of the American Republic*, Washington: Library of Congress, 1998, p. 91.

15. Stephen McDowell and Mark Beliles, *In God We Trust Tour Guide*, Charlottesville, VA: Providence Foundation, 1998, pp. 26-27.

16. *The Tennessee Justice's Manual and Civil Officer's Guide*, Judge James Coffield Mitchell, Nashville: J.C. Mitchell & C.C. Norvell, 1834, pp. 457-458.

17. See Chapters 3, 6, 11.

18. See Beliles and McDowell, *America's Providential History*, pp. 133-135.

19. *Ibid*, pp. 152-153.

20. *Ibid,* pp.121-122.

21. Morris, p. 270.

22. Noah Webster, *Value of the Bible and Excellence of the Christian Religion*, 1834, republished by the Foundation for American Christian Education, San Francisco, 1988, p. 78.

Chapter 9

The Role of Women in History
Preservers and Propagators of Liberty as Teachers of the Human Race

"Dear God, guide me. Make my life count," prayed Susanna Wesley daily. Born the 25th of 25 children to a minister and his wife, she loved God from her youth and had a burning desire to live her life for Him. As a young woman she dreamed, "I hope the fire I start will not only burn all of London but all of the United Kingdom as well. I hope it will burn all over the world."

Susanna was always looking for an opportunity to fulfill that dream and was always asking God what He would have her do. How should she start that fire? Should she become a missionary, a teacher? Or did God have another plan for her? At a young age she married a minister and, like her mother, began having children —19 in all. She devoted most of her time and effort to being a good wife and mother.

Even in the midst of hardship after hardship, she continued to pour herself into her children and inspire them for good. When her children were around five or six-years-old she would set aside one whole day to teach them how to read. She taught the alphabet phonetically and then had her children read the Bible.

She never traveled throughout the world or directly started a spiritual fire in London or elsewhere. But Susanna's dream did become a reality in her 13th and 17th born children, Charles and John Wesley, who spread the Gospel throughout the world.

Susanna Wesley's words, "Dear God, guide me. Make my life count," have echoed down through the centuries as women have tried to discern God's role for them in the advancement of liberty, nations, and His Kingdom. Modern women can look to them as examples for applying Biblical principles to their lives as they strive to leave their own mark on history.

Molding Young Minds

Women in early America saw their most crucial role in society as forming the character of the next generation. They thought that men, in general, could lead the nation, but that they were the ones who would train the leaders. This was primarily carried out in the home.

John Adams wrote in a letter to his wife, Abigail, "I think I have some times observed to you in conversation, that upon examining the biography of illustrious men, you will generally find some female about them, in the relation of mother, or wife, or sister, to whose instigation a great part of their merit is to be ascribed."[1]

In recent years, people have debated whether women can compete with men in public life. Certainly they can, but never forget that no one can compete with a mother in the home. As more mothers have joined the workforce, through choice or necessity, the United States has experienced greater problems because those who can best form the character of the next generation are having less input into the lives of the next generation. Neither the state, nor the school, nor even the church can effectively replace mom or dad in the home.

Daniel Webster said it well in his Remarks to the Ladies of Richmond, October 5, 1840:

> [T]he mothers of a civilized nation . . . [work], not on frail and perishable matter, but on the immortal mind, moulding and fashioning beings who are to exist for ever. . . . They work, not upon the canvas that shall perish, or the marble that shall crumble into dust, but upon mind, upon spirit, which is to last for ever, and which is to bear, for good or evil, throughout its duration, the impress of a mother's . . . hand.[2]

God has ordained certain unique duties for men and women. The primary role of women is as mothers, who are teachers that form and shape the character of the next generation. While all women are not mothers or wives, this is still the primary role of women in life, though they are certainly not limited to only this role.

Mothers comfort and feed their children. They feed not only the physical child, but also the spiritual, mental and emotional child. This feeding nourishes and instructs, strengthens and invigorates, enlivens and comforts. Mothers provide this comfort and nourishment to their children and to society. Teaching naturally flows from this desire.

God describes Himself as a mother to Israel, "As one whom his mother comforteth, so will I comfort you; and ye shall be comforted in Jerusalem" (Is. 66:13). Paul said that they had brought the Gospel to the Thessalonians in a gentle manner, "as a nursing mother tenderly cares for her own children" (1 Thess. 2:7). This heart for their spiritual children caused Paul and those with him to gladly pour out their own lives for the Thessalonian believers. This is the heart God gives mothers for their children. Without this heart, nations are doomed.

There is a statue in Plymouth, Massachusetts, honoring the Pilgrim mother. On the base of that statue these words are engraved, "They brought up their families in sturdy virtue and a living faith in God without which nations p erish." These qualities, imparted in the American home, are the foundation of our existence as a free nation. As the role of mothers is diminished in shaping the godly character of future generations, so will America decline. Mothers who fulfill their primary role will impact society in many ways.

Abigail Adams

Abigail Adams was one of the most inspirational and influential women in history. She was the first woman to be both the wife and mother of an American president, an honor she held solely until Barbara Bush, the wife of former President George H. W. Bush, saw her son George W. Bush sworn in as president.

It is said of Abigail that as a wife and inspiration to John Adams she "strengthened his courage, fired his nobler feelings and nerved his higher purposes. She was the source of his strength and the inspiration that gave him the power to rise above his own weaknesses as often as he did."

An excerpt of a letter to her husband on the day he became president reveals much of her character:

> You have this day to declare yourself head of a nation. "And now, O Lord, my God, thou hast made thy servant ruler over the people. Give unto him an understanding heart that he may know how to go out and come in before this great people, and that he may discern between good and bad. For who is able to judge this thy so great a people" were the words of a royal sovereign; and not less applicable to him who is invested with the chief magistracy of a nation, though he wear not a crown, nor the robes of royalty.
>
> My thoughts and my meditations are with you, though personally absent; and my petitions to Heaven are that the things that make for peace may not be hidden from your eyes. My feelings are not those of pride or

ostentation, upon the occasion. They are solemnized by a sense of the obligations, the important trusts, and numerous duties connected with it. That you may be enabled to discharge them with honor to yourself, with justice and impartiality to your country, and with satisfaction to this great people, shall be the daily prayer of your A.A.[3]

Abigail's influence was not only instrumental to her husband's achievements, but also those of her son, John Quincy Adams. She was responsible for his education — training that produced a great statesmen.

Abigail was John Quincy's primary educator until age 10 or 11. As a 10-year-old, John Quincy knew French and Latin, read Rollins and Smollet, and helped manage the farm with his mother while his father was away serving the nation. At the same age he wrote to his father in a letter, "I wish, sir, you would give me some instructions with regard to my time, and advise me how to proportion my studies and my play, in writing, and I will keep them by me and endeavor to follow them."[4]

At age 11, John Quincy traveled with his father to France, yet Abigail used her letters to continue the education she had so well begun at their home in Braintree, Massachusetts. In June of 1778 she wrote:

> You are in possession of a naturally good understanding, and of spirits unbroken by adversity and untamed with care. Improve your understanding by acquiring useful knowledge and virtue, such as will render you an ornament to society, and honor to your country, and a blessing to your parents. Great learning and superior abilities, should you ever possess them, will be of little value and small estimation, unless virtue, honor, truth, and integrity are added to them. Adhere to those religious sentiments and principles which were early instilled into your mind, and remember, that you are accountable to your Maker for all your words and actions.[5]

In the same letter she encouraged John Quincy to pay attention to the development of his conduct by heeding the instruction of his parents; "for, dear as you are to me, I would much rather you should have found your grave in the ocean you have crossed . . . than see you an immoral, profligate, or graceless child."

When he was 14 he received a U.S. Congressional diplomatic appointment as secretary to the ambassador of the court of Catherine the Great in Russia. Besides serving as president, he also served 18 years in the U.S. House of Representatives, was a U.S. Senator, was Secretary of State, and served as Foreign ambassador to England, France, Holland, Prussia and Russia. In addition to his scholarship and statesmanship, John Quincy had been trained in godly character and thought. He had a providential view of history[6], as seen in his 1837 July 4th Oration[7], where he spoke of America being a link in the progress of the Gospel throughout history, and where he recognized the founding of this nation upon Christian principles.

John Quincy once wrote of his mother:

> My mother was an angel upon earth. She was a minister of blessings to all human beings within her sphere of action. . . . She has been to me more than a mother. She has been a spirit from above watching over me for good, and contributing by my mere consciousness of her existence to the comfort of my life. . . . There is not a virtue that can abide in the female heart but it was the ornament of hers.[8]

Sarah Edwards

Jonathan Edwards was perhaps the greatest theologian/philosopher in America's history and was the leader in sparking the first Great Awakening in the 1730s. Much of his success was due to his wife, Sarah. She managed the household, was instrumental in raising their 11 children, and created an atmosphere of harmony, love and esteem in their home. Visitors frequently stayed overnight in the Edwards' home and were more often affected by the character of the home than any words spoken by Jonathan in conversation.

When George Whitefield visited them, he was deeply impressed with the Edwards' children, with Jonathan and especially with Sarah — her ability to talk "feelingly and solidly of the things of God," and her role of helpmate to her husband. Her example motivated him to marry the next year.[9]

A writer, who knew and visited the Edwards, Samuel Hopkins, wrote of Sarah's training of her children:

> She had an excellent way of governing her children. She knew how to make them regard and obey her cheerfully, without loud, angry words, much less heavy blows. . . . If any correction was necessary, she did not administer it in a passion. . . . In her directions in matters of importance, she would address herself to the reason of her children, that they might not only know her will, but at the same time be convinced of the reasonableness of it. . . . Her system of discipline was begun at a very early age and it was her rule to resist the first as well as every subsequent exhibition of temper or disobedience in the child . . . wisely reflecting that until a child will obey his parents, he can never be brought to obey God.[10]

A study was done of 1,400 descendants of Jonathan and Sarah Edwards. There were 13 college presidents, 65 professors, 100 lawyers, 30 judges, 66 physicians, and 80 holders of public office including three senators, three governors, and a vice president of the United States. Sarah not only affected the lives of many during the time she lived, but through her descendants she has touched all of eternity.

Mercy Otis Warren

Many women carried their role as teachers beyond their families, for example Mercy Otis Warren. Mercy wrote one of the first histories of the American Revolution, *History of the Rise, Progress and Termination of the American Revolution*, which was quite unusual for a woman at that time.

She wrote this work with a desire to be of use to the newly formed American republic. She thought a principal responsibility of her writings was, "to form the minds, to fix the principles[,] to correct the errors, and to beckon by the soft allurements of love, as well as the stronger voice of reason, the young members of society (peculiarly my charge), to tread the path of true glory."[11] True history will inspire youth "to tread the path of true glory."

In her writings, Mercy not only saw an opportunity to benefit her country, but to also fulfill her role as a mother—"to cultivate the sentiments of public and private virtue in whatever falls from her pen."[12] She agreed with the common sentiment of her day that history should train people, especially young people, in "public and private virtue."[13]

Mama West

Benjamin West's mother greatly influenced society through inspiring her son, the father of American painting. Raised in a plain Quaker home in Pennsylvania, Benjamin West (1738-1820) went on to become a very successful painter known throughout America and Europe. While serving as the president of the British Royal Academy, Benjamin gave much support to many of America's first artists. He attributed his success to his mother.

> When Benjamin West was seven years old, he was left one summer day with the charge of an infant niece. As it lay in the cradle and he was engaged in fanning away the flies, the motion of the fan pleased the child and caused it to smile. Attracted by the charms thus created, young West felt his instinctive passion aroused; and seeing paper, pen and some red and black ink on a table, he eagerly seized them and made his first attempt at portrait painting. Just as he had finished his maiden task his mother and sister entered. He tried to conceal what he had done, but his confusion arrested his mother's attention, and she asked him what he had been doing. With reluctance and timidity, he handed her the paper, begging at the same time, that she would not be offended.[14]

His reluctance likely came from the strict Quaker tenets against graven images; and he wasn't sure how his mom would respond. He had never seen a painting or portrait before.

> Examining the drawing for a short time, she turned to her daughter and, with a smile, said, "I declare, he has made a likeness of Sally." She gave him a fond kiss, which so encouraged him that he promised her some drawings of the flowers which she was then holding, if she wished to have them.
>
> The next year a cousin sent him a box of colors and pencils, with large quantities of canvas prepared for the easel, and half a dozen engravings. Early in the morning after their reception, he took all his materials into the garret, and for several days forget all about school. His mother suspected that the box was the cause of his neglect of his books, and going into the garret and finding him busy at a picture, she was about to reprimand him; but her eye fell on some of his compositions, and her anger cooled at once. She was so pleased with them that she loaded him with kisses and promised to secure his father's pardon for his neglect of school.
>
> How much the world is indebted to Mrs. West for her early and constant encouragement of the immortal artist. He often used to say, after his reputation was established, "My mother's kiss made me a painter."[15]

Building Nations Through the Home

Besides the primary source of education, homes are also the seed-beds of the Gospel, civil liberty, civility, health and welfare. They, not the government, are to be the primary provider of health, education, and welfare. Homes are the foundation of society. It is here that women have great influence.

The Gospel is spread primarily through the homes of a nation. After Lydia was converted by Paul (his first convert in Europe), she introduced her household to God and then opened her home to Paul, and hence, to the Gospel (Acts 16:14-15). Christianity first spread into Europe through her home. Women, more than anyone, can make the atmosphere of their home conducive to spreading the Gospel.

Civil liberty is also chiefly spread through homes. Motherhood is critical for the development of the character and self-government necessary to support a free nation. Mother, and educator of women in the 19th century, Lydia Sigourney, said:

> For the strength of a nation, especially of a republican nation, is in the intelligent and well-ordered homes of the people. And in proportion as the discipline of families is relaxed, will the happy organization of communi-

ties be affected, and national character become vagrant, turbulent, or ripe for revolution.[16]

Further, homes provide the foundation of happiness and comfort in a society. It is in homes that morals and true knowledge are imparted. It is there that spiritual and mental health is cultivated, which provide the most important ingredient for physical health. Caring for the elderly, the sick, the orphaned and the needy should also be in the home. Daniel Webster wrote:

> [H]appiness . . . depends on the right administration of government, and a proper tone of public morals. That is a subject on which the moral perceptions of woman are both quicker and juster than those of the other sex. . . . It is by the promulgation of sound morals in the community, and more especially by the training and instruction of the young, that woman performs her part towards the preservation of a free government. It is generally admitted that public liberty, and the perpetuity of a free constitution, rest on the virtue and intelligence of the community which enjoys it. How is that virtue to be inspired, and how is that intelligence to be communicated?. . . . Mothers are, indeed, the affectionate and effective teachers of the human race.[17]

Dolley Madison

As the first lady, Dolley Madison was the facilitator of the nation's business. Because President Thomas Jefferson's wife had died at a young age and he never remarried, Dolley served as White House hostess during his administration.

She continued this role when her husband, James, succeeded Jefferson as president. For 16 years she set a home atmosphere for the White House and the office of the presidency. She was the first to serve state dinners at the White House, where much of the nation's business was, and has been, accomplished. And during the War of 1812 she risked great danger by staying in the White House to save important paintings and documents when the British troops were marching into Washington.

Narcissa Whitman

Narcissa and Marcus Whitman were among the first missionaries and pioneers to the Oregon territory. Narcissa and another missionary's wife were the first two American women to travel over the Rockies. The settlement of the northwest took place through the Whitman home. Narcissa was known for her faith, courage and determination. In the end those she came to serve took Narcissa's life. Indians martyred her and her husband.

Harriet Beecher Stowe

When Harriet Beecher Stowe visited President Abraham Lincoln in the White House he first greeted her with the words, "So this is the little lady who made this big war."[18] He made this statement due to the influence of her book, *Uncle Tom's Cabin*. A runaway best seller in the 1850s, it sold more than 100,000 copies in six months and put her on the forefront of America's abolition movement. She was acclaimed by literary and political leaders throughout the world, from Charles Dickens to Mark Twain to England's Queen Victoria.

Prior to writing the book, Harriet didn't have much time to do anything outside the home, "I am but a mere drudge with few ideas beyond babies and house-keeping." When her husband Calvin's salary was cut in half at the seminary where he worked, Harriet's writing developed out of necessity.

Calvin had always encouraged her in her writing, believing it was part of God's fate for her. He told her to let her writing flow, for as a result her husband and children would call her blessed, like the woman in Proverbs 31 who uses her talents for good.

She began to write some articles and submit them to eastern magazine publishers. Her success was immediate, though she continued to face many personal challenges. With her rapidly growing family, eventually numbering seven children, came an increase in physical sickness, plus all the pressures she faced caused her to feel emotionally drained. After she heard that her brother had been found shot to death outside his home, she broke down physically and emotionally. During a time of recuperation, she began writing a series for a magazine that became *Uncle Tom's Cabin*.

Concerning *Uncle Tom's Cabin*, Harriet said she did not write it, "I was only the instrument. The Lord wrote the book."[19]

Though this book led to international fame and visits with many famous people, Harriet remained faithful to her duties as a wife and mother. She also assumed leadership in the anti-slavery movement. With the help of her husband and brother, she drew up an anti-slavery petition, got 3,000 ministers to sign it, and presented it to the U.S. Congress.

Harriet Beecher Stowe had as much to do with the freeing of the slaves in America as anyone. And she brought about this great social change while fulfilling her duties and responsibilities in the home.

Persevering Through Adversity

Many women have contributed to the advancement of God's purposes with great circumstances to overcome.

Pamela Cunningham

Pamela Cunningham had become an invalid when she fell from a horse as a girl. When her mother visited Mount Vernon in 1853 and reported to Pamela the state of disrepair to which first President George Washington's home had fallen (she had seen its stateliness as a child), Pamela began "to emerge from her sheltered life and participate openly in public affairs." She took it upon herself to preserve the memory of "the Father of our Country."

Elswyth Thane writes in *Mount Vernon is Ours*:

> The Mount Vernon Ladies' Association is not sponsored by nor beholden to the Federal Government or the State of Virginia. It stands alone, its original charter having been granted in 1858, when ladies were not supposed to be capable of conducting anything like public affairs, and it was the creation of one resolute woman who at the age of 37 acquired what even her friends at first considered an impracticable obsession. She had made up her mind that the home, which George Washington loved, should not be allowed to fall down in ruins from neglect. Not the uncooperative Washington family, the skeptical Virginia Legislature, nor her own condition of chronic invalidism could daunt her, nor swerve her from her apparently impossible purpose. As an example of sheer grit and courage, laced with Southern charm, Ann Pamela Cunningham remains unique.[20]

God's providence was evident in all she did to accomplish the task. She enlisted the assistance of Edward Everett (pastor, member of congress, Governor of Massachusetts, senator, President of Harvard, minister to Great Britain, and known for his oratory), raised the money, persuaded John Augustine Washington to sell the land, and obtained the approval of the state of Virginia. In her invalid condition all the travel and work nearly killed her, but she persevered, and her vision was accomplished. The organization which she started, The Mount Vernon Ladies Association, is the oldest non-government sponsored organization for the preservation of an historic site.

Phillis Wheatley

Phillis Wheatley was the first significant black writer in America, and her book of poems was probably the first book published by a black American. Her accomplishments are even more admirable when considering her circumstances in life.

Phillis came as a slave to America from Africa in 1761, at about the age of eight. When she arrived she knew no English and was frail. While she quickly learned English, and much more, she remained frail all her life. John and Susanna Wheatley purchased Phillis and incorporated her into their family life. Susanna and her daughter, Mary, tutored her in the Bible, English, Latin, history, geography and Christian principles. Phillis learned quickly and acquired a better education than most women in Boston had at the time.

Phillis began writing poetry at age 12 and many of her poems reflect her strong Christian faith. At the age of 18, Phillis joined the Old South Congregational Church. She was not only glad to be a Christian but was also proud to be an American. God was her first priority, followed by herself and the Wheatley family.

Shortly after her first book of poems was published in 1773, John Wheatley gave Phillis her freedom. In her short life she gained much renown and met many famous people, including President George Washington, about whom she had written a poem.

The following poem reveals Phillis Wheatley's providential view of life, recognizing God's hand in her own circumstances and history.

On Being Brought From Africa to America

'TWAS mercy brought me from my Pagan land,
Taught my benighted soul to understand
That there's a God, that there's a Saviour too:
Once I redemption neither sought nor knew.
Some view our sable race with scornful eye,
"Their colour is a diabolic die."
Remember, Christians, Negros, black as Cain,
May be refin'd, and join the angelic train.[21]

A Lady of Philadelphia

The following is from *The Women of the American Revolution* by Elizabeth F. Ellet:

> A letter found among some papers belonging to a lady of Philadelphia, addressed to a British officer in Boston, and written before the Declaration of Independence, reads, in part,

"I will tell you what I have done. My only brother I have sent to the camp with my prayers and blessings. I hope he will not disgrace me; I am confident he will behave with honor, and emulate the great examples he has before him; and had I twenty sons and brothers they should go. I have retrenched every superfluous expense in my table and family; tea I have not drunk since last Christmas, nor bought a new cap or gown since your defeat at Lexington; and what I never did before, have learned to knit, and am now making stockings of American wool for my servants; and this way do I throw in my mite to the public good. I know this — that as free I can die but once; but as a slave I shall not be worthy of life. I have the pleasure to assure you that these are the sentiments of all my sister Americans. They have sacrificed assemblies, parties of pleasure, tea drinking and finery, to that great spirit of patriotism that actuates all degrees of people throughout this extensive continent. If these are the sentiments of females, what must glow in the breasts of our husbands, brothers, and sons! They are as with one heart determined to die or be free. It is not a quibble in politics, a science which few understand, that we are contending for; it is this plain truth, which the most ignorant peasant knows, and is clear to the weakest capacity — that no man has a right to take their money without their consent. You say you are no politician. Oh, sir, it requires no Machiavelian head to discover this tyranny and oppression. It is written with a sunbeam. Every one will see and know it, because it will make every one feel; and we shall be unworthy of the blessings of Heaven if we ever submit to it. . . . Heaven seems to smile on us; for in the memory of man, never were known such quantities of flax, and sheep without number. We are making powder fast, and do not want for ammunition."[22]

A Good Lady and Her Two Sons

The following story is from *Annals of the American Revolution* by Jedidiah Morse.

The female part of our citizens contributed their full proportion in every period, towards the accomplishment of the revolution. They wrought in their own way, and with great effect. An anecdote which we have just seen in one of our newspapers, will explain what I mean.

A good lady — we knew her when she had grown old — in 1775, lived on the sea-board, about a day's march from Boston, where the British army then was. By some unaccountable accident, a rumour was spread, in town and country, in and about there, that the *Regulars* were on a full march for the place, and would probably arrive in three hours at farthest. This was after the battle of Lexington, and all, as might be well supposed, was in sad confusion — some were boiling with rage and full of fight, some with fear and confusion, some hiding their treasures, and others flying for life. In this wild moment, when most people, in some way or other, were frightened from their property, our heroine, who had two sons, one about nineteen years of age, and the other about sixteen, was seen by our informant, preparing them to discharge their duty.

This lady had a vision for the cause of liberty and had imparted this to her sons as well. Now, as the cause entered a phase where a greater commitment was required, she was ready to send them to the battle.

The eldest she was able to equip in fine style — she took her husband's fowling-piece, "made for duck or plover," (the good man being absent on a coasting voyage to Virginia) and with it the powder horn and shot bag; but the lad thinking the duck and goose shot not quite the size to kill regulars, his mother took a chisel, cut up her pewter spoons, and hammered them into slugs, and put them into his bag, and he set off in great earnest, but thought he would call one moment and see the parson, who said well done, my brave boy — God preserve you — and on he went in the way of his duty. The youngest was importunate for his equipments, but his mother could find nothing to arm him with but an old rusty sword; the boy seemed rather unwilling to risk himself with this alone, but lingered in the street, in a state of hesitation, when his mother thus upbraided him. "You John H*****, what will your father say if he hears that a child of his is afraid to meet the British, go along; beg or borrow a gun, or you will find one, child — some coward, I dare say, will be running away, then take his gun and march forward, and if you come back and I hear you have not behaved like a man, I shall carry the blush of shame on my face to the grave." She then shut the door, wiped the tear from her eye, and waited the issue; the boy joined the march. Such a woman could not have cowards for her sons.

Instances of refined and delicate pride and affection occurred, at that period, every day, in different places, and in fact this disposition and feeling was then so common, that it now operates as one great cause of our not having more facts of this kind recorded. What few there are remembered should not be lost. Nothing great or glorious was ever achieved which woman did not act in, advise, or consent to.[23]

Making Your Life Count

"Dear God, guide me. Make my life count." A love of God, an understanding of His purpose, a love of learning, a heart to nourish and teach and a burning desire to fulfill God's plan — these are the characteristics you should cultivate to make your life count.

We can see these qualities in Susannah Wesley, Sarah Edwards, Abigail Adams and others. If God has put a desire in your heart, no matter what the nature, don't let it die out, but seek to fan the flames and be responsible to fulfill your duties where God has you.

Katherine Lee Bates

Katherine Lee Bates was a woman who had a burning desire to leave a permanent legacy. She wrote poems and stories from the time she was a young girl. She stated, "If I could only write a poem people would remember after I was dead, I would consider my life had been worth living. That's my dream, to write something worthwhile, something that will live after me."

All through college and her rise as a teacher, then full professor and head of the English Department of a college for women, her life's dream was always burning in her heart. It burned for over two decades. When she was 34 years old Katherine Lee Bates did write those words that would live after her. It was atop Pike's Peak looking out over the mountains, fields, and sky that she felt love for her country such as she had never had before and the words came to her:

> O beautiful for spacious skies
> For amber waves of grain
> For purple mountain majesties
> Above the fruited plain!
> America, America!
> God shed His grace on thee,
> And crown thy good with brotherhood
> From sea to shining sea.

To Godly women in America: the role you play in advancing liberty, nations, and God's Kingdom may be one of renown, as a Harriet Beecher Stowe, or it may be one of support, as a Sarah Edwards, or it may be one where your children become great leaders, as with Susanna Wesley or Abigail Adams, or it may be one where you fulfill God's plan by overcoming adversity, as Pamela Cunningham. It is most likely that history will never take notice of the role you play, but the impact you have is immeasurable, for you are the shapers of the generations to come, you are the preservers of the happiness and freedom of our nation, you are the creators of a new generation. Without you our nation will surely perish, but with you we can have the greatest hopes for the future fortunes of our country and the advancement of God's truth and liberty throughout the nations.

Most of the problems society faces today have their solution in the homes, for here is where a new generation is being formed. We need a generation of great men and women and children who will not be the "creatures" of our age, but the "creators" of it.

Women — as those that form the character of the next generation, as transmitters and preservers of liberty, as teachers of the human race, as co-managers of the homes, as providers of education, health, and welfare — will play a central role in creating a new age, one where God is glorified and His liberty extends to all.

End Notes

1. *The Christian History of the American Revolution, Consider and Ponder,* Verna M. Hall, compiler, San Francisco: Foundation for American Christian Education, 1976, p. 74.

2. Daniel Webster, "Remarks to the Ladies of Richmond, October 5, 1840," *The Works of Daniel Webster,* Boston: Little, Brown, & Co., 1854, 2:107-108.

3. *Nobel Deeds of American Women,* J. Clement, editor, Boston: Lee & Shepherd, 1851, pp. 48-49.

4. Hall, p. 605.

5. Hall, p. 607, quoting from *Life, Administration and Times of John Quincy Adams* by John Robert Irelan, 1887, pp. 20-22.

6. Adams read through Rollins *Ancient History* when he was 10. His mother began reading it to him a few years before. See Hall, p. 605 for Rollins view of history.

7. John Quincy Adams, "An Oration Delivered before the Inhabitants of the Town of Newburyport at their Request on the Sixty-First Anniversary of the Declaration of Independence, July 4, 1837" (Newburyport: Charles Whipple, 1837).

8. John T. Faris, *Historic Shrines of America,* New York: George H. Doran Co., 1918, p. 49.

9. William J. Petersen, *Martin Luther Had a Wife,* Wheaton, Ill.: House Publishers, p. 87.

10. Ibid., p. 82-83.

11. Mrs. Mercy Otis Warren, *History of the Rise Progress and Termination of the American Revolution,* Indianapolis: reprinted by Liberty Classics, 1988, p. xvii.

12. Ibid.

13. Ibid., p. xxi.

14. *Noble Deeds of American Women,* pp. 202-203.

15. *Ibid.*

16. Lydia H. Sigourney, *Letters to Young Ladies* (1852), quoted in *Christian History of the Constitution of the United States of America,* compiled by Verna M. Hall, San Francisco: Foundation for American Christian Education, 1980, p. 410.

17. "Remarks to the Ladies of Richmond, October 5, 1840," *The Works of Daniel Webster,* 2:105-108.

18. William J. Petersen, *Harriet Beecher Stowe Had a Husband,* Wheaton, Ill.: Tyndale House Publishers, 1983, p. 134.

19. *Ibid.,* p. 131.

20. Elswyth Thane, *Mount Vernon Is Ours, The Story of Its Preservation,* New York: Duell, Sloan, and Pearce, 1966, p. 3.

21. *The Poems of Phillis Wheatley,* Julian D. Mason, Jr., editor, Chapel Hill: The University of North Carolina Press, 1989, p. 53.

22. *The Women of the American Revolution,* by Elizabeth F. Ellet, 1849, in Hall, *Consider and Ponder,* p. 74.

23. Jedidiah Morse, *Annals of the American Revolution,* Port Washington, NY: Kennikat Press, 1968. Reprint of original, first published in 1824, p. 233.

Section III

Applying Biblical Principles to Governing the Nations

"All Scripture is inspired by God and profitable for teaching, for reproof, for correction, for training in righteousness; that the man of God may be adequate, eguipped for every good work."

2 Timothy 3:16-17

"You shall thus observe My statutes, and keep My judgments, so as to carry them out, that you may live securely on the land. Then the land will yield its produce, so that you can eat your fill and live securely on it."

Leviticus 25:18-19

Chapter 10

We Hold These Truths

Governmental Principles of America' s Founders

Patrick Henry wrote in a letter to Archibald Blair, January 8, 1799:

And, whilst I see the dangers that threaten ours from her [France's] in-
trigues and her arms, I am not so much alarmed as at the apprehension of
her destroying the great pillars of all government and of social life,—I
mean virtue, morality, and religion. This is the armor, my friend, and this
alone, that renders us invincible. These are the tactics we should study. If
we lose these, we are conquered, fallen indeed.[1]

In this statement, Patrick Henry affirmed the truth adhered to by the
founders of America—that is, they understood that in order for this nation
to remain free, prosperous, and strong it must have its foundation in certain
fundamental principles. These vital principles, or first principles, must be a
part of the citizens' lives, as well as the institutions that comprise society.
George Mason wrote in 1776 that "no free government or the blessing of
liberty can be preserved to any people but by . . . frequent recurrence to fundamental principles."[2]

Henry mentioned three such principles, "virtue, morality, and religion." We will examine these and other foundational governmental principles that were part of the lives and teachings of America's founders.

1. Individuality

America's founders believed that man is created in the image of God
and, therefore, he has value and possesses certain God-given rights. The
Declaration of Independence states it this way:

We hold these truths to be self-evident, that all men are created equal, that they are endowed by their Creator with certain inalienable rights, that among these are life, liberty and the pursuit of happiness.

Our founders also believed that man has a unique purpose in God and that God providentially moves to fulfill His plan for men and nations.

Elias Boudinot was a member of the Continental Congress, serving as President of that body in 1782-83; a signer of the Treaty of Peace; a member of the U.S. House of Representatives from New Jersey; the Director of the National Mint, 1796-1805; and the first president of the American Bible Society, serving from 1816-1821. In an oration given in 1793 he said:

When great events are to be produced in this our world, great exertions generally become necessary; men are therefore usually raised up, with talents and powers peculiarly adapted to the purposes intended by Providence.[3]

George Washington was one such man whom God raised up. God providentially prepared and preserved Washington. One example of this is seen in an incident that occurred in 1755 during the French and Indian War. (We looked at this in more detail in Chapter 2, but it is repeated in part here since it illustrates this principle well.)

Washington was second in command to British General Braddock as the British and Colonial troops marched out into the wilderness to drive the French off British territory. Washington tried to warn Braddock that European military tactics would not work in the American frontier, but the General wouldn't listen and they marched right into an ambush, where they were soundly defeated. Only Washington's fearlessness and leadership saved the day.

During the battle Gen. Braddock was mortally wounded. Washington had four bullets pass through his coat and two horses shot from under him, yet escaped unhurt. He was fired upon numerous times from near point-blank range and remained unharmed. An Indian who took part in the battle later stated, "Washington was not born to be killed by a bullet! For I had seventeen fair fires at him, and after all could not bring him to the ground."[4]

The chief and several of his Indians had singled out Washington to kill him, and when they couldn't they "concluded that he was under the protection of the Great Spirit, had a charmed life, and could not be slain in battle."[5]

In a letter to his brother, Washington wrote:

But by the all-powerful dispensations of Providence, I have been protected beyond all human probability or expectation; for I had four bullets through my coat, and two horses shot under me, yet escaped unhurt, although death was levelling my companions on every side of me.[6]

Rev. Samuel Davies preached a sermon on August 17, 1755, wherein he cites the preservation of young Washington. He spoke of "that heroic youth, Colonel Washington, whom I cannot but hope Providence has hitherto preserved in so signal a manner for some important service to his country."[7]

Our founders not only believed that God has a unique purpose for man but also that God has a plan for nations. From the beginning of America the settlers spoke of the vision they had for establishing new colonies. In 1630 Puritan John Winthrop wrote in *A Model of Christian Charity* of their desire to establish a colony that would be as "a city set on a hill," one that was such an example of a Godly community that all the people of the earth would look at them and say, "Lord, make us like that of New England."[8]

The founders believed God had a unique destiny for America. They felt this nation would play an important role in the advancement of liberty for all mankind. On July 4, 1837, in an oration commemorating the anniversary of the Declaration of Independence, our sixth President, John Quincy Adams, stated:

Is it not that, in the chain of human events, the birthday of the nation is indissolubly linked with the birthday of the Saviour? That it forms a leading event in the progress of the gospel dispensation? Is it not that the Declaration of Independence first organized the social compact on the foundation of the Redeemer's mission upon earth? That it laid the cornerstone of human government upon the first precepts of Christianity and gave to the world the first irrevocable pledge of the fulfillment of the prophecies announced directly from Heaven at the birth of the Saviour and predicted by the greatest of the Hebrew prophets 600 years before?[9]

Adams clearly spoke of the individuality of America as it fit into God's plan for the nations and the spread of Christianity throughout the earth in history.

2. Self-government

Elias Boudinot revealed another fundamental principle upon which our nation was founded:

Another essential ingredient in the happiness we enjoy as a nation, and which arises from the principles of the revolution, is the right that every people have to govern themselves in such manner as they judge best calculated for the common benefit.[10]

This was a new concept, because during most of history people lived under "ruler's law," where the rulers made the laws and the people had no voice in the matter. However, in America, the people made the laws, and everyone, including the rulers, were subject to it.

Our founders understood that a people cannot govern themselves in civil affairs if they do not govern their own lives well. Robert C. Winthrop, speaker of the U.S. House of Representatives from 1847-49, said in 1849:

All societies of men must be governed in some way or other. The less they may have of stringent State Government, the more they must have of individual self-government. The less they rely on public law or physical force, the more they must rely on private moral restraint. Men, in a word, must necessarily be controlled either by a power within them, or by a power without them; either by the Word of God, or by the strong arm of man; either by the Bible or the bayonet.[11]

The basis of the ability for man to govern himself well is rooted in his being in subjection to a higher power. The founders' firm commitment to God, as well as their commitment to govern their lives according to His laws as contained in the Bible, was the foundation for self-government in America. When we examine the scores of constitutions, compacts, and charters written in colonial America we readily see the source of their civil law was found in the Bible. For example, in the Massachusetts Body of Liberties (which was a precursor to our Bill of Rights), written by Rev. Nathaniel Ward in 1641, the Pentateuch (the first five books of the Bible) was the basis for its criminal code, and "in case of the defect of a law in any partecular [sic] case" the standard was "the word of God."[12] Often the colonists would quote directly from the Scriptures and give references to justify their civil laws as seen, for example, in The Laws of the Pilgrims.[13]

Self-government is limited apart from God, therefore, the ability to govern well is limited where the people and leaders do not seek to govern themselves and their nation under God. George Washington said, "It is impossible to govern the universe without the aid of a Supreme Being."[14]

It is important to realize that the foundation for self-government is laid in the families of a nation. Noah Webster wrote in *A Manual of Useful Studies:*

In the family are formed the elements of civil government; the family discipline is the model of all social order; . . . the respect for the law and the magistrate begins in the respect for parents. . . . Families are the nurseries of good and bad citizens. The parent who neglects to restrain and govern his child, or who, by his example, corrupts him, is the enemy of the community to which he belongs; the parent who instructs his child in good principles, and subjects him to correct discipline, is the guardian angel of his child, and the best benefactor of society.[15]

Elias Boudinot agreed:

Good government generally begins in the family, and if the moral character of a people once degenerates, their political character must soon follow.[16]

3. Education

Our founders were very much aware of the relation of education and liberty. They knew that a people cannot be ignorant and free. Jefferson said it this way:

If a nation expects to be ignorant and free, in a state of civilization, it expects what never was and never will be.

Benjamin Franklin said that ignorance produces bondage:

A nation of well informed men who have been taught to know and prize the rights which God has given them cannot be enslaved. It is in the region of ignorance that tyranny begins.

Our founders believed that useful education—that which produces liberty—must have its foundation in Christianity.

Though many may not recognize his name today, Benjamin Rush played a very significant role in our history. Although Rush was a signer of the Declaration of Independence and a member of the Pennsylvania Constitutional Convention, his contributions were not limited to governmental affairs. He was also a professor of medicine, a writer, a principal founder of Dickinson College, and a leader in education. In addition, he served on many Bible and medical societies, and societies for the abolition of slavery. He wrote in 1806:

In contemplating the political institutions of the United States, I lament that we waste so much time and money in punishing crimes and take so little pains to prevent them. We profess to be republicans, and yet we neglect the only means of establishing and perpetuating our republican forms of government, that is, the universal education of our youth in the principles of christianity by the means of the bible. For this Divine book, above all others, favors that equality among mankind, that respect for just laws, and those sober and frugal virtues, which constitute the soul of republicanism[17]

Education in colonial America was primarily centered in the home and church, with the Bible the focal point of all education. Schools were started to provide a Christian education to those who were not able to receive such training at home and to supplement home education. The first schools were started by the church. The first common schools originated with the school law of 1647 in Massachusetts, which stated:

It being one chief project of that old deluder, Satan, to keep men from the knowledge of the Scriptures.[18]

Our founders recognized that Satan wants to keep people ignorant. If he can keep them ignorant, he can keep them in bondage. This motivated them to not only start schools but also colleges.

Colleges and universities were started as seminaries to train a godly and literate clergy. In fact, 106 of the first 108 colleges were founded on the Christian faith. One of the original rules and precepts of Harvard College stated:

Let every Student be plainly instructed, and earnestly pressed to consider well, the end of his life and studies is, to know God and Jesus Christ which is eternall life, (John 17:3), and therefore to lay Christ in the bottome, as the only foundation of all sound knowledge and Learning.[19]

The Father of the American Revolution, Samuel Adams, declared that education in the principles of the Christian religion is the means of renovating our age. He wrote in a letter October 4, 1790, to John Adams, then vice-president of the United States:

Let divines and philosophers, statesmen and patriots, unite their endeavors to renovate the age, by impressing the minds of men with the importance of educating their little boys and girls, of inculcating in the minds of youth the fear and love of the Deity and universal philanthropy, and, in subordination to these great principles, the love of their country; of instructing them in the art of self-government, without which they never can act a wise part in the government of societies, great or small; in short, of leading them in the study and practice of the exalted virtues of the Christian system.[20]

Knowledge apart from God and His truth is little better than complete ignorance, because the most important aspect of education is the imbuing of moral principles. All education is religious—it imparts a basic set of principles and ideals, a worldview. How the youth are educated today, will determine the course our nation takes in the future.

Noah Webster understood this very well. He spent his entire adult life working to reform America and to provide a foundation of liberty, happiness, and prosperity for all citizens. Education from a Christian perspective was key. In 1839 he wrote:

> Practical truths in religion, in morals, and in all civil and social concerns, ought to be among the first and most prominent objects of instruction. Without a competent knowledge of legal and social rights and duties, persons are often liable to suffer in property or reputation, by neglect or mistakes. Without religious and moral principles deeply impressed on the mind, and controlling the whole conduct, science and literature will not make men what the laws of God require them to be; and without both kinds of knowledge, citizens can not enjoy the blessings which they seek, and which a strict conformity to rules of duty will enable them to obtain.[21]

Numerous people in America today agree that a lack of moral values is the root of our problems, yet, without a standard of moral absolutes rooted in a Sovereign God and His Truth, and without these being taught and lived in the homes, in the schools, in our government, and in the media, we, as a nation, will not be able to impart these needed morals.

The people behind the French Revolution believed virtue was necessary for their efforts to succeed, but they thought they could be virtuous on their own apart from God. Our founders knew this could never be. Washington, in his Farewell Address, specifically addressed this belief when he said:

> And let us with caution indulge the supposition, that morality can be maintained without religion. . . . [R]eason and experience both forbid us to expect, that national morality can prevail in exclusion of religious principles.[22]

4. Property (Conscience)

James Madison revealed the founders understanding that property is both internal and external when he wrote:

> Property. . . . In the former sense, a man's land, or merchandise, or money, is called his property. In the latter sense, a man has a property in

his opinions and the free communication of them. He has a property of peculiar value in his religious opinions, and in the profession and practice
dictated by them. . . . He has an equal property in the free use of his facul-
ties, and free choice of the objects on which to employ them. In a word, as
a man is said to have a right to his property, he may be equally said to have
a property in his rights.[23]

A person's property is whatever he has exclusive right to possess and
control. Property is first internal. Madison said that "Conscience is the
most sacred of all property." A person's conscience is his most precious aspect of property because it tells him what is right and wrong in his actions.
Each person in a free government must be a good steward of his conscience
and keep it clear. By doing so, he will know what is right and wrong from
within and, therefore, he will be able to live his life in a right manner.

Freedom of conscience and freedom of religion were of primary importance to our founders. They incorporated these ideas in their constitutions and laws, for example, the Virginia Bill of Rights, Sec. 16, first
adopted June 12, 1776:

> That religion, or the duty which we owe our Creator, and the manner of
> discharging it, can be directed only by reason and convictions, not by force
> or violence; and therefore all men are equally entitled to the free exercise
> of religion, according to the dictates of conscience; and that it is the mutual
> duty of all to practice Christian forbearance, love, and charity towards
> each other.

Over the generations, our founders were leading the way in establishing freedom of worship and conscience as an inalienable right of man.
While many today present our forefathers as religious bigots and the epit-
ome of intolerance, they were in reality on the forefront of incorporating
freedom of conscience into civil society. This is exemplified by such men
as Thomas Hooker, Roger Williams, and William Penn.

Penn, who was the founder of Pennsylvania, established that colony as
a "holy experiment," where people of all sects of Christianity could come
and freely worship God. As a Quaker in England he had experienced much
persecution for his beliefs and he did not want such persecution to occur in
Pennsylvania. Penn led the way for many religious and civil reforms. His
actions at a trial he faced in 1670 in London helped to secure the rights of
juries and did much to promote freedom of worship.

Our founders also recognized the importance of the external aspect of
the principle of property. James Madison wrote in 1792:

Government is instituted to protect property of every sort. . . . This being the end of government, that is NOT a just government, . . . nor is property secure under it, where the property which a man has . . . is violated by arbitrary seizures of one class of citizens for the service of the rest.[24]

The Boston Tea Party took place as a result of the people acting upon the principle of property. Beginning with the Stamp Act in 1764, the government of England attempted to tax the colonists without their consent. An outcry from the colonists forced Britain to repeal the measure, but over the years the king and parliament continued to try to exert what they felt was their right to tax the colonists even though they were not represented in the body that imposed the taxes. The colonists' slogan "no taxation without representation" was based upon the principle of property, for if someone could take another man's property without his consent, then he really had no property rights. Since the tea that was shipped to Boston in 1773 had a tax upon it, the colonists refused to buy it. When the authorities threatened to confiscate the privately owned British ship unless it unloaded the tea, the colonists felt their only recourse was to dump the tea in the harbor. They were not going to violate their principles and submit to tyranny.

The principle of property lead Noah Webster to work for copyright legislation on the state and national level. He said, "the production of genius and the imagination are if possible more really and exclusively property than houses and lands, and are equally entitled to legal security."[25]

5. Union (Covenant)

The people of a free nation will not only be self-governed but will also voluntarily work in union with each other for the common good of the entire nation. The external union of a people results from an internal unity of ideas and principles residing in the hearts of the people. Compulsory union, that imposed by external force and fear, will never last (as seen by the former Soviet Union). Union cannot be forced externally, but must arise from internal unity.

Christianity provided the basis of a "community united, not by external bonds, but by the vital force of distinctive ideas and principles." Civil covenants started in America in 1620 when English Pilgrims drew up the Mayflower Compact, which states:

Having undertaken for the glory of God and advancement of the Christian faith, and the honor of our king and country, a voyage to plant the first colony in the northern parts of Virginia; do by these presents solemnly and mutually in the presence of God, and one of another, covenant and combine ourselves together into a civil body politic, for our better ordering and preservation and furtherance of the ends aforesaid.[26]

The Pilgrims were able to covenant to live together in civil society because some years earlier they had covenanted to join themselves together in a church body (via the Scrooby Covenant). In fact, American constitutionalism (which has affected constitutions in most nations) is based upon the Biblical idea of covenant.

There are many other examples of the early founders of America forming civil covenants, such as in the formation of the colony of Connecticut (see the Fundamental Orders of Connecticut, 1639) and in the New England Confederation of 1643, which was the first union among English colonies.

The 13 original colonies were able to form an external union together because of a common internal unity of ideas and principles produced by Christianity. The churches and clergy had been sowing common seeds of truth for generations. The Great Awakening (1740-1760) also did much to promote unity among the colonists. Not surprisingly, it was a minister, Rev. Jonathan Mayhew, who first proposed the idea of union among the colonies.

As conflict with England began to increase in the early 1770s, the colonists' unity of ideas began to be followed by a unity of action. When the English authorities closed the port of Boston in response to the "tea party" the other colonies came to the aid of their Boston neighbors. Their first action was to pray. Days of Prayer and Fasting were declared by Massachusetts, Connecticut and Virginia. Jefferson penned the resolve in Virginia "to invoke the divine interposition to give to the American people one heart and one mind to oppose by all just means every injury to American rights."[27] Material assistance began to flow in as well. George Washington headed the list of contributors from Virginia.

Steps toward union began to follow their unity of ideas and action. On September 5, 1774, the first Continental Congress convened in Philadelphia where representatives of 12 of the colonies met to discuss how they could unite in their resistance to the Intolerable Acts of the British Parliament. One of their first resolves was to ask the Rev. Jacob Duché to open the Congress in prayer, which he did with great effect on the morning of the 7th as recorded by John Adams in a letter to his wife.[28]

A later Continental Congress, with representatives from all 13 colonies, would approve a Declaration of Independence, cementing a civil covenant (union) of the united colonies.

6. Virtue or Christian Character

No nation can long endure without virtue or morality in the people. A loss of principles and manners is the greatest threat to a free people and will cause a nation's downfall more surely than any foreign enemy.

John Adams said while President in 1798:

> [W]e have no government armed with power capable of contending with human passions unbridled by morality and religion. Avarice, ambition, revenge, or gallantry, would break the strongest cords of our Constitution as a whale goes through a net. Our Constitution was made only for a moral and religious people. It is wholly inadequate to the government of any other. [29]

Only a moral and religious people can supply the power necessary to support the form of our government. The founders of America saw that our virtue was rooted in Christianity. In 1838 the Legislature of New York said:

> Our Government depends for its being on the virtue of the people,— on that virtue that has its foundation in the morality of the Christian religion; and that religion is the common and prevailing faith of the people. [30]

The founders of America not only taught the value of morality and Christian character, but they also lived it. They were great examples in word and deed.

Take for example George Washington. As he was disbanding the army that he had commanded during the Revolution, he wrote a letter to the Governors of all the States on June 8, 1783, giving his advice on what needed to be done to assure the success of the newly formed nation. He wrote:

> I now make it my earnest prayer, that God would have you, and the State over which you preside, in his holy protection . . . that he would most graciously be pleased to dispose us all to do justice, to love mercy, and to demean ourselves with that charity, humility, and pacific temper of mind, which were the characteristics of the Divine Author of our blessed religion, and without an humble imitation of whose example in these things, we can never hope to be a happy nation. [31]

His advice to the Governors? Imitate Jesus Christ and His character. Washington himself reflected the Divine Author of his blessed religion in many ways. One example is seen in his response to the attempt to make him king.

After the war ended, many people were looking for a way to deal with the problems the new nation of America faced. Members of the military were especially aware of the weaknesses of the congress to handle the difficulties since many of them had not received the payment promised to them. A group of officers proposed making Washington king as the best means of averting national collapse. The people loved him and the officers would support him, and both knew he would act in a benevolent manner. Colonel Lewis Nicola presented this idea to Washington in a letter in the spring of 1782. Washington's reply reveals his character:

> Sir, With a mixture of great surprise and astonishment, I have read with attention the sentiments you have submitted to my perusal. Be assured, Sir, no occurrence in the course of the war has given me more painful sensations, than your information of their being such ideas existing in the army, as you have expressed, and I must view with abhorrence and reprehend with severity. . . .
>
> I am much at loss to conceive what part of my conduct could have given encouragement to an address, which to me seems big with greatest mischiefs, that can befall my country. If I am not deceived in the knowledge of my self, you could not have found a person to whom your schemes are more disagreeable.[32]

It is easy to see how the character of the father of our country helped to assure our survival and success. Both our leaders and citizens must practice "private and public Virtue," which according to John Adams, "is the only Foundation of Republics."[33]

7. Faith

The most important principle to form the foundation of a nation, and that from which all the other principles flow, is faith or religion. We have already seen in previous quotes how our Founders firmly believed this. Consider also the following:

George Washington wrote in 1797: "Religion and Morality are the essential pillars of Civil society."[34] In his farewell address in 1796, Washington wrote:

> Of all the dispositions and habits which lead to political prosperity, religion and morality are indispensable supports.[35]

James Madison wrote in 1825:

> [T]he belief in a God All Powerful wise and good, is . . . essential to the moral order of the World and to the happiness of man.[36]

On June 28, 1787, at the Constitutional Convention, 81 year-old Benjamin Franklin said:

> I have lived, Sir, a long time, and the longer I live, the more convincing proofs I see of this truth—that God Governs in the affairs of men. And if a sparrow cannot fall to the ground without His notice, is it probable that an empire can rise without His aid? We have been assured, Sir, in the sacred writings, that "except the Lord build the House they in vain that build it." I firmly believe this; and I also believe that without His concurring aid we shall succeed in this political building no better, than the Builders of Babel.[37]

Thomas Jefferson said:

> Among the most inestimable of our blessings is that . . . of liberty to worship our Creator in the way we think most agreeable in His will; a liberty deemed in other countries incompatible with good government and yet proved by our experience to be its best support.[38]

The Constitution of New Hampshire of June 2, 1784 stated:

> morality and piety, rightly grounded on evangelical principles, will give the best and greatest security to government, and will lay in the hearts of men the strongest obligations to due subjection; . . . the knowledge of these, is most likely to be propagated through a society by the institution of the public worship of the DEITY, and of public instruction in morality and religion.[39]

And we could go on and on with statements from our Founders and from the early civil documents revealing their firm conviction of this principle. They believed that the supreme civil power was not rooted in a president, or king, or a parliament, or elected legislature, but in God. James Otis wrote:

> The supreme power in a state . . . belongs alone to God. Parliaments are in all cases to declare what is for the good of the whole; but it is not the declaration of Parliament that makes it so: There must be in every instance a higher authority, viz. God. Should an Act of Parliament be against any of His natural laws, which are immutably true, their declaration would be contrary to eternal truth, equity, and justice, and consequently void.[40]

Our founders believed that it was not just faith in any god or religion that formed the foundation of free societies, but it was specifically the Christian religion and faith in the only true God and His Word, the Bible. In a letter to James Madison from 16 October 1829, Noah Webster wrote:

The christian religion, in its purity, is the basis or rather the source of all genuine freedom in government. . . . I am persuaded that no civil government of a republican form can exist & be durable, in which the principles of that religion have not a controlling influence.[41]

In the Preface to his *United States History* book, Webster wrote:

The brief exposition of the constitution of the United States, will unfold to young persons the principles of republican government; and it is the sincere desire of the writer that our citizens should early understand that the genuine source of correct republican principles is the Bible, particularly the New Testament or the Christian religion.[42]

Benjamin Rush wrote in 1806:

Christianity is the only true and perfect religion, and that in proportion as mankind adopt its principles and obeys its precepts, they will be wise and happy.[43]

The father of American Geography, Jedidiah Morse wrote:

To the kindly influence of Christianity we owe that degree of civil freedom, and political and social happiness which mankind now enjoys.[44]

The U.S. House of Representatives declared in 1854:

[T]he great vital and conservative element in our system is the belief of our people in the pure doctrines and divine truths of the gospel of Jesus Christ.[45]

This principle was exemplified in their actions as well as their words. About seven months after the first Continental Congress met in Philadelphia, Paul Revere set out on his famous ride to warn the colonists, and in particular two leaders of the "rebellion," Samuel Adams and John Hancock (who were at Rev. Jonas Clark's home), that the British were coming. The shot that was heard around the world occurred on the morning of April 19, 1775. Rev. Jonas Clark (upon whose Church lawn fighting began and whose parishioners took part) declared: "From this day will be dated the liberty of the world!"[46]

About one month before the Battle of Lexington, the Governor of Connecticut had called upon the colony to observe a

Day of public Fasting and Prayer . . . that God would graciously pour out his Holy Spirit on us, to bring us to a thorough repentance and effectual reformation; . . . That He would restore, preserve and secure the liberties of this, and all the other American Colonies, and make this land a mountain of Holiness and habitation of Righteousness forever. . . . That God would preserve and confirm the Union of the Colonies in the pursuit and practice of that Religion and virtue which will honour Him.[47]

What day had Governor Jonathan Trumbull selected for them to be praying?

Wednesday, the nineteenth Day of April![48]

Martial law was declared by England in response to the fighting. In response to the declaration of martial law, the Continental Congress declared a Day of Fasting and Prayer, recommending Christians of all denominations in all colonies to observe it. It is estimated that two of the three million people living in America observed that day.

In the years that followed, America's situation often looked bleak, but our war for independence was won. This was mainly due to the Providence of God and the Christian character and faith of our founders. These men recognized the battle was the Lord's, and gave Him thanks when He moved on their behalf.

Take for example the defeat of Burgoyne at Saratoga. Due to the Providence of God, General Burgoyne and his 11,000 were forced to surrender at Saratoga. In response to the victory, the Continental Congress proclaimed a Day of Thanksgiving and Praise to God. They stated:

> Forasmuch as it is the indispensable duty of all men to adore the superintending providence of Almighty God, . . . and it having pleased Him in His abundant mercy. . . to crown our arms with most signal success. . . it is therefore recommended . . . to set apart Thursday, the 18th day of December, for solemn thanksgiving and praise.[49]

They recommended for everyone to confess their sins and humbly ask God, "through the merits of Jesus Christ, mercifully to forgive and blot them out of remembrance" and thus He then would be able to pour our His blessings upon every aspect of the nation.[50]

Congress and Washington recognized the providence of God in the events leading to the surrender of Cornwallis at Yorktown as well. Congress went to Church together to "return thanks to Almighty God, for crowning the allied arms . . . with success, by the surrender of the Earl of Cornwallis.[51]

These are only a few words and examples that reveal the Christian faith of our founders and their belief that faith in God and conformity to His principles are the foundation of freedom.

The Power and Form of Free Nations

These seven principles comprised the power of America from our beginning. They provided the foundation upon which our form of government could be built. Without these foundational principles in the lives of Americans, our nation would never have been established nor have become the most free, just, and prosperous nation in history. Likewise, we will never remain a free and prosperous nation without this power or spirit. If the power is removed, the form will become corrupt.

The great statesmen Daniel Webster gave us this warning:

> If we and our posterity shall be true to the Christian religion, if we and they shall live always in the fear of God and shall respect His Commandments,. . . we may have the highest hopes of the future fortunes of our country; . . . . But if we and our posterity neglect religious instruction and authority, violate the rules of eternal justice, trifle with the injunctions of morality, and recklessly destroy the political constitution which holds us together, no man can tell how sudden a catastrophe may overwhelm us that shall bury all our glory in profound obscurity.[52]

We must seek, as our Founders did, to infuse these principles into every aspect of the life of our nation, and in so doing clothe our nation with armor that will make us invincible and assure the future fortunes of our country.

End Notes

1. *Patrick Henry*, Moses Coit Tyler, Boston: Houghton, Mifflin, and Co., 1893, p. 365.

2. George Mason, *Bill of Rights of Virginia*, June, 1776, in *Sources of Our Liberties*, edited by Richard L. Perry, Chicago: American Bar Foundation, 1978, p. 312.

3. Elias Boudinot, "Oration at Elizabethtown, New Jersey, on the Fourth of July, 1793." *American Eloquence: A Collection of Speeches and Addresses, by the Most Eminent Orators of America*, New York: D. Appleton and Company, 1858, Vol. 1, p. 264.

4. William J. Johnson, *George Washington the Christian*, Reprinted by Mott Media, Milford, MI, 1976, p. 40.

5. Washington Irving, *The Life of Washington*, Vol. 1, New York: G.P. Putnam's Sons, 1857.

6. *Ibid.*, p. 259.

7. *Ibid*, p. 268-269.

8. *Old South Leaflets*, Boston: Old South Association.

9. John Quincy Adams, *An Oration Delivered before the Inhabitants of the Town of Newburyport on the Sixty-First Anniversary of the Declaration of Independence, July 4th, 1837*, Charles Whipple, Newburyport, 1837, pp. 5-6.

10. Boudinot, p. 265.

11. Robert C. Winthrop, "Address to Massachusetts Bible Society Meeting, May 28, 1849", *Addresses and Speeches on Various Occasions*, Boston: Little, Brown & Co., 1852, p. 172.

12. Richard Morris, editor, *Significant Documents in United States History*, Vol. 1, New York: Van Nostrand Reinhold Co., 1969, p. 15-16.

13. *The Laws of the Pilgrims, 1672 & 1685*, A Facsimile Edition, Pulbished by Michael Glazier and the Pilgrim Society, 1977

14. *Maxims of Washington*, compiled by John Frederick Schroeder, New York: D. Appleton & Co., 1854, p. 341.

15. Noah Webster, *A Manual of Useful Studies*, New Haven: S. Babcock, 1839, p. 77-78.

16. Boudinot, p. 266.

17. *Benjamin Rush*, Essays, Literary, Moral and Philosophical, Philadelphia: printed by Thomas and William Bradford, 1806, p. 113.

18. Richard Morris, p. 20.

19. From *New Englands First Fruits, 1643*, in *Teaching and Learning America's Christian History* by Rosalie Slater, San Francisco: Foundation for American Christian Education, 1980, p. vii.

20. *The Life and Public Services of Samuel Adams*, by William V. Wells, Boston: Little, Brown & Co., 1865, Vol. III, p. 301.

21. Webster, p. vi.

22. George Washington's Farewell Address, September 17, 1796. *A Compilation of the Messages and Papers of the Presidents*, by James D. Richardson, Washington: Bureau of National Literature and Art, 1910, 1:205-216.

23. *The Christian History of the Constitution of the United States*, compiled by Verna Hall, San Francisco: Foundation for American Christian Education, 1980, p. 248A.

24. *Our Ageless Constitution*, David Stedman and LaVaughn Lewis, editors. Asheboro, NC: W. David Stedman Assoc., 1987, p. 34, 274.

25. Quoted in article on Webster by Rosalie Slater, in preface to reprint of Webster's original dictionary (1828), San Francisco: Foundation for American Christian Education, 1980, p. 15.

26. Richard Morris, pp. 1-2.

27. Mark Beliles and Stephen McDowell, *America's Providential History*, Charlottesville: Providence Foundation, 1989, p. 131.

28. *Ibid.*, pp. 133-135.

29. "A Letter to the Officers of the First Brigade of the Third Division of the Militia of Massachusetts, Oct. 11, 1798," in *The Works of John Adams, Second President of the United States*, Boston: Little, Brown and Co., 1854, 9:228-229.

30. B.F. Morris, *Christian Life and Character of the Civil Institutions of the United States*, Philadelphia: George W. Childs, 1864, p. 239.

31. *Circular Letter Addressed to the Governors of all the States on Disbanding the Army*, 1783. Old South Leaflets, No. 15.

32. George Washington, Letter to Colonel Lewis Nicola, Newburg, 22 May 1782. *The Writings of George Washington*, Vol. 8, Jared Sparks, Ed., Boston, 1835.

33. *The Christian History of the American Revolution, Consider and Ponder*, Verna Hall, compiler, San Francisco: Foundation for American Christian Education, 1976, p. 615.

34. *Letter to the Clergy of Different Denominations Residing in and near the City of Philadelphia*, March 3, 1797.

35. *Messages and Papers of the Presidents*, 1:205-216.

36. Letter to Frederick Beasley, Nov. 20, 1825.

37. *Notes of Debates in the Federal Convention of 1787*, reported by James Madison. New York: W.W. Norton & Co., 1987, pp. 209-210.

38. Beliles and McDowell, p. 178.

39. *Sources of Our Liberties*, p. 382.

40. *Ibid.*, pp. 264-265.

41. Madison Papers, Series 2, Library of Congress

42. *History of the United States*, New Haven: Durrie & Peck, 1833, p. v.

43. Rush, p. 93.

44. Election Sermon given at Charleston, MA on April 25, 1799.

45. Cited in B.F. Morris, p. 328.

46. Franklin Cole, editor, *They Preached Liberty*, Indianapolis: Liberty Press, p. 39.

47. *The Christian History of the American Revolution*, p. 40.

48. *Ibid.*

49. *Ibid.*, pp. 530-531.

50. *Ibid.*

51. Beliles and McDowell, p. 167.

52. B.F. Morris, p. 270.

Chapter 11

The Changing Nature of Law in America

Many Americans use Jefferson's phrase, "a wall of separation between Church and S tate," t o describe what they believe the Constitution prescribes for the relationship of religion and civil government. Recent authors[1] have aptly pointed out how many today misapply or do not understand the "wall" metaphor — how it has been cut off from its historical meaning and made to communicate ideas contrary to Jefferson and the founders of America. The phrase "separation of church and state" has been repeated so often in an improper context that many incorrectly believe that our Constitution mandates a strict separation, meaning a restriction of religious influence upon civil government and the public square. Many present the framers of the Constitution and the founders of America as irreligious men who were strict separationists, thus, giving us "a separation of church and state."

The founders certainly believed in a jurisdictional separation of Church and state, where these two legitimate institutions had specific responsibilities and authority in their jurisdictions, and neither should encroach upon the other. But to the founders both of these were under the same Higher Authority who, as we will see, prescribed His will for man and the human institutions of family, church, and state through the laws of nature and nature's God.

Honest examination shows that the founders were extremely religious men, who, not only had no qualms about letting their religious beliefs flow to civil matters, but considered, in the words of Washington, religion and morality the foundation of free governments. Even one of the least orthodox of the founders, Thomas Jefferson, mixed religion and civil matters in a way that would produce violent convulsions from modern separationists

— writing laws punishing Sabbath breakers, granting the governor the authority to issue "days of public fasting and humiliation, or thanksgiving," (including the punitive provision of a 50 pound fine on ministers failing to perform divine service on the appointed day), supporting the use of the Bible as a text in public schools, suggesting and approving the use of tax dollars to support missionaries.

A strict separationist view has produced many judicial rulings and actions of public and private figures that, while claimed as constitutional, would have been viewed as dangerous and subversive of liberty by those who gave us the Constitution. Some have been so ludicrous that almost everyone has reacted strongly, for example, the recent federal court ruling that it is unconstitutional for public school students to say "under God" in the Pledge of Allegiance. Strong reaction against the ruling came from many Democrats and Republicans, liberals and conservatives.

But others just as contrary to the views of the founders have passed with much less reaction, yet with the usual claim of their constitutionality, and accepted by many Americans a s what our founders wanted. Thus, some things the courts have ruled as unconstitutional include: posting the Ten Commandments in schools (Stone v. Graham, 1980) and public buildings (Harvey v. Cobb County, 1993); having a prayer at a school graduation ceremony (Harris v. Joint School District, 1994); having a planter in the shape of a cross at a public cemetery (Warsaw v. Tehachapi, 1990); having a classroom library contain books which deal with Christianity, or for a teacher to be seen with a personal copy of the Bible at school (Roberts v. Madigan, 1990); displaying religious artwork in schools (Washegesic v. Bloomingdale Public Schools, 1993).

Even a cursory look at history shows many actions of the Founding Fathers, Jefferson included, would be considered unconstitutional by modern courts, and that the modern concept of separation of church and state has limited (if any) historical support. So then, why do so many people (citizens, judges, legislators, educators) not understand or misapply the "wall" metaphor (and similar ideas)?

There are various reasons for this. Certainly lack of knowledge or bad history is one chief reason. As Chief Justice Rehnguist wrote (dissenting in Wallace v. Jaffree, 1985):

> The "wall of separation between church and State" is a metaphor based on bad history, a metaphor which has proved useless as a guide to judging. It should be frankly and explicitly abandoned.[2]

Personal presuppositions (such as Justice Black's view of Catholicism) is another, but it is not my intent to give an exhaustive list.

One fundamental reason, which also explains why those who have knowledge of the founders' actions and thinking yet still embrace a strict separationist view claiming its constitutionality, is that America has been undergoing a change in the foundation of law and a change in the view of the nature and purpose of law. Modern rulings and actions reflect this philosophical change in law.

America's founders generally had a Christian view of law, where law is rooted in the absolutes of a Supreme Creator who reveals His will (law) to man, while modern man generally has a humanistic or evolutionary view of law, seeing that it originates in man. This is evidenced not only in the legal and political arena, but in all areas of life. The differing views can be encapsulated by comparing the definition of *immoral* from the founding era with that of today.

Noah Webster, in his *An American Dictionary of the English Language* (1828), writes under his definition of immoral: "Every action is immoral which contravenes any divine precept, or which is contrary to the duties men owe to each other." The standard for immoral action is "divine precept." A modern *Webster's New World Dictionary* defines immoral as "not in conformity with accepted principles of right and wrong behavior."[3] Thus, the consensus of man — not divine precept — determines right and wrong behavior.

The Founders' Christian View of Law

To determine the founders' view of law, we can examine: 1) the ideas of the political writers that shaped their thinking, 2) their own words, 3) the seminal constitutions, compacts, and charters of the colonies, 4) early laws written by the colonists, 5) documents in the early American republic, 6) court rulings, 7) the content of education in the schools, colleges, and textbooks.

Influential Political Writers

Dr. Donald Lutz conducted an exhaustive ten-year research of about 15,000 political documents of the Founders' Era (1760-1805), and, from 916 of these items, recorded every reference our founders made to other sources. This list of 3154 citations reveals those writings and men that most shaped the political ideas of our founders. By far, the most quoted source of their political ideas was the Bible, 34% of citations. The next most quoted sources were individuals who had a Christian view of law — Montesquieu (8.3%), Blackstone (7.9%), and Locke (2.9%).[4]

Montesquieu

Baron De Montesquieu begins his *The Spirit of Laws* (1748) by commenting on laws in general, stating:

> God is related to the universe, as Creator and Preserver; the laws by which He created all things are those by which He preserves them. He acts according to these rules, because He knows them; He knows them, because He made them; and He made them, because they are in relation of His Wisdom and power. [5]

He says of the laws of the Creator used to govern the world: "These rules are a fixed and invariable relation."[6] Writing that all of creation are subject to God's fixed laws, he points out how man "incessantly transgresses the laws established by God" setting up his own laws in place of God's that flow from "a thousand impetuous passions." To keep from forgetting his Creator, Montesquieu says that "God has therefore reminded him of his duty by the laws of religion . . .; philosophy . . . [and] by political and civil laws." Then he speaks of the Laws of Nature: "The law which, impressing on our minds the idea of a Creator, inclines us towards Him, is the first in importance . . . of natural laws."[7]

Sir William Blackstone

Blackstone was the next most quoted source. In his *Commentaries on the Laws of England* (1765), which was studied by lawyers in America for a century and a half, he writes:

> [W]hen the supreme being formed the universe, and created matter out of nothing, he impressed certain principles upon that matter, from which it can never depart, and without which it would cease to be. When he put that matter into motion, he established certain laws of motion, to which all moveable bodies must conform. . . .
>
> If we farther advance . . . to vegetable and animal life, we shall find them still governed by laws; . . . [As operations of inanimate and organic processes] are not left to chance, or the will of the creature itself, but are performed i n a wondrous involuntary manner, and guided by unerring rules laid down by the great creator. . . .
>
> Man, considered as a creature, must necessarily be subject to the laws of his creator, for he is an entirely dependent being. . . . And consequently as man depends absolutely upon his maker for every thing, it is necessary that he should in all points conform to his maker's will.

This will of his maker is called the law of nature. . . .

This law of nature, being co-eval with mankind and dictated by God himself, is of course superior in obligation to any other. It is binding over all the globe, in all countries, and at all times: no human laws are of any validity, if contrary to this; and such of them as are valid derive all their force, and all their authority, mediately or immediately, from this original. . . .

The doctrines thus delivered we call the revealed or divine law, and they are to be found only in the holy scriptures. These precepts, when revealed, are found upon comparison to be really a part of the original law of nature. . . . As then the moral precepts of this law are indeed of the same original with those of the law of nature. . . . the revealed law . . . is the law of nature expressly declared to be so by God himself. . . .

Upon these two foundations, the law of nature and the law of revelation, depend all human laws; that is to say, no human laws should be suffered to contradict these.[8]

John Locke

The third most quoted source was John Locke who stated in "The Second Treatise of Government, ch. 1,":

The rules that they [the legislators] make for other men's actions must . . . be conformable to the law of nature — i.e., the will of God, of which that is a declaration — and the fundamental law of nature being the preservation of mankind, no human sanction can be good or valid against it.[9]

In his "Essay Concerning Human Understanding" he states his view on the source of truth:

The holy Scripture is to me, and always will be, the constant guide of my belief; and I shall always hearken to it, as containing infallible truth relating to things of the highest concernment. . . . [W]here I lack the evidence of things, there yet is ground enough for me to believe, because God has said it: and I shall immediately condemn and quit any opinion of mine, as soon as I am shown that it is contrary to any revelation in the holy scripture.[10]

Pufendorf

Samuel von Pufendorf (1.3% of citations) stated: "Our Saviour reduced the essence of the law to two heads: Love God and love your neighbor. To these heads can be referred the entire natural law."[11]

Pufendorf was clear that "God . . . is the cause and origin of all things."[12] He wrote that "God is the author of the natural law"[13] To understand natural law, "it is necessary to presuppose that God exists, and by His providence rules all things; also that He has enjoined upon the human race that they observe those dictates of the reason, as laws promulgated by Himself by means of our natural light."[14] "[M]an has been obliged by God to keep the same [natural law], as a means not devised by will of man, and changeable at their discretion, but expressly ordained by God Himself, in order to insure this end."[15]

This is contrary to the modern view that law evolves as society changes and man can change the law at his discretion. These writers, as did America's founders, believed that any law that is contrary to God's law is no law at all.

When the founders wrote of "the laws of nature and of nature's God" they understood this to mean what Locke, Blackstone, Montesquieu and others had presented; i.e. "the laws of nature" is the will of God revealed in creation and the conscience of man, and "the laws of nature's God" is the will of God revealed in the Scriptures.

Sir Edward Coke

There were many prominent political writers who presented this view of law long before Montesquieu and Blackstone, including Sir Edward Coke and Hugo Grotius. These men were also quoted by America's founders — Coke 1.3% of citations and Grotius, 0.9%. Coke, a noted English jurist, wrote in Calvin's Case (c. 1610):

> The law of nature is that which God at the time of creation of the nature of man infused into his heart, for his preservation and direction; and this is *lex aeterna*, the moral law, called also the law of nature. And by the law, written with the finger of God in the heart of man, were the people of God a long time governed, before the law was written by Moses, who was the first reporter or writer of law in the world. The Apostle in the Second Chapter to the Romans saith, *Cum enim gentes quae legem non habent naturaliter ea quae legis sunt faciunt* [While the nations who do not have the law do naturally the things of the law]. And this is within the command of the moral law, *honora patrem*, which doubtless doth extend to him that is *pater patriae*. And that the Apostle saith, *Omnis anima potestatibus subdita sit* [Let every person be subject to authorities]. And these be the words of the Great Divine, *Hoc Deus in Sacris Scripturis jubet, hoc lex naturae dictari, ut quilibet subditus obediat superio. . . .* [This God commands in Sacred Scripture, this the law of nature dictates, in order that

anyone who is a subject might render obedience to the superior]. (T)herefore the law of God and nature is one to all.... This law of nature, which indeed is the eternal law of the Creator, infused into the heart of the creature at the time of his creation, was two thousand years before any laws written, and before any judicial or municipal laws. [16]

Grotius

Hugo Grotius (1583-1645) was a Dutch political writer who systematized the law of nations. His view of law can be summarized in his statement: "What God has shown to be His will that is law."[17]

Vattel

Quoted less often by the founders (.5%), yet a prominent writer who also adhered to a Christian view of law, Vattel, in *The Law of Nations*, said "all men . . . are to live conformably to their nature and to the designs of their common Creator." [18] Vattel stated:

> Piety and religion have an essential influence on the happiness of a Nation. . . . By piety I mean a disposition of soul which leads us to refer all our actions to God, and to seek, in everything that we do, to be pleasing to the Supreme Being. This virtue is an indispensable obligation upon all men;. . . . A Nation ought, therefore, to be pious. . . . An enlightened piety in the people is the firmest support of lawful authority. . . .
>
> Piety should be enlightened. It is idle to propose to please God if one does not know the means to be taken. . . .
>
> Every man is bound to endeavor to obtain correct ideas of God, to know His laws, His purpose with respect to His creatures, and the lot He has appointed to them."[19]

All of these writers, while adhering to the basic premise that law was rooted in a being superior to man and who had a set of fixed moral laws, were certainly not uniform in their political or religious philosophy. For example, **Thomas Hobbes** (cited 1.0%), saw the "Holy Scripture" as the source "of what is law throughout all Christendom, both natural and civil,"[20] but he believed, contrary to Reformation doctrine and the view of most early Americans, that the earthly religious and civil rulers were the sovereigns God used to establish His law in their dominion.[21] The difference was not in the recognition of higher law, but in how such law would flow into society.

British philosopher **David Hume** (1711-1776) was the most quoted writer with a non-Christian view of law (at 2.7%). Citations were overwhelmingly from *The History of England* rather than from his works containing his views that the founders opposed. Even then, there were many who wrote negatively of Hume. James Madison considered him a "bungling lawgiver."[22] John Adams called him an "atheist, deist, and libertine."[23] Thomas Jefferson found him "endeavoring to mislead by either the suppression of a truth or by giving it a false coloring,"[24] and he lamented any influence Hume's *Treatise of Human Nature* (1739-40) had had upon his thinking:

> I remember well the enthusiasm with which I devoured it when young, and the length of time, the research and reflection which were necessary to eradicate the poison it had instilled into my mind.[25]

There were other writers (classical, rationalistic and atheistic enlightenment) cited by the founders who did not have a Christian view of law, such as Rousseau (0.9%), and Voltaire (0.5%). They were a very small minority of the total citations.[26]

The Words of the Founders

To substantiate that the founders held a Christian view of law, consider the words of early leaders, lawyers, and judges.

James Otis, an early leader in the struggle for independence, presented the colonists' view of the laws of nature in his famous pamphlet "The Rights of the British Colonies Asserted and Proved":

> To say the Parliament is absolute and arbitrary is a contradiction. The Parliament cannot make 2 and 2, 5: Omnipotency cannot do it. The supreme power in a state . . . strictly speaking, belongs alone to God. Parliaments are in all cases to declare what is for the good of the whole; but it is not the declaration of Parliament that makes it so: There must be in every instance a higher authority, viz. God. Should an Act of Parliament be against any of His natural laws, which are immutably true, their declaration would be contrary to eternal truth, equity, and justice, and consequently void.[27]

Samuel Adams: "In the supposed state of nature, all men are equally bound by the laws of nature, or to speak more properly, the laws of the Creator."[28]

John Jay, first chief-justice of the U.S. Supreme Court: "[T]he . . . natural law was given by the Sovereign of the Universe to all mankind."[29]

James Wilson (1742-1798), signer of the Declaration and the Constitution, U.S. Supreme Court Justice (1789-1798, appointed by Washington); professor of law at Philadelphia College (1790 ff), published with

Thomas McKean "Commentaries on the Constitution of the United States" (1792):

> God . . . is the promulgator as well as the author of natural law.[30]

> All [laws], however, may be arranged in two different classes. 1) Divine. 2) Human. . . . But it should always be remembered that this law, natural or revealed, made for men or for nations, flows from the same Divine source: it is the law of God. . . . Human law must rest its authority ultimately upon the authority of that law which is Divine.[31]

John Quincy Adams: "[T]he laws of nature and of nature's God . . . of course presupposes the existence of a God, the moral ruler of the universe, and a rule of right and wrong, of just and unjust, binding upon man, preceding all institutions of human society and of government."[32]

Alexander Hamilton, quoting Blackstone: "[T]he law of nature, 'which, being coeval with mankind and dictated by God himself, is, of course, superior in obligation to any other. It is binding over all the globe, in all countries, and at all times. No human laws are of any validity, if contrary to this." [33]

Noah Webster, in his definition of *law*: The " 'Law of nature' is a rule of conduct arising out of the natural relations of human beings established by the Creator and existing prior to any positive precept [human law]. . . . These . . . have been established by the Creator and are, with a peculiar felicity of expression, denominated in Scripture, 'ordinances of heaven.'"[34]

Rufus King, signer of the Constitution: "[T]he . . . law established by the Creator . . . extends over the whole globe, is everywhere and at all times binding upon mankind. . . . [This] is the law of God by which he makes his way known to man and is paramount to all human control." [35]

William Findley, U.S. Congress, Revolutionary Soldier: "The law of nature being coeval with mankind and dictated by God Himself is of course superior to [and] the foundation of all other laws."[36]

In Federalist 43, **James Madison** responds to the question, On what principle can the federation be superseded without the unanimous consent of the parties to it? (asked in 43.29), by replying:

> The first question is answered at once by recurring to the absolute necessity of the case; to the great principle of self-preservation; to the transcendent law of nature and of nature's God. (43.30)[37]

Jefferson is less explicit in stating his belief in the origin of law, but he was clear in his belief that rights do not originate from rulers or from man but from God and the universal law of nature: "The God who gave us life gave us liberty at the same time."[38] In the Declaration he speaks of "the laws of nature and of nature's God" and "that all men . . . are endowed by their Creator with certain unalienable rights."[39]

The first Americans to write law commentaries presented this same viewpoint.

Zephaniah Swift (1759-1823), lawyer, congressman, judge, Chief Justice of the Connecticut Supreme Court (1806-19), assisted in revising the laws of Connecticut and wrote the first law commentary in 1795-96 (*A System of the Laws of the State of Connecticut*), in which he stated:

> [T]he transcendent excellence and boundless power of the Supreme Deity . . . [has] impressed upon them those general and immutable laws that will regulate their operation through the endless ages of eternity. . . . These general laws . . . are denominated the laws of nature.[40]

James Kent's *Commentaries on American Law* (1826-30) served as the standard general treatise on law in the United States for many decades. Kent wrote in his commentaries:

> Vattel . . . and all the other great masters of ethical and national juris-prudence, place the foundation of the law of nature in the will of God, discoverable by right reason, and aided by Divine revelation. . . .
>
> The law of nature, by the obligations of which individuals and states are bound, is identical with the will of God, and that will is ascer-tained. . . either by consulting Divine revelation, where that is declama-tory, or by the application of human reason where revelation is silent.[41]

Kent agreed with the "masters of jurisprudence" that law is rooted in Divine revelation. Joseph Story, Supreme Court Justice and author of a commentary on the Constitution, presents the same ideas in some of his writings.

Textbooks in schools also presented the view that law is rooted in Divine revelation. **Andrew Young**'s First Lessons in Civil Government (1846) states:

> The will of the Creator is the law of nature which men are bound to obey. But mankind in their present imperfect state are not capable of dis-covering in all cases what the law of nature requires; it has therefore pleased Divine Providence to reveal his will to mankind, to instruct them in their duties to himself and to each other. This will is revealed in the Holy Scriptures, and is called the law of revelation, or the Divine law.[42]

There were those Americans who who did not have this Christian view of law, for example Thomas Paine. In the *Declaration of Rights* (1794, from prison in France) Paine wrote "the Law . . . is the expression of the general will. . . . [T]he rights of man rests on the national sovereignty. This sovereignty . . . resides essentially in the whole people."[43] Paine's ideas on law, as well as his anti-Christian views, were not well accepted in America.[44]

The Seminal Constitutions, Compacts, and Charters of the Colonies

In the *Colonial Origins of the American Constitution*, Donald Lutz includes 80 foundational civil documents written in the American colonies. Even a brief examination of these confirms that all 13 colonies embraced a Biblical view of law. In his outline of "some of the things that a reading of these documents together leads us to conclude," Lutz gives number one as: "Political covenants were derived in form and content from religious covenants used to found religious communities." He writes that one element of a political covenant is "an oath calling on God as a witness or partner."[45]

Quoting from just a few of these shows the Christian motives for founding the colonies and the recognition of God as the highest authority and source of law:

- First Charter of Virginia (1606): The third paragraph of the charter speaks of their desire to propagate the "Christian Religion to such People, as yet live in Darkness and miserable Ignorance of the true Knowledge and Worship of God, and in time bring the Infidels and Savages, living in those parts, to human Civility, and to a settled and quiet Government."[46]
- The Mayflower Compact was written by a small group of English separatists seeking religious and civil freedom, who were undertaking the planting of a colony "for the Glory of God, and Advancement of the Christian Faith."[47]
- Adopted January 14, 1639, the Fundamental Orders of Connecticut began with the inhabitants covenanting together under God "to maintain and preserve the liberty and purity of the gospel of our Lord Jesus which we now profess." It gave the governor and magistrates "power to administer justice according to the Laws here established, and for want thereof according to the rule of the word of God."[48]
- The Charter of Maryland (1632) revealed the motive of Catholic proprietor Cecil Calvert, Lord Baltimore, in establishing the colony of Maryland — "being animated with a laudable, and pious Zeal for extending the Christian religion."[49]
- Charter of Rhode Island (1663): The charter mentioned their intentions of "godlie edifieing themselves, and one another, in the holie Christian ffaith

and worshipp" and their desire for the "conversione of the poore ignorant Indian natives."[50]

- The Salem Covenant of 1629: "We Covenant with the Lord and one with an other; and doe bynd our selves in the presence of God, to walke together in all his waies, according as he is pleased to reveale himselfe unto us in his Blessed word of truth."[51]

- Frame of Government of Pennsylvania (1682): The Preamble begins: "When the great and wise God had made the world, of all his creatures, it pleased him to chuse man his Deputy to rule it: and to fit him for so great a charge and trust, he did not only qualify him with skill and power, but with integrity to use them justly."[52]

- Section one of the Pennsylvania Charter of Privileges (1701) contains qualifications of officers where "all Persons who also profess to believe in Jesus Christ, the Saviour of the World, shall be capable (notwithstanding their other Persuasions and Practices in Point of Conscience and Religion) to serve this Government in any Capacity, both legislatively and exec-utively."[53]

Early Laws Written by the Colonists

- "Laws Divine, Morall, and Martiall, etc." written in Virginia between, 1609-1612: The colonists were required to serve God, to attend divine serves, to not speak against God or blaspheme God's holy name, and to not speak or act in any way that would "tend to the derision, or despight [open defiance] of Gods holy word upon paine of death."[54]

- Laws of the Pilgrims (1636, revised 1658, 1671, 1685): The preface to the 1671 Book of Laws states that "Laws . . . are so far good and wholesome, as by how much they are derived from, and agreeable to the ancient Platform of Gods Law."[55] The specific statutes reflected their Biblical philosophy of life. They even quoted Scriptures to support many of their Capital Laws.

- Massachusetts Body of Liberties (1641): Section 1 states that no man's life or property can be taken except by some express law that has been suffi-ciently published, "or in case of the defect of a law in any parteculer case by the word of god."[56]

- What became know as The Blue Laws of Connecticut acknowledged "that the supreme power of making laws, and of repealing them, belong to God only, and that by him, this power is given to Jesus Christ, as Mediator, Math. 28:19. Joh. 5:22. And that the Laws for holinesse, and Righteous-ness, are already made, and given us in the scriptures."[57]

- The Frame of Government of Pennsylvania recognized the Lord's Day (the Sabbath), Biblical standards for marriage — "all marriages (not forbidden by the law of God, as to nearness of blood and affinity by marriage) shall be encouraged,"— and Biblical qualifications for civil officials — "all . . .

shall be such as possess faith in Jesus Christ."[58] All offenses against God were to be discouraged and punished, and many were listed. Religious freedom was granted to all persons "who confess and acknowledge the one Almighty and eternal God, to be the Creator, Upholder and Ruler of the world."[59]

Documents in the Early American Republic

After independence the state constitutions acknowledged God as the Supreme Power and provided for the protection of God-given inalienable rights of man. Most required elected officials to take a Christian oath of office, thus subordinating themselves to the Highest Authority.

- The Declaration of Independence, 1776: "the laws of nature and of nature's God"; "all men are created equal, that they are endowed by their Creator with certain unalienable Rights"; "appealing to the Supreme Judge of the world for the rectitude of our intentions"; "with a firm reliance on the Protection of Divine Providence."
- The Constitution of Maryland (1776) states: "it is the duty of every man to worship God in such manner as he thinks most acceptable to him; all persons, professing the Christian religion, are equally entitled to protection in their religious liberty." The oath of office included "a declaration of a belief in the Christian religion."[60]
- The Constitution of Massachusetts (1780) acknowledged "the goodness of the great Legislator of the universe . . . His providence. . . . and devoutly imploring His direction." It declared: "It is the right as well as the duty of all men in society, publicly, and at stated seasons, to worship the SUPREME BEING, the great Creator and Preserver of the universe." It also recognized that "the happiness of a people, and the good order and preservation of civil government, essentially depend upon piety, religion, and morality."[61]
- The Constitution of New Hampshire (1784) recognized "morality and piety, rightly grounded on evangelical principles" as the "best and greatest security to government."[62]
- The Constitution of South Carolina (1776): "The qualifications of electors shall be that [he] . . . acknowledges the being of a God and believes in a future state of rewards and punishments."[63]
- The Constitution of Tennessee (1797): "No person who denies the being of God, or a future state of rewards and punishments, shall hold any office in the civil department of this State."[64]
- The U.S. Constitution requires a Christian oath, acknowledges the Christian Sabbath, and is dated in the year of our Lord.[65]

- The Northwest Ordinance (1789), Article III: "Religion, morality, and knowledge being necessary to good government and the happiness of mankind, schools and the means of education shall forever be encouraged."[66]

Court Rulings

- *Church of the Holy Trinity v. United States* (1892): In its ruling, the U.S. Supreme Court declared "this is a Christian nation" and presented much historical evidence for this.[67]

- *Updegraph v. The Commonwealth* (1824): Supreme Court of Pennsylvania rules, "Christianity, general Christianity, is and always has been a part of the common law. . . ; not Christianity with an established church . . . but Christianity with liberty of conscience to all men."[68]

- *The People v. Ruggles* (1811): In this decision delivered by Chief Justice James Kent, the Supreme Court of New York said "we are a Christian people and the morality of the country is deeply engrafted upon Christianity and not upon the doctrines or worship of those impostors [other religions]."[69]

- *Vidal v. Girard's Executors* (1844): "It is also said, and truly, that the Christian religion is a part of the common law."[70]

- *Runkel v. Winemiller* (1799): the Supreme Court of Maryland ruled, "By our form of government, the Christian religion is the established religion."[71]

- *City of Charleston v. Benjamin* (1846): "Christianity is a part of the common law of the land." "What constitutes the standard of good morals? Is it not Christianity? There certainly is none other. . . . The day of moral virtue in which we live would, in an instant, if that standard were abolished, lapse into the dark and murky night of Pagan immorality."[72]

- *Lindenmuller v. The People* (1860): The Supreme Court of New York ruled, "All agreed that the Christian religion was engrafted upon the law and entitled to protection as the basis of our morals and the strength of our government."[73]

- *Shover v. State* (1850): the Supreme Court of Arkansas ruled "the Christian religion . . . is recognized as constituting a part and parcel of the common law."[74]

A look at education — most colleges and schools were Christian and the texts reflected their Biblical worldview[75] — reinforces the idea that early America had a Christian view of law and life. As John Marshall, Chief Justice of the U.S. Supreme Court, said:

The American population is entirely Christian, & with us, Christianity & Religion are identified. It would be strange, indeed, if with such a people, our institutions did not presuppose Christianity, & did not often refer to it, & exhibit relations with it.[76]

In relation to law, early Americans certainly viewed it from a Christian perspective. But over the years that gradually began to change so that now most Americans have a humanistic view of law.

Humanistic View of Law

Time does not permit examining in any detail how this change occurred, but many things have contributed to the changing philosophical foundation of American society — changes in theological thought, educational systems, personal belief, et cetera. The changing view of law can be summarized by the actions and words of Roscoe Pound.

In his *Spirit of the Common Law*, Roscoe Pound, who was President of Harvard Law School in the 1920s, revealed the nature of the changing view of law in America. Pound recognized the Christian foundation of law in the United States but did not directly attack it. In fact, he said that the old Christian legal foundation was good and produced many good results; but, he went on to say that this foundation was not good enough to bring us into the modern era. According to him, we needed a new law system, one founded on a different premise. Pound and others claimed that law was rooted in the best that society had to offer—in the consensus of the society and what they deemed best for mankind—and as society grew and became better, the law would change with it. Evolving law and the sovereignty of the state replaced the absolutes of God's law. Pound said "the state takes the place of Jehovah."

Many in the judicial system began to embrace this evolving view of law and rejected the Christian understanding of absolute law rooted in a Higher Power. For example Supreme Court justice Benjamin Cardozo (appointed in 1932) said:

> If there is any law which is back of the sovereignty of the state, and superior thereto, it is not law in such a sense as to concern the judge or lawyer, however much it concerns the statesmen or the moralist.[77]

Relativism began to affect judicial philosophy and constitutional interpretation, as reflected in the words of Charles Evans Hughes, Supreme Court Chief Justice from 1930 to 1941: "We are under a Constitution, but the Constitution is what the judges say it is."[78]

A humanistic view of law and life, and moral relativism have spread to the point where today a majority of Americans embrace this idea. Its dissemination and influence is such that, according to one recent poll even a majority of those who claim to be Christian reject moral absolutes.[79]

The Importance of a Nation's View of Law

What is the impact of the changing view of law in America? A person's and nation's view of law is very important, for it determines what the people perceive as the purpose of law, and consequently what they will attempt to have the law and government do. A brief contrast of a Biblical and humanistic view of law reveals some of the potential impact of this change.

Contrast of Biblical and Humanistic View of Law

There is obviously no universal agreement on what a Biblical or humanistic philosophy of law is. The opponents of each view often present the other in an extreme manner. Hence, proponents of a Biblical view of law are presented as narrow extremists who want to take control of government and the judiciary and impose their moral code upon the nation. Humanists have been presented much in the way Jefferson was by his political opponents when he ran for President, as wanting to confiscate everyone's Bibles and restrict religious worship. Neither are accurate representations of the majority. But the general nature of law from the two views is clear.

Law, from a Christian perspective and as the Founders of America viewed it, originates in the will of God, revealed in general to man through nature and his conscience, and more specifically in the revelation of the Scriptures. Law from a humanistic view is rooted in man, ultimately autonomous man, but practically in the state, and in the consensus of the majority, or of a powerful minority.

From a Biblical perspective man is fallen and fallible, has a sinful nature, and thus needs to be restrained. The Biblical purpose of civil law is to restrain the evil action of men in society. True law reveals what is right and wrong, and hence, exposes law-breakers. But law in itself cannot produce what is right, it cannot change the heart or attitude of man, therefore, the Christian acknowledges the inability to legislate good, or to make people moral by passing laws. However, the Christian recognizes the moral basis of all laws. All laws everywhere are based upon the moral presuppositions of the law-makers. Laws against murder reflect a moral belief. Laws against theft are based upon the command to not steal. All law has a moral concern. The important question to the Christian is whose morality does it legislate.

From a Christian presupposition then, the law cannot change or reform man; this is a spiritual matter. Man can only be changed by the grace of God. He cannot be legislated into a new morality.

Humanists see the evils in society and in man, but explain them differently than Christians. To the humanist there is no higher being than man. There is no incarnate Savior. From a humanistic perspective there is no hope of internal regeneration to save man, therefore, any salvation or transformation that occurs in men or nations must come from man. Historically, humanistic man has tended to use the instrument of law and government to attempt to bring such a transformation or "salvation."

Having no other means of provision, of salvation, or of peace, humanistic man attempts to regulate and provide all things through government and law. It is only through the force of law that evil will be eliminated and utopia established on earth. Humanistic law is used to promote and advance humanistic morals. Such law, in conjunction with a corresponding educational system, is the only hope humanistic man has of establishing a "saved" or "righteous" — that is, good and progressing — society.

To restate this, if there is no God who redeems man internally, then any elimination of problems brought on by what is in the heart of man must be done by man — often collective man and his government. The attempt will thus be made by government (at least those that have a vision for a progressing society) to use the instrument of law to bring more peace and goodwill among men and to eliminate all that is negative, such as poverty, crime, war, disease, prejudice, and ignorance.

From a Christian perspective, law can restrain sinful man from acting evilly, for the fear of punishment is a deterrent, but he cannot be changed by law. Unless the evil heart of man is changed, there will be no advancement toward a better society. Humanistic law seeks to save and change man internally. Since the government (and laws issued thereby) is the instrument for such change, the government becomes the savior in a humanistic society.

Therefore, there is a great potential for the humanist to see law (and the state from which it comes) as savior. This might not be overtly proclaimed, but is demonstrated by actions. Certainly man is the highest authority and the source of law in a humanistic society, and hence he is the god of that society, for the source of law of a society is the god of a society — and man will look to his god to assist him, to provide for him, and to save him.

To the founders, who had a predominantly Christian worldview, they saw God, through His Son, as their savior. The state served a legitimate but limited purpose to protect the life, liberty, and property of the citizens.

From a Christian perspective the state is limited. America's founders certainly saw the state in this manner. As an example, in 1792 Congress considered a bill that would have given subsidies to cod fishermen in New England. Some few argued Congress had power to do so under the general welfare clause. Speaking against the bill, James Madison said first, this is a limited government with only the specified powers listed in the Constitution belonging to Congress, the executive, and judiciary, then:

> If Congress can employ money indefinitely to the general welfare, and are the sole and supreme judges of the general welfare, they may take the care of religion into their own hands; they may appoint teachers in every state, county, and parish, and pay them out of their public treasury; they may take into their own hands the education of children, establishing in like manner schools throughout the Union; they may assume the provision for the poor; they may undertake the regulation of all roads other than post-roads.[80]

Imagine the reaction Madison would receive today for proposing no government involvement in schools, providing for the poor, and regulation of all roads.

There are people with a humanistic view of law who are for limited government. However, in nations that have embraced a humanistic view of law, the state generally acts as the sovereign, where all spheres of life come under its authority and direction (for example, ancient Rome, the former U.S.S.R., and present day China). Similarly, there have been nations that have verbally embraced a Christian view of law but did not practice limited government. But those who founded America would argue that correct and consistent Christian thought would produce limited and free government. The history of America is a great confirmation of this.

Thus, one reason a people's view of law is important is that it affects the scope and extent of civil government in a nation. It also affects the form of government.

The source and origin of law has to do with sovereignty, with ultimate authority, with a people's view of "God," for the source of law of a society is the God of that society. A people's religion, by which is meant their ultimate source of authority, determines their view of law and everything else.

Christianity: the Support of Free Governments

America's founder's believed that religion affects the form of government in a nation. In a general sense they saw Christianity as the only support for a free, self-governed, and happy society.

John Adams said while President in 1798:

[W]e have no government armed with power capable of contending with human passions unbridled by morality and religion. Avarice, ambition, revenge, or gallantry, would break the strongest cords of our Constitution as a whale goes through a net. Our Constitution was made only for a moral and religious people. It is wholly inadequate to the government of any other.[81]

In 1838 the Legislature of New York said:

Our Government depends for its being on the virtue of the people, – on that virtue that has its foundation in the morality of the Christian religion; and that religion is the common and prevailing faith of the people.[82]

George Washington wrote in 1797: "Religion and Morality are the essential pillars of Civil society."[83] In his farewell address in 1796, he wrote:

Of all the dispositions and habits which lead to political prosperity, religion and morality are indispensable supports.[84]

James Madison wrote in 1825: "[T]he belief in a God All Powerful wise and good, is...essential to the moral order of the World and to the happiness of man."[85] In his *Memorial and Remonstrance*, he said:

Before any man can be considered as a member of Civil Society, he must be considered as a subject of the Governor of the Universe.[86]

Noah Webster wrote in his History of the United States:

[T]he genuine source of correct republican principles is the Bible, particularly the New Testament or the Christian religion.[87]

Benjamin Rush wrote in 1806:

Christianity is the only true and perfect religion, and that in proportion as mankind adopt its principles and obeys its precepts, they will be wise and happy.[88]

The father of American Geography, **Jedidiah Morse** wrote:

To the kindly influence of Christianity we owe that degree of civil freedom, and political and social happiness which mankind now enjoys.[89]

The Constitution of New Hampshire of June 2, 1784 stated:

[M]orality and piety, rightly grounded on evangelical principles, will give the best and greatest security to government, and will lay in the hearts of men the strongest obligations to due subjection.[90]

James McHenry, signer of the Constitution said:

The Holy Scriptures . . . can alone secure to society, order and peace, and to our courts of justice and constitutions of government, purity, stability, and usefulness. In vain, without the Bible, we increase penal laws and draw entrenchments around our institutions.[91]

Samuel Adams stated: "Religion and good morals are the only solid foundations of public liberty and happiness."[92]

Charles Carroll, Signer of the Declaration, wrote: "Without morals a republic cannot subsist any length of time; they therefore who are decrying the Christian religion whose morality is so sublime and pure . . . are undermining the solid foundation of morals, the best security for the duration of free governments."[93]

Thomas Jefferson wrote in 1809: "The practice of morality being necessary for the well-being of society, He [God] has taken care to impress its precepts so indelibly on our hearts that they shall not be effaced by the subtleties of our brain. We all agree in the obligation of the moral precepts of Jesus and nowhere will they be found delivered in greater purity than in his discourses."[94]

Many other founders could be quoted to show that the generally accepted view of early America was that the Christian religion was the foundation of liberty and our free republican form of government. Early courts and congresses declared the same thing. For example, the **U.S. House of Representatives** resolved in 1854:

[T]he great vital and conservative element in our system is the belief of our people in the pure doctrines and divine truths of the gospel of Jesus Christ.[95]

Why did early Americans believe Christianity was essential to free government? They believed it contained the principles of liberty, and also the power to transform men from within to live as self-governed citizens. The Supreme Court of New York ruled (in People v. Ruggles, 1811): "[W]hatever strikes at the root of Christianity tends manifestly to the dissolution of civil government . . . because it tends to corrupt the morals of the people, and to destroy good order."[96]

Thomas Jefferson noted: "The precepts of philosophy, and of the Hebrew code, laid hold of actions only. [Jesus] pushed his scrutinies into the heart of man, erected his tribunal in the region of his thoughts, and purified the waters at the fountain head."[97]

To our founders, the religion of a people affected their civil and religious liberty. To them, Christianity laid the support for free governments in general, but it also affected the specific form of government. In *The Spirit of Laws*, Montesquieu presented the idea that a nation's form of civil government is directly determined by its religion. Under the section on "Of Laws in Relation to Religion Considered in Itself, and in its Doctrines," he writes:

> The Christian religion, which ordains that men should love each other, would, without doubt, have every nation blest with the best civil, the best political laws; because these, next to this religion, are the greatest good that men can give and receive.[98]

He goes on to make the points, under titled sections: 1) "That a moderate Government is most agreeable to the Christian Religion, and a despotic Government to the Mahommedan" and 2) "That the Catholic Religion is most agreeable to a Monarchy, and the Protestant to a Republic"[99] This is an important idea that should be explored by nations seeking to be free.

The foundation of law and government was important to our founders. Most of them would believe that the abandoning of "the laws of nature and nature's God" for "the laws of men," would lead to loss of liberty and a detrimental change in the scope, form, and function of our government.

Pound believed that the nation could not continue to advance if it retained the Christian foundation of law; the consensus of man must be the new source of law. The founders believed the "Supreme Judge of the World" must be the source, and that it was this foundation that produced a liberty and happiness unlike any in history.

Many today would disagree with our founders and their view of law, but most Americans are not aware of the founders view or of the changing nature of law in America and its importance for our future. Both views of law and the arguments for which view is preferable need to be clearly presented so people can more accurately decide what standard of law we will embrace; or who will be the source of law, and hence the God, our nation.

End Notes

1. See Daniel L. Dreisbach, *Thomas Jefferson and the Wall of Separation between Church and State,* New York: New York University Press, 2002; Daniel L. Dreisbach, "'Sowing Useful Truths and Principles': The Danbury Baptists, Thomas Jefferson, and the 'Wall of Separation'", *Journal of Church and State,* Vol. 39, Summer 1997, pp. 455-501; *Religion and Political Culture in Jefferson's Virginia,* Garrett Ward Sheldon and Daniel L. Dreisbach, editors, New York: Rowman & Littlefield Publishers, 2000; Robert L. Cord, *Separation of Church and State,. New York: Lambeth Press, 1982; David Barton, Original Intent,* Aledo, Tex.: WallBuilder Press, 1996.

2. *Wallace v. Jaffree,* 472 U.S. 38 (1985) at 92, 106-107 (Rehnquist, J., dissenting).

3. Noah Webster, *An American Dictionary of the English Language,* New York: S. Converse, 1828, definition of immoral. *Webster's New World Dictionary of the American Language,* David B. Guralnik, editor, Nashville: The Southwestern Company, 1969, p. 373.

4. Donald S. Lutz, "The Relative Influence of European Writers on Late Eighteenth-Century American Political Thought," *The American Political Science Review,* vol. 78, 1984, pp. 189-197.

5. Baron De Montesquieu, *The Spirit of Laws,* translated from the French by Thomas Nugent, 2 Vols., New York: the Colonial Press, 1899, Vol. 1, p. 1.

6. Ibid., p. 2.

7. Ibid., p. 3.

8. Sir William Blackstone, *Commentaries on the Laws of England,* Philadelphia: Robert Bell, Union Library, 1771, vol. 1, 38-42.

9. From, *The Second Treatise of Government, ch. 1,* quoted in Gary T. Amos, *Defending the Declaration, How the Bible and Christianity Influenced the Writing of the Declaration of Independence,* Charlottesville, Vir.: Providence Foundation, 1994.

10. From, *An Essay Concerning Human Understanding,* vol.1, quoted in Amos, p. 55.

11. Samuel von Pufendorf, *On the Duty of Man and Citizen According to Natural Law,* translation by Frank Gardner Moore of the 1682 edition, New York: Oxford University Press, 1927, reprinted by the Legal Classics Library, 1993, p. X.

12. Ibid., p. 23.

13. Ibid., p. 19.

14. Ibid., p. 19.

15. Ibid., p. 20.

16. From *Calvin's Case* (circa 1610), quoted in Gary Amos, *Defending the Declaration,* p. 43.

17. Hugo Grotius, *Commentary on the Law of Prize and Booty,* translated from the original manuscript of 1604 by Gwladys L. Williams, Oxford: Clarendon Press, 1950, vol. 1, p. 8.

18. E. De Vattel, *The Law of Nations or the Principles of Natural Law Applied to the Conduct and to the Affairs of Nations and of Sovereigns,* translation of the first edition of 1758 by Charles G. Fenwick, Washington: The Carnegie Institution, 1916, reprinted by the Legal Classics Library, 1993, p. 5.

19. Ibid., p. 53.

20. Thomas Hobbes, *Leviathan,* with selected variants from the Latin edition of 1668, Edwin Curley, editor, Indianapolis: Hackett Publishing Co., 1994, "Of the Number, Antiquity, Scope, Authority, and Interpreters of the Books of Holy Scripture," Chapter XXXIII, p. 250.

21. Ibid.

22. James Madison, *Letters and Other Writings of James Madison,* New York: R. Worthington, 1884, Vol. IV, p. 58, to N.P. Trist in February 1830.

23. John Adams, *Diary and Autobiography of John Adams,* L.H. Butterfield, editor, Cambridge, MA: Belknap Press, 1962, Vol. II, p. 391, diary entry of June 23, 1779.

24. Thomas Jefferson, *Memoir, Correspondence, and Miscellanies, From the Papers of Thomas Jefferson,* Thomas Jefferson Randolph, editor, Boston: Gray and Bowen, 1830, vol. IV, p. 80, to John Norvell on June 11, 1807.

25. Thomas Jefferson, *The Writings of Thomas Jefferson,* Washington, D.C.: The Thomas Jefferson Memorial Association, 1904, vol. XII, p. 405, to Col. William Duane on August 12, 1810.

26. See Lutz, p. 194.

27. *Sources of Our Liberties*, Richard L. Perry, editor, New York: American Bar Foundation, 1952, pp. 264-265.

28. Samuel Adams, *The Writings of Samuel Adams*, Harry Alonzo Cushing, editor, New York: G.P. Putnam's Sons, 1908, vol. IV, p. 356, to the Legislature of Massachusetts on January 17, 1794.

29. John Jay, *The Life of John Jay*, William Jay, editor, New York: J. & J. Harper, 1833, Vol. II, p. 385, to John Murray on April 15, 1818.

30. James Wilson, *The Works of the Honourable James Wilson*, Bird Wilson, editor, Philadelphia: Lorenzo Press, 1804, Vol. I, p. 64, "Of the General Principles of Law and Obligation."

31. James Wilson, *Works*, Vol. 1, pp. 103-105, "Of the General Principles of Law and Obligation."

32. John Quincy Adams, *The Jubilee of the Constitution*, New York: Published by Samuel Colman, 1839, pp. 13-14.

33. Alexander Hamilton, *The Papers of Alexander Hamilton*, Harold Syrett, editor, NY: Columbia University Press, 1961, Vol. I, p. 87, from "The Farmer Refuted," February 23, 1775.

34. Noah Webster, *An American Dictionary of the English Language*, New York: S. Converse, 1828, definition of law, #3 and #6.

35. Rufus King, *The Life and Correspondence of Rufus King*, Charles R. King, editor, New York: G.P. Putnam's Sons, 1900, Vol. VI, p. 276, to C. Gore on February 17, 1820.

36. William Findley, Observations on "The Two Sons of Oil," Pittsburgh: Patterson and Hopkins, 1812, p. 35.

37. *The Federalist*, Edited by Michael Loyd Chadwick, Washington, D.C.: Global Affairs, p. 238.

38. *Writings of Thomas Jefferson*, ed. By Paul Leicester Ford, New York: G.P. Putnam's Sons, 1892-1899, Vol. I, p. 447.

39. In his original draft Jefferson wrote of man as created with certain inherent and inalienable rights. The drafting committee changed this to the present wording, which Jefferson embraced.

40. Zephaniah Swift, *A System of the Laws of the State of Connecticut*, Windham: John Byrne, 1795, Vol. I, pp. 6-7.

41. James Kent, *Commentaries on American Law*, seventh edition, New York: William Kent, 1851, p. 2, 4.

42. Andrew W. Young, *First Lessons in Civil Government*, Auburn, N.Y.: H. And J.C. Ivison, 1846, p. 16.

43. Thomas Paine, "Declaration of Rights," *The Writings of Thomas Paine*, Collected and edited by Daniel Conway, New York: G.P. Putnam's Sons, Vol.3 , p. 129-130.

44. Even Benjamin Franklin, who was not an orthodox Christian, said Paine's anti-Christian writings would only result in evil and should not be published (see *The Works of Benjamin Franklin*, Jared Sparks, editor. Boston: Tappan, Whittemore, and Mason, 1840, pp. 281-282.)

45. *Colonial Origins of the American Constitution*, edited by Donald S. Lutz, Indianapolis: Liberty Fund, 1998, pp. xxxv-xxxvi.

46. *Sources of Our Liberties*, Richard L. Perry, editor, New York: American Bar Foundation, 1952, p. 40.

47. *Sources of Our Liberties*, p. 60.

48. *Sources of Our Liberties*, p. 120.

49. The Charter of Maryland, June 20, 1632, in *Sources of Our Liberties*, p. 105.

50. *Sources of Our Liberties*, p. 169

51. *Colonial Origins of the American Constitution*, p. 35.

52. *Sources of Our Liberties*, p. 209.

53. *Sources of Our Liberties*, p. 256.

54. *For the Colony in Virginea Britannia, Lawes Divine, Morall and Martiall, etc.*, compiled by William Strachey, edited by David H. Flaherty, Charlottesville: University Press of Virginia, 1969, pp. 10-11.

55. *The Laws of the Pilgrims, A Facsimile Edition of The Book of the General Laws of the Inhabitants of the Jurisdiction of New-Plimouth, 1672 & 1685*, Wilmington, Del.: Pilgrim Society, 1977, p. 1.

56. *Sources of Our Liberties*, p. 148.

57. *The Blue Laws of New Haven Colony*, usually called Blue Laws of Connecticut . . . , By an antiquarian, Hartford: printed by Case, Tiffany & Co., 1838, p. 145.

58. *Sources of Our Liberties,* p. 216, 218, 220.

59. *Sources of Our Liberties,* p. 220.

60. *Sources of Our Liberties,* pp. 349, 350.

61. *Sources of Our Liberties,* pp. 373, 374.

62. *Sources of Our Liberties,* p. 382.

63. *The Constitutions of the Several Independent States of America,* Boston: Norman and Bowen, 1785, p. 146, South Carolina, 1776, Section 13.

64. *The Constitutions of the Sixteen States,* Boston: Manning and Loring, 1797, p. 274, Tennessee, 1796, Article VIII, Section II.

65. For a discussion of Christianity and the Constitution see Daniel L. Dreisbach, "In Search of a Christian Commonwealth: An Examination of Selected Nineteenth-Century Commentaries on References to God and the Christian Religion in the United States Constitution", *Baylor Law Review,* Fall 1996, Vol. 48, Number 4, pp. 928-1000. See also Barton, *Original Intent.*

66. *Sources of Our Liberties,* p. 396.

67. *Church of the Holy Trinity v. U.S.;* 143 U.S. 457, 458 (1892).

68. *Updegraph v. The Commonwealth;* 11 Serg & R. 393, 394 (Sup. Ct. Penn. 1824).

69. *People v. Ruggles;* 8 Johns 545 (Sup. Ct. NY. 1811).

70. *Vidal v. Girard's Executors;* 8 Johns 545 (Sup. Ct. NY. 1811).

71. *Runkel v. Winemiller;* 4 Harris & McHenry 256, 259 (Sup. Ct. Md. 1799).

72. *City Council of Charleston v. S.A. Benjamin;* 2 Strob. 508, 518-520, 522-524 (Sup. Ct. S.C. 1846).

73. *Lindenmuller v. The People,* 33 Barb 548, (Sup. Ct. NY 1861).

74. *Shover v. State;* 10 English 259, 263 (Sup. Ct. Ark. 1850).

75. See Stephen McDowell, *Restoring America's Christian Education,* Charlottesville, Vir.: Providence Foundation, 2000.

76. Daniel L. Dreisbach, *Religion and Politics in the Early Republic,* Lexington, KY: The University Press of Kentucky, 1996, p. 113.

77. Benjamin Cardozo, *The Growth of Law,* New Haven: Yale University Press, 1924, p. 49.

78. Charles Evans Hughes, *The Autobiographical Notes of Charles Evans Hughes,* David J. Danelski and Joseph S. Tulchin, editors, Cambridge: Harvard University Press, 1973, p. 144, speech at Elmira on May 3, 1907.

79. Barna Poll conducted in the Spring of 2002. In a survey of adults and teenagers, people were asked if they believed that there are moral absolutes that are unchanging, or that moral truth is relative; 64% of adults said truth is relative to the person and situation. Among teenagers, 83% said moral truth is relative; only 6% said it is absolute. Among born-again Christians 32% of adults and 9% of teens expressed a belief in absolute truth. The number one answer as to what people believe is the basis for moral decisions was doing whatever feels right (believed by 31% of adults and 38% of teens).

80. "On the Cod Fishery Bill, granting Bounties," February 7, 1792, in *The Debates of the Several State Conventions on the Adoption of the Federal Constitution as Recommended by the General Convention at Philadelphia in 1787. . . ,* in Five Volumes, by Jonathan Elliot, New York: Burt Franklin R, Vol. IV, p. 429.

81. "A Letter to the Officers of the First Brigade of the Third Division of the Militia of Massachusetts, Oct. 11, 1798." In *The Works of John Adams, Second President of the United States,* Boston: Little, Brown and Co., 1854, 9:228-229.

82. B.F. Morris, *Christian Life and Character of the Civil Institutions of the United States,* Philadelphia: George W.Childs, 1864, p. 239.

83. George Washington, Letter to the Clergy of Different Denominations Residing in and near the City of Philadelphia, March 3, 1797.

84. A Compilation of the *Messages and Papers of the Presidents,* By James D. Richardson, Washington: Bureau of National Literature and Art, 1910, 1:205-216.

85. James Madison, Letter to Frederick Beasley, Nov. 20, 1825.

86. James Madison, *Memorial and Remonstrance,* 1785, in Norman Cousins, *"In God We Trust," the Religious Beliefs and Ideas of the American Founding Fathers,* New York: Harper & Brothers, 1958, p. 301.

87. Noah Webster, *History of the United States*, New Haven: Durrie & Peck, 1833, p. v.

88. Benjamin Rush, *Essays, Literary, Moral and Philosophical*, Philadelphia: printed by Thomas and William Bradford, 1806, p. 93.

89. Jedidiah Morse, Election Sermon given at Charleston, MA on April 25, 1799.

90. *Sources of Our Liberties*, p. 382.

91. Bernard C. Steiner, *One Hundred and Ten Years of Bible Society Work in Maryland*, Baltimore: Maryland Bible Society, 1921, p. 14.

92. Samuel Adams, *The Writings of Samuel Adams*, Harry Alonzo Cushing, editor, New York: G.P. Putnam's Sons, 1905, Vol. IV, p. 74, to John Trumbull on October 16, 1778.

93. Bernard C. Steiner, *The Life and Correspondence of James McHenry*, Cleveland: The Burrows Brothers Company, 1907, p. 475, Charles Carroll to James McHenry on November 4, 1800.

94. Thomas Jefferson, *The Writings of Thomas Jefferson*, Albert Ellery Bergh, editor, Washington, D.C.: The Thomas Jefferson Memorial Association, 1904. Vol. XII, p. 315, to James Fishback, September 27, 1809.

95. Cited in B.F. Morris, p. 328.

96. *Ruggles* at 546.

97. Thomas Jefferson, *Memoir, Correspondence, and Miscellanies, From the Papers of Thomas Jefferson*, Thomas Jefferson Randolph, editor, Boston: Gray and Bowen, 1830, Vol. III, p. 509, to Benjamin Rush on April 21, 1803, Jefferson's "Syllabus of an Estimate of the Merit of the Doctrines of Jesus, Compared with Those of Others."

98. Montesquieu, Vol. 2, p. 27.

99. Ibid., pp. 29, 30.

Chapter 12

The Bible, Slavery, and America's Founders

America's Founding Fathers are seen by some people today as unjust and hypocrites, for while they talked of liberty and equality, they at the same time were enslaving hundreds of thousands of Africans. Some allege that the Founders bear most of the blame for the evils of slavery. Consequently, many today have little respect for the Founders and turn their ear from listening to anything they may have to say. And, in their view, to speak of America as founded as a Christian nation is unthinkable (for how could a Christian nation tolerate slavery?).

It is certainly true that during most of America's history most blacks have not had the same opportunities and protections as whites. From the time of colonization until the Civil War most Africans in America (especially those living in the South) were enslaved, and the 100 years following emancipation were marked with segregation and racism. Only in the last 30 years has there been closer to equal opportunities, though we still need continued advancement in equality among the races and race relations. But is the charge against the Founders justified? Are they to bear most of the blame for the evils of slavery? Can we speak of America as founded as a Christian nation, while at it's founding it allowed slavery?

Understanding the answer to these questions is important for the future of liberty in America and advancement of racial equality. The secular view of history taught in government schools today does not provide an adequate answer. We must view these important concerns from a Biblical and providential perspective.

America's Founders were predominantly Christians and had a Biblical worldview. If that was so, some say, how could they allow slavery, for isn't slavery sin? As the Bible reveals to man what is sin, we need to examine what it has to say about slavery.

The Bible and Slavery

The Bible teaches that slavery, in one form or another (including spiritual, mental, and physical), is always the fruit of disobedience to God and His law-word. (This is not to say that the enslavement of any one person, or group of people, is due to their sin, for many have been enslaved unjustly, like Joseph and numerous Christians throughout history.) Personal and civil liberty is the result of applying the truth of the Scriptures. As a person or nation more fully applies the principles of Christianity, there will be increasing freedom in every realm of life. Sanctification for a person, or nation, is a gradual process. The fruit of changed thinking and action, which comes from rooting sin out of our lives, may take time to see. This certainly applies historically in removing slavery from the Christian world.

Slavery is a product of the fall of man and has existed in the world since that time. Slavery was not a part of God's original created order, and as God's created order has gradually been re-established since the time of Christ, slavery has gradually been eliminated. Christian nations (those based upon Biblical principles) have led the way in the abolition of slavery. America was at the forefront of this fight. After independence, great steps were taken down the path of ending slavery — probably more than had been done by any other nation up until that time in history (though certainly more could have been done). Many who had settled in America had already been moving toward these ends. Unfortunately, the generations following the Founders did not continue to move forward in a united fashion. A great conflict was the outcome of this failure.

When God gave the law to Moses, slavery was a part of the world, and so the law of God recognized slavery. But this does not mean that slavery was God's original intention. The law of Moses was given to fallen man. Some of the ordinances deal with things not intended for the original creation order, such as slavery and divorce. These will be eliminated completely only when sin is eliminated from the earth. God's laws concerning slavery provided parameters for treatment of slaves, which were for the benefit of all involved. God desires all men and nations to be liberated. This begins internally and will be manifested externally to the extent internal change occurs. The Biblical slave laws reflect God's redemptive desire, for men and nations.

Types of Slavery Permitted by the Bible

The Mosaic law permitted some types of slavery. These include:

1. Voluntary servitude by the sons of Israel (indentured servants)

Those who needed assistance, could not pay their debts, or needed protection from another were allowed under Biblical law to become indentured servants (see Ex. 21:2-6; Deut. 15:12-18). They were dependent on their master instead of the state. This was a way to aid the poor and give them an opportunity to get back on their feet. It was not to be a permanent subsidy. Many early settlers to America came as indentured servants. These servants were well treated and when released, given generous pay.

2. Voluntary permanent slaves

If indentured servants so chose, they could remain a slave (Ex. 21:2-6; Deut. 15:16-17). Their ear was pierced to indicate this permanent subjection. The law recognized that some people want the security of enslavement.

Today, there are some people who would rather be dependent upon government to provide their needs (and with that provision accepting their commands) than do what is necessary to live free from its provision and direction. Some even act in a manner that puts them in jail, desiring the care and provision they get more than personal freedom.

3. Thief or criminal making restitution

A thief who could not, or did not, make restitution was sold as a slave: "If a man steals . . . he shall surely make restitution; if he owns nothing, then he shall be sold for his theft" (Ex. 22:1,3). The servitude ceased when enough work was done to pay for the amount due in restitution.

4. Pagans could be permanent slaves

Leviticus 25:44-46 states:

As for your male and female slaves whom you may have — you may acquire male and female slaves from the pagan nations that are around you. Then, too, it is out of the sons of the sojourners who live as aliens among you that you may gain acquisition, and out of their families who are with you, whom they will have produced in your land; they also may become your possession. You may even bequeath them to your sons after you, to receive as a possession; you can use them as permanent slaves. But in respect to your countrymen [brother], the sons of Israel, you shall not rule with severity over one another.

In the Sabbath year all Hebrew debtors/slaves were released from their debts. This was not so for foreigners (Deut. 15:3). Theologian R.J. Rushdoony writes, "since unbelievers are by nature slaves, they could be held as life-long slaves"[1] without piercing the ear to indicate their voluntary servitude (Lev. 25:44-46). This passage in Leviticus says that pagans could be permanent slaves and could be bequeathed to the children of the Hebrews. However, there are Biblical laws concerning slaves that are given for their protection and eventual redemption. Slaves could become part of the covenant and part of the family, even receiving an inheritance. Under the new covenant, a way was made to set slaves free internally, which should then be following by external preparation enabling those who were slaves to live at liberty, being self-governed under God.

Involuntary Servitude is Not Biblical

Exodus 21:16 says: "He who kidnaps a man, whether he sells him or he is found in his possession, shall surely be put to death." Deuteronomy 24:7 states: "If a man is caught kidnapping any of his countrymen of the sons of Israel, and he deals with him violently, or sells him, then that thief shall die; so you shall purge the evil from among you."

Kidnapping and enforced slavery are forbidden and punishable by death. This was true for any man (Ex. 21:16), as well as for the Israelites (Deut. 24:7). This was stealing a man's freedom. While aspects of slavery are Biblical (for punishment and restitution for theft, or for those who prefer the security of becoming a permanent bondservant), the Bible strictly forbids involuntary servitude.

Any slave that ran away from his master (thus expressing his desire for freedom) was to be welcomed by the Israelites, not mistreated, and not returned. Deuteronomy 23:15-16 states:

> You shall not hand over to his master a slave who has escaped from his master to you. He shall live with you in your midst, in the place which he shall choose in one of your towns where it pleases him; you shall not mistreat him.

This implied slaves must be treated justly, plus they had a degree of liberty. Other slave laws confirm this. In addition, such action was a fulfillment of the law of love in both the Old and New Testaments. The law of God declares: "you shall love your neighbor as yourself" (Lev. 19:17-18). Leviticus 19:33-34 clearly reveals that this applies to strangers and aliens as well: "The stranger, . . . you shall not do him wrong. . . . you shall love him as yourself."

It was forbidden to take the life or liberty of any other man. Rushdoony writes:

> Thus, the only kind of slavery permitted is voluntary slavery, as Deuteronomy 23:15,16 makes very clear. Biblical law permits voluntary slavery because it recognizes that some people are not able to maintain a position of independence. To attach themselves voluntarily to a capable man and to serve him, protected by law, is thus a legitimate way of life, although a lesser one. The master then assumes the role of the benefactor, the bestower of welfare, rather that the state, and the slave is protected by the law of the state. A runaway slave thus cannot be restored to his master: he is free to go. The exception is the thief or criminal who is working out his restitution. The Code of Hammurabi decreed death for men who harbored a runaway slave; the Biblical law provided for the freedom of the slave.[2]

Rushdoony also says that

> the selling of slaves was forbidden. Since Israelites were voluntary slaves, and since not even a foreign slave could be compelled to return to his master (Deut. 23:15, 16), slavery was on a different basis under the law than in non-Biblical cultures. The slave was a member of the household, with rights therein. A slave-market could not exist in Israel. The slave who was working out a restitution for theft had no incentive to escape, for to do so would make him an incorrigible criminal and liable to death.[3]

When slaves (indentured servants) were acquired under the law, it was their labor that was purchased, not their person, and the price took into account the year of freedom (Lev. 25:44-55; Ex. 21:2; Deut. 15:12-13).

Laws related to slaves

There are a number of laws in the Bible related to slavery. They include:

1. Hebrew slaves (indentured servants) were freed after 6 years.

> If you buy a Hebrew slave, he shall serve for six years; but on the seventh he shall go out as a free man without payment (Ex. 21:2).

> If your kinsman, a Hebrew man or woman, is sold to you, then he shall serve you six years, but in the seventh year you shall set him free. And when you set him free, you shall not send him away empty-handed (Deut. 15:12-13).

Hebrew slaves were to be set free after six years. If the man was married when he came, his wife was to go with him (Ex. 21:3).

This law did not apply to non-Hebrew slaves (see point 4 under "Types of slavery permitted by the Bible" above), though, as mentioned, any slave showing a desire for freedom was to be safely harbored if they ran away. In violation of this law, many Christian slaves in America were not given the option of freedom after six years (and many escaped slaves were forcefully returned). To comply with the spirit and law of the Old and New Testament, non-Christian slaves should have been introduced by their master to Christianity, equipped to live in liberty, and then given the opportunity to choose to live free. Christianity would have prepared them to live in freedom.

2. Freed slaves were released with liberal pay.

When these slaves were set free they were not to be sent away empty handed. They were to be furnished liberally from the flocks, threshing floor, and wine vat (Deut. 15:12-15).

3. Slaves were to be responsible.

We have mentioned that some people prefer the security of enslavement to the uncertainty of living free. People who live free have certain responsibilities they must maintain. They cannot have the fruit of freedom without the responsibilities of freedom. It is within this context that the following law can be understood:

> If he [a Hebrew slave] comes alone, he shall go out alone; if he is the husband of a wife, then his wife shall go out with him. If his master gives him a wife, and she bears him sons or daughters, the wife and her children shall belong to her master, and he shall go out alone (Ex. 21:3-4).

Rushdoony comments:

> The bondservant, however, could not have the best of both worlds, the world of freedom and the world of servitude. A wife meant responsibility: to marry, a man had to have a dowry as evidence of his ability to head a household. A man could not gain the benefit of freedom, a wife, and at the same time gain the benefit of security under a master.[4]

Marrying as a slave required no responsibility of provision or need of a dowry. He gained the benefits of marriage without the responsibilities associated with it. Rushdoony continues:

If he married while a bondservant, or a slave, he knew that in so doing he was abandoning either freedom or his family. He either remained permanently a slave with his family and had his ear pierced as a sign of subordination (like a woman), or he left his family. If he walked out and left his family, he could, if he earned enough, redeem his family from bondage. The law here is humane and also unsentimental. It recognizes that some people are by nature slaves and will always be so. It both requires that they be dealt with in a godly manner and also that the slave recognize his position and accept it with grace. Socialism, on the contrary, tries to give the slave all the advantages of his security together with the benefits of freedom, and, in the process, destroys both the free and the enslaved.[5]

4. Runaway slaves were to go free.

As mentioned earlier, Deuteronomy 23:15-16 says that a runaway slave was to go free. He was to be welcomed to live in any of the towns of Israel he chose. The Israelites were not to mistreat him.

Rushdoony says that, "Since the slave was, except where debt and theft were concerned, a slave by nature and by choice, a fugitive slave went free, and the return of such fugitives was forbidden (Deut. 23:15,16)." This aspect of Biblical law was violated by American slavery and the United States Constitution (see Art. IV, Sec. 2, Par. 3). "Christians cannot become slaves voluntarily; they are not to become the slaves of men (1 Cor. 7:23), nor 'entangled again with the yoke of bondage' (Gal. 5:1)."[6] Those who became Christians while slaves were to become free if they could (1 Cor. 7:21). If they could not, they were to exemplify the character of Christ (Eph. 6:5-9; Col. 4:1; 1 Tim. 6:1-2). Eventually, Christianity would overthrow slavery, not so much by denouncing it, but by promoting the equality of man under God, and teaching the principles of liberty and the brotherhood of mankind under Christ. It would be the responsibility of Christians, especially those who found themselves in a place of owning slaves (for example, many Christian Americans in the past inherited slaves) to teach such ideas, and then act accordingly. Many Christians in early America did just this. Phyllis Wheatley was introduced to Christianity by her masters, educated, and given her freedom. Many American Christians, in both North and South, at the time of the Civil War did much to educate slaves Biblically. Stonewall Jackson, who never owned slaves himself and was against slavery, conducted many classes in his church to educate slaves.

5. Excessive punishment of slaves was forbidden.

A slave could be punished by striking with a rod (Ex. 21:20-21), but if the punishment was excessive, the slave was to be given his freedom (Ex. 21:26-27; Lev. 24:17). This included knocking out the tooth or damaging the eye. This applied to indentured servants as well as other slaves. Since the owner would lose his investment in such a situation, there was a financial incentive for just treatment.

Just treatment of slaves was required of the masters. Paul writes: "Masters, grant to your slaves justice and fairness, knowing that you too have a Master in heaven" (Col. 4:1).

6. Slaves could be brought into the covenant.

Slaves could be circumcised (brought into the covenant) and then eat of the Passover meal (Ex. 12:43-44; Gen. 17:12-13). Slaves could also eat of holy things (Lev. 22:10-11).

7. Slaves had some rights and position in the home and could share in the inheritance.

(See Gen. 24:2 and Prov. 17:2.)

8. Slaves were to rest on the Sabbath like everyone else.

The Fourth Commandment applied to all (Ex. 20:8-11).

9. Female slave laws were for their protection.

Exodus 21:4-11 gives some laws about female slaves, which served for their protection. These Hebrew female slaves were without family to assist them in their need or to help to provide security for them. These slaves laws were a way to protect them from abuse not faced by males and to keep them from being turned out into the street, where much harm could come to them.

Examination of the Biblical view of slavery enables us to more effectively address the assertion that slavery was America's original sin. In light of the Scriptures we cannot say that slavery, in a broad and general sense, is sin. But this brief look at the Biblical slave laws does reveal how fallen man's example of slavery has violated God's laws, and America's form of slavery in particular violated various aspects of the law, as well as the general spirit of liberty instituted by Christ.

The Christian foundation and environment of America caused most people to seek to view life from a Biblical perspective. Concerning slavery, they would ask "Is it Biblical?". While most of the Founders saw it was God's desire to eliminate the institution, others attempted to justify it. At the time of the Civil War some people justified Southern slavery by appealing to the Bible. However, through this brief review of the Old Testament slave laws we have seen that American slavery violated some of these laws, not to mention the spirit of liberty instituted by the coming of Christ.

Slavery and the New Testament

When Paul wrote how slaves and masters were to act (Eph. 6:5-9; Col. 4:1; 1 Tim. 6:1-2; Col. 3:22-25; Titus 2:9-10), he was not endorsing involuntary slavery or the Roman slave system. He was addressing the attitudes, actions, and matters of the heart of those Christians who found themselves in slavery or as slave owners. This encompassed many people, for half the population of Rome and a large proportion of the Roman Empire were slaves. Many people were converted to Christianity while slaves or slave owners, and many Christians were enslaved.

It is in this context that we can better understand the example of Paul, Onesimus, and Philemon. Onesimus, a slave of Philemon who apparently stole s ome money from his master and ran away, encountered P aul in Rome and became a Christian. Paul sent him back to his master carrying the letter to Philemon. Author of the famous *Bible Handbook*, Henry Halley writes:

> The Bible gives no hint as to how the master received his returning slave. But there is a tradition that says his master did receive him, and took Paul's veiled hint and gave the slave his liberty. That is the way the Gospel works. Christ in the heart of the slave made the slave recognize the social usages of his day, and go back to his master determined to be a good slave and live out his natural life as a slave. Christ in the heart of the master made the master recognize the slave as a Christian brother and give him his liberty. There is a tradition that Onesimus afterward became a bishop of Berea.[7]

The Mosaic slave laws and the writings of Paul benefitted and protected the slaves as best as possible in their situation. God's desire for any who are enslaved is freedom (Luke 4:18; Gal. 5:1). Those who are set free in Christ then need to be prepared to walk in liberty. Pagan nations had a much different outlook toward slaves, believing slaves had no rights or privileges. Because of the restrictions and humane aspect of the Mosaic laws on slavery, it never existed on a large scale in Israel, and did not exhibit the cruelties seen in Egypt, Greece, Rome, Assyria and other nations.

Sinful man will always live in some form of bondage and slavery, as a slave to the state, to a lord or noble, or to other men. As a step in man's freedom, God's laws of slavery provided the best situation for those who find themselves in bondage. God's ultimate desire is that all walk in the liberty of the gospel both internally and externally.

As the gospel principles of liberty have spread throughout history in all the nations, man has put aside the institution of overt slavery. However, since sinful man tends to live in bondage, different forms of slavery have replaced the more obvious system of past centuries. The state has assumed the role of master for many, providing aid and assistance, and with it more and more control, to those unable to provide for themselves. The only solution to slavery is the liberty of the gospel.

Brief History of Slavery

Slavery has existed throughout the world since after the fall of man. Egypt and other ancient empires enslaved multitudes. Greece and Rome had many slaves, taken from nations they conquered. Slavery was a part of almost every culture. While some Christian nations had taken steps to end slavery, it was still an established part of most of the world when America began to be settled.

Many of the early settlers came to America as indentured servants, indebted to others for a brief period of time to pay for their passage. England at this time recognized the forced labor of the apprentice, the hired servant, convicts, and indentured servants. Some of these laborers were subject to whippings and other forms of punishment. These forms of servitude were limited in duration and "transmitted no claim to the servant's children."[8]

According to Hugh Thomas in *The Slave Trade*, about 11,328,000 Africans were transported to the new world between 1440 and 1870. Of these about 4 million went to Brazil, 2.5 million to Spanish colonies, 2 million to the British West Indies, 1.6 million to the French West Indies, and 500,000 went to what became the United States of America.[9]

A Dutch ship, seeking to unload its human cargo, brought the first slaves to Virginia in 1619. Over the next century a small number of slaves were brought to America. In 1700 there were not more than 20 to 30 thousand black slaves in all the colonies. There were some people who spoke against slavery (e.g. the Quakers and Mennonites)[10] and some political efforts to check slavery (as in laws of Massachusetts and Rhode Island), but these had little large scale effect. The colonies' laws recognized and protected slave property. Efforts were made to restrict the slave trade in several colonies, but the British government overruled such efforts and the trade went on down to the Revolution.

When independence was declared from England, the legal status of slavery was firmly established in the colonies, though there were plenty of voices speaking out against it, and with independence those voices would increase.

America's Founders and Slavery

Some people suggest today that all early Americans must have been despicable to allow such an evil as slavery. They say early America should be judged as evil and sinful, and anything they have to say should be discounted. But if we were to judge modern America by this same standard, it would be far more wicked — we are not merely enslaving people, but we are murdering tens of millions of innocent unborn children through abortion. These people claim that they would not have allowed slavery if they were alive then. They would speak out and take any measures necessary. But where is their outcry and action to end slavery in the Sudan today? (And slavery there is much worse than that in early America.)

Some say we should not listen to the Founders of America because they owned slaves, or at least allowed slavery to exist in the society. However, if we were to cut ourselves off from the history of nations that had slavery in the past we would have to have nothing to do with any people because almost every society has had slavery, including African Americans, for many African societies sold slaves to the Europeans; and up to ten percent of blacks in America owned slaves.

The Founders Believed Slavery Was Fundamentally Wrong.

The overwhelming majority of early Americans and most of America's leaders did not own slaves. Some did own slaves, which were often inherited (like George Washington at age eleven), but many of these people set them free after independence. Most Founders believed that slavery was wrong and that it should be abolished. William Livingston, signer of the Constitution and Governor of New Jersey, wrote to an anti-slavery society in New York (John Jay, the first Chief Justice of the U.S. Supreme Court and President of the Continental Congress, was President of this society):

> I would most ardently wish to become a member of it [the anti-slavery society] and . . . I can safely promise them that neither my tongue, nor my pen, nor purse shall be wanting to promote the abolition of what to me appears so inconsistent with humanity and Christianity. . . . May the great

and the equal Father of the human race, who has expressly declared His abhorrence of oppression, and that He is no respecter of persons, succeed a design so laudably calculated to undo the heavy burdens, to let the oppressed go free, and to break every yoke.[11]

John Quincy Adams, who worked tirelessly for years to end slavery, spoke of the anti-slavery views of the southern Founders, including Jefferson who owned slaves:

The inconsistency of the institution of domestic slavery with the principles of the Declaration of Independence was seen and lamented by all the southern patriots of the Revolution; by no one with deeper and more unalterable conviction than by the author of the Declaration himself. No charge of insincerity or hypocrisy can be fairly laid to their charge. Never from their lips was heard one syllable of attempt to justify the institution of slavery. They universally considered it as a reproach fastened upon them by the unnatural step-mother country and they saw that before the principles of the Declaration of Independence, slavery, in common with every other mode of oppression, was destined sooner or later to be banished from the earth. Such was the undoubting conviction of Jefferson to his dying day. In the Memoir of His Life, written at the age of seventy-seven, he gave to his countrymen the solemn and emphatic warning that the day was not distant when they must hear and adopt the general emancipation of their slaves. "Nothing is more certainly written," said he, "in the book of fate, than that these people are to be free."[12]

The Founding Fathers believed that blacks had the same God-given inalienable rights as any other peoples. James Otis of Massachusetts said in 1764 that "The colonists are by the law of nature freeborn, as indeed all men are, white or black."[13]

There had always been free blacks in America who owned property, voted, and had the same rights as other citizens.[14] Most of the men who gave us the Declaration and the Constitution wanted to see slavery abolished. For example, George Washington wrote in a letter to Robert Morris:

I can only say that there is not a man living who wishes more sincerely than I do to see a plan adopted for the abolition of it [slavery].[15]

Charles Carroll, Signer of Declaration from Maryland, wrote:

Why keep alive the question of slavery? It is admitted by all to be a great evil.[16]

Benjamin Rush, Signer from Pennsylvania, stated:

Domestic slavery is repugnant to the principles of Christianity. . . . It is rebellion against the authority of a common Father. It is a practical denial of
the extent and efficacy of the death of a common Savior. It is an usurpation
of the prerogative of the great Sovereign of the universe who has solemnly
claimed an exclusive property in the souls of men.[17]

Father of American education, and contributor to the ideas in the Constitution, Noah Webster wrote:

Justice and humanity require it [the end of slavery] — Christianity commands it. Let every benevolent . . . pray for the glorious period when the
last slave who fights for freedom shall be restored to the possession of that
inestimable right.[18]

Quotes from John Adams reveal his strong anti-slavery views:

Every measure of prudence, therefore, ought to be assumed for the eventual total extirpation of slavery from the United States. . . . I have, through
my whole life, held the practice of slavery in . . . abhorrence.[19]

My opinion against it [slavery] has always been known. . . . [N]ever in my
life did I own a slave.[20]

When Benjamin Franklin served as President of the Pennsylvania Society of Promoting the Abolition of Slavery he declared: "Slavery is . . . an
atrocious debasement of human nature."[21]

Thomas Jefferson's original draft of the Declaration included a strong
denunciation of slavery, declaring the king's perpetuation of the slave trade
and his vetoing of colonial anti-slavery measures as one reason the colonists were declaring their independence:

He [King George III] has waged cruel war against human nature itself,
violating its most sacred rights of life and liberty in the persons of a distant
people who never offended him, captivating and carrying them into slavery in another hemisphere. . . . Determined to keep open a market where
MEN should be bought and sold, he has prostituted his negative for sup-
pressing every legislative attempt to prohibit or restrain this execrable
commerce.[22]

Prior to independence, anti-slavery measures by the colonists were
thwarted by the British government. Franklin wrote in 1773:

A disposition to abolish slavery prevails in North America, that many of
Pennsylvanians have set their slaves at liberty, and that even the Virginia
Assembly have petitioned the King for permission to make a law for pre-
venting the importation of more into that colony. This request, however,

will probably not be granted as their former laws of that kind have always been repealed.[23]

The Founders took action against slavery.

The founders did not just believe slavery was an evil that needed to be abolished, and they did not just speak against it, but they acted on their beliefs. During the Revolutionary War black slaves who fought won their freedom in every state except South Carolina and Georgia.[24]

Many of the founders started and served in anti-slavery societies. Franklin and Rush founded the first such society in America in 1774. John Jay was president of a similar society in New York. Other Founding Fathers serving in anti-slavery societies included: William Livingston (Constitution signer), James Madison, Richard Bassett, James Monroe, Bushrod Washington, Charles Carroll, William Few, John Marshall, Richard Stockton, Zephaniah Swift, and many more.[25]

As the Founders worked to free themselves from enslavement to Britain, based upon laws of God and nature, they also spoke against slavery and took steps to stop it. Abolition grew as principled resistance to the tyranny of England grew, since both were based upon the same ideas. This worked itself out on a personal as well as policy level, as seen in the following incident in the life of William Whipple, signer of the Declaration of Independence from New Hampshire. Dwight writes:

> When General Whipple set out to join the army, he took with him for his waiting servant, a colored man named Prince, one whom he had imported from Africa many years before. He was a slave whom his master highly valued. As he advanced on his journey, he said to Prince, "If we should be called into an engagement with the enemy, I expect you will behave like a man of courage, and fight like a brave soldier for your country." Prince feelingly replied, "Sir, I have no inducement to fight, I have no country while I am a slave. If I had my freedom, I would endeavor to defend it to the last drop of my blood." This reply of Prince produced the effect on his master's heart which Prince desired. The general declared him free on the spot.[26]

The Founders opposed slavery based upon the principle of the equality of all men. Throughout history many slaves have revolted but it was believed (even by those enslaved) that some people had the right to enslave others. The American slave protests were the first in history based on principles of God-endowed liberty for all. It was not the secularists who spoke out against slavery but the ministers and Christian statesmen.

Before independence, some states had tried to restrict slavery in different ways (e.g. Virginia had voted to end the slave trade in 1773), but the English government had not allowed it. Following independence and victory in the war, the rule of the mother country was removed, leaving freedom for each state to deal with the slavery problem. Within about 20 years of the 1783 Treaty of Peace with Britain, the northern states abolished slavery: Pennsylvania and Massachusetts in 1780; Connecticut and Rhode Island in 1784; New Hampshire in 1792; Vermont in 1793; New York in 1799; and New Jersey in 1804.

The Northwest Ordinance (1787, 1789), which governed the admission of new states into the union from the then northwest territories, forbid slavery. Thus, Ohio, Indiana, Illinois, Michigan, Wisconsin, and Iowa all prohibited slavery. This first federal act dealing with slavery was authored by Rufus King (signer of the Constitution) and signed into law by President George Washington.

Although no Southern state abolished slavery, there was much anti-slavery sentiment. Many anti-slavery societies were started, especially in the upper South. Many Southern states considered proposals abolishing slavery, for example, the Virginia legislature in 1778 and 1796. When none passed, many, like Washington, set their slaves free, making provision for their well being. Following independence, "Virginia changed her laws to make it easier for individuals to emancipate slaves,"[27] though over time the laws became more restrictive in Virginia.

While most states were moving toward freedom for slaves, the deep South (Georgia, South Carolina, North Carolina) was largely pro-slavery. Yet, even so, the Southern courts before around 1840 generally took the position that slavery violated the natural rights of blacks. For example, the Mississippi Supreme Court ruled in 1818:

> Slavery is condemned by reason and the laws of nature. It exists and can only exist, through municipal regulations, and in matters of doubt,...courts must lean *in favorem vitae et libertatis* [in favor of life and liberty].[28]

The same court ruled in 1820 that the slave "is still a human being, and possesses all those rights, of which he is not deprived by the positive provisions of the law."[29]

Free blacks were citizens and voted in most Northern states and Virginia, North Carolina, and South Carolina. In Baltimore prior to 1800, more blacks voted than whites; but in 1801 and 1809, Maryland began to restrict black voting and in 1835 North Carolina prohibited it. Other states made similar restrictions, but a number of Northern states allowed blacks to vote and hold office. In Massachusetts this right was given nearly a decade before the American Revolution and was never taken away, either before or after the Civil War.

Slavery and the Constitution

The issue of slavery was considered at the Constitutional Convention. Though most delegates were opposed to slavery, they compromised on the issue when the representatives from Georgia and South Carolina threatened to walk out. The delegates realized slavery would continue in these states with or without the union. They saw a strong union of all the colonies was the best means of securing their liberty (which was by no means guaranteed to survive). They did not agree to abolish slavery as some wanted to do, but they did take the forward step of giving the Congress the power to end the slave trade after 20 years.[30] No nation in Europe or elsewhere had agreed to such political action.

Even so, many warned of the dangers of allowing this evil to continue. George Mason of Virginia told the delegates:

> Every master of slaves is born a petty tyrant. They bring the judgement of heaven upon a country. As nations cannot be rewarded or punished in the next world, they must be in this. By an inevitable chain of causes and effects, Providence punishes national sins by national calamities.[31]

Jefferson had written some time before this:

> The whole commerce between master and slave is a perpetual exercise of the most boisterous passions, the most unremitting despotism on the one part, and degrading submissions on the other. . . . And with what execration should the statesman be loaded, who permitting one half the citizens thus to trample on the rights of the other. . . . And can the liberties of a nation be thought secure when we have removed their only firm basis, a conviction in the minds of the people that these liberties are of the gift of God? That they are not to be violated but with his wrath? Indeed I tremble for my country when I reflect that God is just: that his justice cannot sleep forever.[32]

Constitutional Convention Delegate, Luther Martin, stated:

> [I]t ought to be considered that national crimes can only be and frequently are punished in this world by national punishments; and that the continuance of the slave-trade, and thus giving it a national sanction and encouragement, ought to be considered as justly exposing us to the displeasure

and vengeance of Him who is equally Lord of all and who views with equal eye the poor African slave and his American master.[33]

Some today misinterpret the Constitutional provision of counting the slaves as three-fifths for purposes of representation as pro-slavery or black dehumanization. But it was a political compromise between the north and the south. The three-fifths provision applied only to slaves and not free blacks, who voted and had the same rights as whites (and in some southern states this meant being able to own slaves). While the Southern states wanted to count the slaves in their population to determine the number of congressmen from their states, slavery opponents pushed to keep the Southern states from having more representatives, and hence more power in congress.

The Constitution did provide that runaway slaves would be returned to their owners (We saw previously that returning runaway slaves is contrary to Biblical slave laws, unless these slaves were making restitution for a crime.) but the words slave and slavery were carefully avoided. "Many of the framers did not want to blemish the Constitution with that shameful term." The initial language of this clause was "legally held to service or labor," but this was deleted when it was objected that *legally* seemed to favor "the idea that slavery was legal in a moral view."[34]

While the Constitution did provide some protection for slavery, this document is not pro-slavery. It embraced the situation of all 13 states at that time, the Founders leaving most of the power to deal with this social evil in the hands of each state. Most saw that the principles of liberty contained in the Declaration could not support slavery and would eventually overthrow it. As delegate to the Constitutional Convention, Luther Martin put it:

> Slavery is inconsistent with the genius of republicanism, and has a tendency to destroy those principles on which it is supported, as it lessens the sense of the equal rights of mankind, and habituates us to tyranny and oppression.[35]

We have seen that after independence the American Founders actually took steps to end slavery. Some could have done more, but as a whole they probably did more than any group of national leaders up until that time in history to deal with the evil of slavery. They took steps toward liberty for the enslaved and believed that the gradual march of liberty would continue, ultimately resulting in the complete death of slavery. The ideas they infused in the foundational civil documents upon which America was founded — such as Creator endowed rights and the equality of all men before the law — eventually prevailed and slavery was abolished. But not without great difficulty because the generations that followed failed to carry out the gradual abolition of slavery in America.

The View of Slavery Changes

Most of America's Founders thought slavery would gradually be abolished. Roger Sherman said that "the abolition of slavery seemed to be going on in the U.S. and that the good sense of the several states would probably by degrees complete it."[36] But it was not. Why?

1. Succeeding generations did not have the character and worldview necessary to complete the task started by the Founders. Eternal vigilance is the price of liberty. Each generation must take up the cause of liberty, which is the cause of God, and fight the battle. While the majority view of the Founders was that American slavery was a social evil that needed to be abolished, many in later generations attempted to justify slavery, often appealing to the Scriptures (though, I believe, in error at many points, as mentioned earlier).

2. American slavery was not in alignment with Biblical slave laws and God's desire for liberty for all mankind. This inconsistency produced an institution that proved too difficult to gradually and peacefully abolish. Some Founders (like Henry and Jefferson) could not see how a peaceful resolution was possible and gave the "necessary evil" argument. Henry said: "As much as I deplore slavery, I see that prudence forbids its abolition."[37]

Jefferson was opposed to slavery yet he thought that once the slaves gained freedom, a peaceful coexistence of whites and blacks would be very difficult to maintain. Jefferson predicted that if the slaves were freed and lived in America,

> Deep-rooted prejudices entertained by the whites' ten thousand recollections, by the blacks, of the injuries they have sustained; new provocations; the real distinctions which nature has made and many other circumstances, will divide us into parties, and produce convulsions which will probably never end but in the extermination of the one or the other race.[38]

This is why many worked (especially many from Virginia, like James Monroe and James Madison) to set up a country in Africa (Liberia) where the freed slaves could live. Some at this time did not see integration as possible, and apart from the power of God, history has shown it is not possible, as there have been and are many ethnic wars. The church must lead the way in race relations, showing all believers are brothers in Christ, and all men have a common Creator.

3. The invention of the cotton gin, which revived the economic benefit of slavery, also contributed to a shift in the thinking of many Americans. At the time of independence and the constitutional period most people viewed slavery as an evil that should and would be abolished. But by the 1830s, many people, including some Southern ministers, began to justify it. Some, like Calhoun, even said it was a positive thing. Others justified it by promoting the inequality of the races. Stephen Douglas argued that the Declaration only applied to whites, but Lincoln rejected that argument and sought to bring the nation back to the principles of the Declaration. In the end these principles prevailed.

The Civil War

It is not the intent of this article to examine the War between the States.[39] The causes behind the war were many. Certainly slavery was a part of the cause (and for a small number of wealthy and influential Southern slave owners, it was probably primary), but slavery was not the central issue for all people in the South. Most Southerners did not own slaves and most of those who did had only a small number.[40]

States rights and perceived unconstitutional taxes were also motivations for secession. There were many abolitionists in the North, both Christian and non-Christian, who pushed for the war, seeing it as a means to end slavery. Though slavery was not initially the reason Lincoln sent troops into the South, he did come to believe that God wanted him to emancipate the slaves.

In all the complexities and tragedy of the war, God was at work fulfilling His providential purposes. Due to the sin of man, to his inability to deal with slavery in a Christian manner, and to other factors, a war erupted. Both good and bad in the root causes, produced good and bad fruit in the outcome of the war.[41]

Though America's Founders failed to accomplish all of their desires and wishes in dealing with the issue of slavery, the principles of equality and God-given rights they established in the American constitutional republic set into motion events leading to the end of slavery in the United States and throughout the world. That America was founded upon such Biblical principles is what made her a Christian nation, not that there was no sin in the Founders. It is because of the Christian foundations that America has become the most free, just, and prosperous nation in history. The

Godly principles infused in her laws, institutions, and families have had immense impact in overthrowing tyranny, oppression, and slavery throughout the world.

End Notes

1. Rousas John.Rushdoony, *Institutes of Biblical Law*, Vol. 1, The Presbyterian and Reformed Publishing Co., p. 137.

2. Rushdoony, p. 286.

3. Rushdoony, pp. 485-486.

4. Rushdoony, p. 251.

5. Rushdoony, p. 251.

6. Rushdoony, p. 137.

7. Henry H. Halley, *Halley's Bible Handbook*, Grand Rapids: Zondervan, 1965, p. 645.

8. Albert Bushnell Hart, *The American Nation: A History, vol. 16, Slavery and Abolition, 1831-1841*, New York: Harper & Brothers, 1906, p. 50.

9. "History of slavery is wide-ranging saga", book review by Gregory Kane of *The Slave Trade* by Hugh Thomas (Simon and Schuster), in The Daily Progress, Charlottesville, Va., December 7, 1997.

10. The earliest known official protest against slavery in America was the *Resolutions of Germantown, Pennsylvania Mennonites, February 18, 1688*. See *Documents of American History*, Henry Steele Commager, editor, New York: F.S. Crofts & Co., 1944, 37-38.

11. William Livingston, *The Papers of William Livingston*, Carl E. Prince, editor, New Brunswick: Rutgers University Press, 1988, Vol. V, p. 255, to the New York Manumission Society on June 26, 1786. In "The Founding Fathers and Slavery" by David Barton, unpublished paper, p. 5.

12. John Quincy Adams, *An Oration Delivered Before the Inhabitants of the Town of Newburyport, at Their Request, on the Sixty-First Anniversary of the Declaration of Independence, July 4th, 1837*, Newburyport: Charles Whipple, 1837, p. 50.

13. *Rights of the Colonies*, in Bernard Bailyn, ed., *Pamphlets of the American Revolution*, Cambridge: Harvard University Press, 1965, p. 439. In "Was the American Founding Unjust? The Case of Slavery," by Thomas G. West, *Principles*, a quarterly review of The Claremont Institute, Spring/Summer 1992, p. 1.

14. Hart, p. 53.

15. Letter to Robert Morris, April 12, 1786, in *George Washington: A Collection*, ed. W.B. Allen, Indianapolis: Liberty Fund, 1988, p. 319.

16. Kate Mason Rowland, *Life and Correspondence of Charles Carroll of Carrollton*, New York & London: G.P. Putnam's Sons, 1898, Vol. II, p. 321, to Robert Goodloe Harper, April 23, 1820. In Barton, p. 3.

17. Benjamin Rush, *Minutes of the Proceedings of a Convention of Delegates from the Abolition Societies Established in Different Parts of the United States Assembled at Philadelphia*, Philadelphia: Zachariah Poulson, 1794, p. 24. In Barton, p. 4.

18. Noah Webster, *Effect of Slavery on Morals and Industry*, Hartford: Hudson and Goodwin, 1793, p. 48. In Barton, p. 4.

19. Adams to Robert J. Evans, June 8, 1819, in Adrienne Koch and William Peden, eds., *Selected Writings of John and John Quincy Adams*, New York: Knopf, 1946, p. 209. In West, p. 2.

20. John Adams, *The Works of John Adams, Second President of the United States*, Charles Francis Adams, ed., Boston: Little, Brown, and Co., 1854, Vol. IX, pp. 92-93, to George Churchman and Jacob Lindley on January 24, 1801. In Barton, p. 3.

21. "An Address to the Public from the Pennsylvania Society for Promoting the Abolition of Slavery" (1789), in Franklin, *Writings*, New York: Library of America, 1987, p. 1154. In West, p. 2.

22. *The Life and Selected Writings of Thomas Jefferson*, Adrienne Koch and William Peden, eds., New York: Random House, 1944, p. 25.

23. Benjamin Franklin, *The Works of Benjamin Franklin*, Jared Sparks, ed., Boston: Tappan, Whittemore, and Mason, 1839, Vol. VIII, p. 42, to the Rev. Dean Woodward on April 10, 1773.

24. Benjamin Quarles, *The Negro and the American Revolution*, Chapel Hill: University of North Carolina Press, 1961, chaps. 4-6. In West, p. 2.

25. Barton, p. 5.

26. N. Dwight, *The Lives of the Signers of the Declaration of Independence*, New York: A.S. Barnes & Burr, 1860, p. 11.

27. West, p. 4.

28. *Harry v. Decker & Hopkins* (1818), in West, p. 4.

29. *Mississippi v. Jones* (1820), in West, p. 4.

30. Congress banned the exportation of slaves from any state in 1794, and in 1808 banned the importation of slaves. The individual states had passed similar legislation prior to 1808 as well. However, several Southern states continued to actively import and export slaves after their state ban went into effect.

31. Mark Beliles and Stephen McDowell, *America's Providential History*, Charlottesville, Va.: Providence Foundation, 1991, p. 227.

32. Thomas Jefferson, *Notes on the State of Virginia*, Trenton: Wilson & Blackwell, 1803, Query XVIII, pp. 221-222.

33. Luther Martin, *The Genuine Information Delivered to the Legislature of the State of Maryland Relative to the Proceedings of the General Convention Lately Held at Philadelphia*, Philadelphia: Eleazor Oswald, 1788, p. 57. In Barton, p. 4.

34. West, p. 5. See Max Farrand, ed. *The Records of the Federal Convention of 1787*, New Haven: Yale University Press, 1937, vol. 2, p. 417 (remarks on August 25), and pp. 601 (report of Committee of Style), 628 (Sept. 15). See also Madison's *Notes of Debates in the Federal Convention of 1787*, August 25.

35. Luther Martin, *Genuine Information* (1788), in Herbert J. Storing, ed., *The Complete Anti-Federalist*, Chicago: University of Chicago Press, 1981, vol. 2, p. 62. In West, p. 6.

36. Remarks at the Constitutional Convention, August 22, Farrand, vol. 2, pp. 369-72. In West, pp. 7-8.

37. Henry to Robert Pleasants, Jan. 18, 1773, in Philip B. Kurland and Ralph Lerner, eds. *The Founders' Constitution*, Chicago: University of Chicago Press, 1987, vol. 1, p. 517; Elliot, *Debates*, vol. 3, p. 590. In West, p. 6.

Henry also pointed out that convenience contributed to the continuation of slavery. He said:

"Is it not surprising that at a time when the rights of humanity are defined with precision in a country above all others fond of liberty — that, in such an age, and in such a country, we find men, professing a religion the most humane and gentle, adopting a principle as repugnant to humanity as it is inconsistent with the Bible and destructive to liberty? Believe me, I honor the Quakers for their noble efforts to abolish slavery. Every thinking, honest man regrets it in speculation, yet how few in practice from conscientious motives. Would any man believe that I am master of slaves of my own purchase? I am drawn along by the general inconvenience of living without them. I will not, I cannot justify it. For however culpable my conduct, I will so far pay my devoir to virtue as to won the excellence and rectitude of her precepts, and to lament my own non-conformity to them." In John Hancock, *Essays on the Elective Franchise; or, Who Has the Right to Vote?*, Philadelphia: Merrihew & Son, 1865, pp. 31-32.

38. Jefferson's *Notes*, Query XIV, p. 188.

39. See *America's Providential History*, chapter 16 for more on a providential view of the war.

40. See Hart, pp. 67 ff. Hart records that in 1860 only about 5% of the white population made a substantial profit of slave-keeping (a direct profit; many others benefited from the commerce associated with slavery). About 2% of this number (0.1% of the total white population) were large plantation owners who exerted much political influence.

Some people have pointed out that only 3% of Southerners owned slaves. While this is technically true in some measure, it is misleading. The 3% reflects ownership by the head of the household and does not include all its inhabitants. Taking this into account, at the time of the Civil War about 19% of the population lived in households with slaves; and this was 19% of total population which included a large number of slaves. When you consider that in 6 Southern states (Alabama, Georgia, Florida, Louisiana, Mississippi, South Carolina), there were almost as many or more slaves than whites, this 19% figure actually represents 35%-45% of the white population (in those states) having a direct relation to a home that had slaves.

41. See *America's Providential History*, chapter 16 for some positive and negative effects of the war.

Chapter 13

Qualifications for Godly Officials

It is very important who we choose to govern us. When the righteous rule the people will rejoice, but when the wicked govern they will groan (Proverbs 29:2). Life is like a beautiful day when those who fear God rule, as 2 Samuel 23:3-4 states:

> The God of Israel said, the Rock of Israel spoke to me, He who rules over men righteously, Who rules in the fear of God, is as the light of the morning when the sun rises, a morning without clouds, when the tender grass springs out of the earth, through sunshine after rain.

Our nation's welfare and stability — our continuance as a nation of liberty, justice, and prosperity — will be greatly affected by whom we choose to lead us in the legislative, judicial, and executive departments of state. The qualifications of those who rule is of utmost importance. In choosing those who govern, we must compare their qualifications to those that the Bible says are of most importance.

How Can We Know Who Will Govern Righteously?

If you could ask one question of a candidate for office to help you decide if you would vote for him, what would that question be?

Many people would seek an answer to the question: What are you going to do for me if you are elected? The first time I voted in a presidential election was in 1972. This was before I became a Christian (in heart or head). I voted for the liberal losing candidate George McGovern because I thought his election would more enable me to live the immoral lifestyle that I pursued at that time. This is a typical motivation for many as they vote for those who govern.

Having put aside immorality, some Christians would ask candidates: Are you a Christian? Are you born again? Do you believe the Bible is the inspired word of God? Or any similar religious question. The answers to such questions are important; however, the answer can be positive but the person not be an effective ruler at all. By the 1976 election I had become a believer, though I lacked a Biblical governmental worldview, and I considered this type of question to be most important. As I read about Jimmy Carter, the answer seemed "yes" for the questions above. He unashamedly spoke of being born again in *Time Magazine* and I thought it would be great to have a Christian as President. While having some good qualities, Carter was not a good President. He did not govern in a Biblical manner. He did not have the qualifications necessary to be a Godly civil leader.

In the years following the 1976 election I began to grow in Biblical knowledge and began to learn how to think governmentally. Now, in attempting to discern if a candidate is qualified to govern Biblically, one question I would ask is: What is your philosophy of government? How a ruler governs is as important as the faith he proclaims. True Biblical faith requires a Biblical worldview.

Jimmy Carter may have been sincere in his claim as a born again Christian, but he was sincerely ignorant of Biblical principles of government. His worldview, which affected his actions and policies, was more humanistic than Biblical. That, coupled with a congress with the same worldview, produced the misery index, America held hostage (444 days), increased size and scope of civil government, and a movement of our nation toward more statism. His pagan philosophy of government did not help to bring liberty, justice and rejoicing by the people — the nation was not becoming more like "the light of the morning when the sun rises."

Biblical Qualifications for Governing Officials

When Moses told the children of Israel to select from among them those who would govern them, he set forth a number of Biblical qualifications. He said: "You shall select out of all the people, able men who fear God, men of truth, those who hate dishonest gain" (Ex. 18:21). "Choose wise and discerning and experienced men" (Deut. 1:13). He put forth three general qualifications for governing officials.

1. Knowledge — "men of truth", "wise," "discerning"

As Matthias Burnet stated in an Election Sermon before the Connecticut Assembly in 1803, we should choose "men of good natural understanding and competent acquired knowledge."[1] Knowledge is more important than belief for daily living out your life. Many people say, "I believe in Christ," but this means different things for different people. Your knowledge determines your actions and belief, for as a man "thinks in his heart, so is he" (Prov. 23:7).

A few years ago I ruptured my achilles tendon playing basketball. The first question I asked my family doctor about the various specialists who could perform surgery was, "who is best able to repair it?", not "which, if any, doctor is a Christian?". Now, if two were equally skilled, I would certainly choose the Christian.

The same concept applies to rulers. We want those who best know how to govern Biblically — those who have a Biblical philosophy of government. Some non-Christians' governmental philosophy is more Biblical than some Christians'. Most rulers will not have all Biblical qualifications, so we must weigh all factors. Mature Christians should have mature Biblical knowledge. Unfortunately, many Christians never develop mature Biblical knowledge. I would rather elect an unregenerate man with a Biblical view of governance than a believer who thinks like a pagan, for your knowledge determines your actions.

Some people say that having a good heart and right intentions is of first importance. "If he means well, that is of most importance." Yet, if a man cannot discern the proper actions he is to take, he will always be in danger of being influenced by those who claim to be lovers of liberty and country, but are really more concerned with SELF and private interest; or he may be misguided in how to do good.

As an example, the Bible says we are to help the poor. To some Christians that means using the force of government to make everyone fulfill this duty. Those with this philosophy would tax all citizens and take this money to give to others. This is really socialism, justified under the guise of fulfilling our Biblical duty. History has shown socialism does not work, and I believe that a study of the Scriptures reveals our duty to the poor must be fulfilled voluntarily by individual choice, and in a Biblical manner. Considering that one third of our tax dollars is spent on social programs, the governmental philosophy of our rulers matters greatly.

The qualification of knowledge is not as the world sees knowledge. In the last presidential election one media leader was arguing that Al Gore was the better candidate because he had more knowledge — he went to Harvard, had a high IQ, and read a lot. Just being a knowledgeable person is not enough though. A ruler must have appropriate knowledge, related to fulfilling his duties. First, he must have a Biblical philosophy of government.

Biblical Philosophy of Government

The first aspect of a Biblical philosophy of government that a Godly ruler must understand is the purpose of government.

(1) The purpose of government

The Biblical purpose of government and civil law is to restrain the evil action of men in society (Rom. 13; 1 Pet. 2). True law reveals what is right and wrong, and hence, exposes law-breakers. But law in itself cannot produce what is right, therefore, you cannot legislate good. However, you can legislate morality for, in fact, all law legislates morality. Some people declare "you can't legislate morality," which is true if they mean you cannot make people moral by passing laws. If we could make people moral by law alone, then law makers could simply enact legislation to produce a perfect society. They could bring salvation by law. However, every law reflects someone's morality. All laws everywhere are based upon the moral presuppositions of the law makers. Laws against murder reflect a moral belief. Laws against theft are based upon the command to not steal. All law has a moral concern. The important question is whose morality does it legislate.

From a humanistic perspective, the attempt is made to regulate and provide all things through government and law. Humanists believe that it is through the force of law that evil will be eliminated and utopia established on earth. Judges, legislators, and others have attacked and struck down Biblical law, saying morality cannot be legislated, but have themselves legislated morality — a new morality based on men's selfish desires. But even worse, they have attempted to bring salvation by law, which is contrary to Christian belief. The law cannot save us; it is not the purpose of the law to do so.

The law cannot change or reform man; this is a spiritual matter. Man can only be changed by the grace of God. He cannot be legislated into a new morality. From a pagan perspective there is no hope of internal regeneration to save man, therefore, a pagan view attempts to bring salvation to man and society through the instrument of law. Humanists cry out the loudest about not legislating morality, but they are the ones trying to save mankind through law and government.

The goal of many of our laws (and governmental actions) today is a "saved" society, where there is more peace and goodwill among men and that all that is negative is eliminated, such as poverty, crime, war, disease, prejudice, ignorance. Law can restrain sinful man from acting evilly, for the fear of punishment is a deterrent, but he cannot be changed by law. Unless the evil heart of man is changed, there will be no advancement toward a better society. Humanistic law seeks to save and change man internally. Since the government (and laws issued thereby) is the instrument for such change, the government becomes the savior in a humanistic society.[2]

We need rulers who understand the purpose of law and government so they will not try to make the law do what God never intended it to do, that is, save us.

(2) Jurisdictional authority

A second aspect of a Biblical philosophy of government is understanding jurisdictional authority. Jesus taught this in Matthew 22 when he said "render to Caesar the things that are Caesar's and to God the things that are God's." He was saying that the state has a legitimate function, but that it is limited and should not usurp the authority He gave to individuals, the family, and the church.

We briefly examined the purpose and responsibilities of the individual, family, church, and state in Chapter 3.[3] It is essential that our elected officials understand to whom God has given authority to do what. The result of usurpation of authority by the civil government from the family and church is tyranny.

Government is not to provide the health, education, and welfare of citizens. Government is limited in what it is to do. Today about 2/3 of money spent by civil government is outside its jurisdiction. That is why we have a 40% tax rate, encroachment by government into our lives, regulation of all kinds of things — all of which leads to lose of individual liberty. This situation is a result of having civil rulers who do not understand jurisdictional authority.

A Biblical view of jurisdictional authority and limited government was incorporated into the law of the land by the Founders of America. The men who set up this constitutional republic saw it as very limited. The national government was given only 18 enumerated powers in the Constitution—that was all the authority they had. The national government was not to be involved in anything else. Today we have this turned around, where Washington thinks they have all power unless restricted in some way by the Constitution. A statement by James Madison, our fourth President and chief architect of the Constitution, shows how far we have gone.

In 1792 Congress considered a bill that would have given subsidies to cod fishermen in New England. Some few argued Congress had power to do so under the general welfare clause. Speaking against the bill, James

Madison said first, this is a limited government with only the specified powers listed in the Constitution belonging to Congress, the executive, and judiciary, then:

> If Congress can employ money indefinitely to the general welfare, and are the sole and supreme judges of the general welfare, they may take the care of religion into their own hands; they may appoint teachers in every state, county, and parish, and pay them out of their public treasury; they may take into their own hands the education of children, establishing in like manner schools throughout the Union; they may assume the provision for the poor; they may undertake the regulation of all roads other than post-roads.[4]

Imagine how the media would present Madison today if he proposed no government involvement in schools, providing for the poor, and regulation of all roads.

People for abortion will often say that they are for limited government, that government should leave a woman's body alone and let them decide themselves what to do with their own body. But government is to be limited in its jurisdiction, and its proper jurisdiction is in the protecting of the life, liberty, and property of all the citizens, including the unborn child. Many humanistic thinkers want government to be limited in the areas where it should be acting, and acting in areas where it should be limited. For example, many want government limited in executing justice with swift and appropriate punishment for crime—e.g. no death penalty, no restitution, letting criminals loose in society. I am for limited government, but I am not for limiting government from appropriately punishing criminals. Many people also seek to limit the strength of the military, including having no civilian military. Knowledgeable rulers are needed to discern the proper jurisdiction of civil government.

Understanding the limited role of government is very important, because the tendency of fallen man is to centralize and increase power, and this is often done in the name of good. Most rulers in the world today are statists or socialists. Those with a statist philosophy see civil government as the primary authority in the world—the state (and its law) is the savior. In a statist world, there is no other savior; government much save man for there is no supreme God to do so.

While there is some difference in the Republican and Democratic parties, most of America's national elected officials are socialists or statists, as evidenced by spending appropriations of tax dollars. A minority of principled representatives adhere to the limited jurisdiction of government, but most go along with uncontrolled spending (look, for example, at the pork barrel spending by recent Congresses, both Democratic and Republican). Ever increasing spending by government is done in the name of helping society and the citizens, and is considered legitimate since, to many, the law or government is savior. This often takes the form of taking from one group of citizens to give to others. This is stealing and violates the 8th command. Government is to protect its citizens, not plunder them. We can learn an important lesson regarding these matters from the life of Davy Crockett.

Davy Crockett and Governmental Usurpation

While Davy Crockett was a member of the U.S. House of Representatives a bill was presented appropriating money for a widow of a distinguished naval officer. The officer had recently died and the widow was in financial need. A number of congressmen had spoken in support of the bill, pointing out the great service the officer had made and the need of the widow. The Speaker was about to put the bill to a vote when Crockett arose. He spoke of his respect for the deceased and his sympathy for the widow, but he said:

> We must not permit our respect for the dead or our sympathy for a part of the living to lead us into an act of injustice to the balance of the living. I will not go into an argument to prove that Congress has no power to appropriate this money as an act of charity. Every member upon this floor knows it. We have the right, as individuals, to give away as much of our own money as we please in charity; but as members of Congress we have no right so to appropriate a dollar of the public money.[5]

He pointed out how the government had met every financial obligation to the officer and owed him no debt.

> Mr. Speaker, I have said we have the right to give as much money of our own as we please. I am the poorest man on this floor. I cannot vote for this bill, but I will give one week's pay to the object, and if every member of Congress will do the same, it will amount to more than the bill asks.

He took his seat. Nobody replied. The bill was voted on, and instead of passing, which would have happened had Crockett not said anything, it received but few votes, and failed.

A friend later asked Crockett why he opposed the bill. He explained:

> Several years ago I was one evening standing on the steps of the Capitol with some other members of Congress, when our attention was attracted by a great light over in Georgetown. It was evidently a large fire.

We jumped into a hack and drove over as fast as we could. In spite of all that could be done, many houses were burned and many families made houseless, and, besides, some of them had lost all but the clothes they had on. The weather was very cold, and when I saw so many women and children suffering, I felt that something ought to be done for them. The next morning a bill was introduced appropriating $20,000 for their relief. We put aside all other business and rushed it through as soon as it could be done.

The next summer when Crockett was running for reelection he was riding around campaigning in his district. One day he came upon a farmer plowing his field and spoke to him.

He replied politely, but, as I thought, rather coldly.

I began: "Well, friend, I am one of those unfortunate beings called candidates, and . . ."

"Yes, I know you; you are Colonel Crockett. I have seen you once before, and voted for you the last time you were elected. I suppose you are out electioneering now, but you had better not waste your time or mine. I shall not vote for you again."

This was a sockdolager [a decisive blow or answer]. . . . I begged him to tell me what was the matter.

"Well, Colonel, it is hardly worth-while to waste time or words upon it. I do not see how it can be mended, but you gave a vote last winter which shows that either you have not capacity to understand the Constitution, or that you are wanting in the honesty and firmness to be guided by it. In either case you are not the man to represent me. But I beg your pardon for expressing it in that way. I did not intend to avail myself of the privilege of the constituent to speak plainly to a candidate for the purpose of insulting or wounding you. I intend by it only to say that your understanding of the Constitution is very different from mine; and I will say to you what, but for my rudeness, I should not have said, that I believe you to be honest. . . . But an understanding of the Constitution different from mine I cannot overlook, because the Constitution, to be worth anything, must be held sacred, and rigidly observed in all its provisions. The man who wields power and misinterprets it is the more dangerous the more honest he is."

"I admit the truth of all you say, but there must be some mistake about it, for I do not remember that I gave any vote last winter upon any constitutional question."

"No, Colonel, there's no mistake. Though I live here in the backwoods and seldom go from home, I take the papers from Washington and read very carefully all the proceedings of Congress. My papers say that last winter you voted for a bill to appropriate $20,000 to some sufferers by a fire in Georgetown. Is that true?"

"Well, my friend; I may as well own up. You have got me there. But certainly nobody will complain that a great and rich country like ours should give the insignificant sum of $20,000 to relieve its suffering women and children, particularly with a full and overflowing Treasury, and I am sure, if you had been there, you would have done just as I did."

"It is not the amount, Colonel, that I complain of; it is the principle. In the first place, the government ought to have in the Treasury no more than enough for its legitimate purposes. But that has nothing to do with the question. The power of collecting and disbursing money at pleasure is the most dangerous power that can be intrusted to man, particularly under our system of collecting revenue by a tariff, which reaches every man in the country, no matter how poor he may be, and the poorer he is the more he pays in proportion to his means. What is worse, it presses upon him without his knowledge where the weight centers, for there is not a man in the United States who can ever guess how much he pays to the government. So you see, that while you are contributing to relieve one, you are drawing it from thousands who are even worse off than he. If you had the right to give anything, the amount was simply a matter of discretion with you, and you had as much right to give $20,000,000 as $20,000. If you have the right to give to one, you have the right to give to all; and, as the Constitution neither defines charity nor stipulates the amount, you are at liberty to give to any and everything which you may believe, or profess to believe, is a charity, and to any amount you may think proper. You will very easily perceive what a wide door this would open for fraud and corruption and favoritism, on the one hand, and for robbing the people on the other. No, Colonel, Congress has no right to give charity. Individual members may give as much of their own money as they please, but they have no right to touch a dollar of the public money for that purpose. If twice as many houses had been burned in this county as in Georgetown, neither you nor any other member of Congress would have thought of appropriating a dollar for our relief. There are about two hundred and forty members of Congress. If they had shown their sympathy for the sufferers by contributing each one weeks pay, it would have made over $13,000. There are plenty of wealthy men in and around Washington who could have given $20,000 without depriving themselves of even a luxury of life. The congressmen chose to keep their own money, which, if reports be true, some of them spend not very creditably; and the people about Washington, no doubt, applauded you for relieving them from the necessity of giving by giving what was not yours to give. The people have delegated to Congress, by the Constitution, the power to do certain things. To do these, it is authorized to collect and pay moneys, and for nothing else. Everything beyond this is usurpation, and a violation of the Constitution."

"So you see, Colonel, you have violated the Constitution in what I consider a vital point. It is a precedent fraught with danger to the country, for when Congress once begins to stretch its power beyond the limits of the Constitution, there is no limit to it, and no security for the people. I have no doubt you acted honestly, but that does not make it any better, except as far as you personally are concerned, and you see that I cannot vote for you."

Being enlightened by this farmer, Crockett replied:

"Well, my friend, you hit the nail upon the head when you said I had not sense enough to understand the Constitution. I intended to be guided by it, and thought I had studied it fully. I have heard many speeches in Congress about the powers of Congress, but what you have said here at your plow has got more hard, sound sense in it than all the fine speeches I ever heard. If I had ever taken the view of it that you have, I would have put my head into the fire before I would have given that vote; and if you will forgive me and vote for me again, if I ever vote for another unconstitutional law I wish I may be shot."

He laughingly replied: "Yes, Colonel, you have sworn to that once before, but I will trust you again upon one condition. You say that you are convinced that your vote was wrong. Your acknowledgment of it will do more good than beating you for it. If, as you go around the district, you will tell people about this vote, and that you are satisfied it was wrong, I will not only vote for you, but will do what I can to keep down opposition, and, perhaps, I may exert some little influence in that way."

Crockett said he would do this, and he would even come back to the area and give a speech to anybody that this man could gather together. The farmer, whose name was Horatio Bunce, said he would gather a group together in a week or so. Bunce was a Christian, and a good example of what a Christian citizen ought to be. He was a man of character and principle, and one with much knowledge who kept an eye on his elected officials. Crockett relates:

At the appointed time I was at his house, having told our conversation to every crowd I had met, and to every man I stayed all night with, and I found that it gave the people interest and a confidence in me stronger than I had ever seen manifested before.

Crockett stayed the night with Bunce and was up until midnight talking "about the principles and affairs of government, and got more real, true knowledge of them than I had got all my life before."

I have known and seen much of him since, for I respect him — no, that is not the word — I reverence and love him more than any living man, and

I go to see him two or three times every year; and I will tell you, sir, if every one who professes to be a Christian lived and acted and enjoyed it as he does, the religion of Christ would take the world by storm.

The next morning they went to a barbecue that was attended by about 1000 men. Crockett opened his speech:

"Fellow-citizens — I present myself before you today feeling like a new man. My eyes have lately been opened to truths which ignorance or prejudice, or both, had heretofore hidden from my view. I feel that I can today offer you the ability to render you more valuable service that I have ever been able to render before. I am here today more for the purpose of acknowledging my error than to seek your votes. That I should make this acknowledgment is due to myself as well as to you. Whether you will vote for me is a matter for your consideration only."

I went on to tell them about the fire and my vote for the appropriation and then told them why I was satisfied it was wrong. I closed by saying:

"And now, fellow-citizens, it remains only for me to tell you that the most of the speech you have listened to with so much interest was simply a repetition of the arguments by which your neighbor, Mr. Bunce, convinced me of my error.

"It is the best speech I ever made in my life, but he is entitled to the credit for it. And now I hope he is satisfied with his convert and that he will get up here and tell you so."

He came upon the stand, and said:

"Fellow-citizens — It affords, me great pleasure to comply with the request of Colonel Crockett. I have always considered him a thoroughly honest man, and I am satisfied that he will faithfully perform all that he has promised you today."

He went down, and there went up from that crowd such a shout for Davy Crockett as his name never called forth before.

I am not much given to tears, but I was taken with a choking then and felt some big drops rolling down my cheeks. And I tell you now that the remembrance of those few words spoken by such a man, and the honest, hearty shout they produced, is worth more to me than all the honors I have received and all the reputation I have ever made, or ever shall make, as a member of Congress.

"Now, sir," concluded Crockett, "you know why I made that speech yesterday."

"There is one thing now to which I will call your attention. You remember that I proposed to give a weeks pay. There are in that House many very wealthy men — men who think nothing of spending a week's pay, or a dozen of them, for a dinner or a wine party when they have something to accomplish by it. Some of those same men made beautiful speeches upon the great debt of gratitude which the country owed the deceased — a debt which could not be paid by money — and the insignificance and worthlessness of money, particularly so insignificant a sum as $10,000, when weighed against the honor of the nation. Yet not one of them responded to my proposition. Money with them is nothing but trash when it is to come out of the people. But it is the one great thing for which most of them are striving, and many of them sacrifice honor, integrity, and justice to obtain it."

Other Aspects of a Biblical Philosophy of Government

In addition to understanding the purpose of government and jurisdictional authority, there are many other aspects of a Biblical philosophy of government that Godly leaders should embrace. These include being pro-life, pro-liberty, and pro-property rights; having knowledge of inalienable rights, the laws of nature, and the laws of nature's God; and knowing the U.S. and their state Constitutions. Today, most of our rulers have a limited knowledge of the Constitution, especially the original intent. Leaders should understand the power and form of free nations[6] and that self-government under God is the foundation of all earthly government. Having an understanding of principles is more important than holding certain views on issues because a man trained in fundamental Biblical governmental principles and a Biblical philosophy of government will know how to reason to specific issues.

It is also important for Godly leaders to have knowledge of specific application of civil law. They should understand God's civil laws and how they apply. For example, understanding and applying the appropriate penalties God sets forth in the Bible for violating criminal law would alleviate many of our criminal problems today. In brief, penalties for violating the civil law were: 1) Restitution for theft. 2) Corporal punishment and/or fines for minor offenses. 3) Death for serious offenses against life or incorrigibility. 4) City of refuge for accidental death.

The governmental philosophy of officials is important. This determines their position on specific issues and on what laws they will enact, or not enact, how they will spend tax dollars, how they will protect the law-abiding citizens, etc. But knowledge in itself is not enough. They also need wisdom to apply the spirit of the law.

Wisdom to Apply Knowledge and Skill in Governing

Solomon received from God a wise and an understanding heart, which was necessary for him to be able to govern well. In general he brought

much good to the nation, but he also displayed wisdom in specific judgments. Solomon's judgment in the situation of the women arguing over the
baby is an excellent example of Godly wisdom. Godly rulers need such
wisdom.

Godly officials will be "able and experienced men" — they will be
skillful. Effective rulers will have the specific knowledge, talents, and
skills necessary to fulfill their specific governing roles. For example, a
president needs executive skills, which may differ from skills needed to be
a congressman or a judge.

Officials may have correct knowledge, but they need something much
more to assure they will act upon what they know to be right, and that they
will resist the temptations that come with power and influence. They need
Godly character to assure they will govern rightly and with humility.

2. Morality or Christian Character — "men of truth," "hate dishonest gain"

A second qualification for Godly officials is morality. They should be
"men truly honest and upright in their principles and views, not actuated
and governed by the sordid motives of self interest and aggrandizement in
their desire and execution of office, but by a sincere regard to the public
good."[7]

There are many examples in history where corrupt and unprincipled
rulers (such as Hitler, Stalin, Idi Amin) have brought on all kinds of miseries to mankind—including loss of liberty and the downfall of nations.

Chandler Robbins, in an Election Sermon in 1791, said:

> Nothing will so surely, so rapidly bring on the dissolution of society,
> and the loss of the liberties of a people, as a want of virtue and integrity in
> their rulers.[8]

Some specific character qualities needed by rulers include:

Honesty / Integrity

Honesty is obviously important in a ruler. Proverbs 29:12 says "if a
ruler pays attention to falsehood [hearkens to lies], all his ministers become
wicked." If a man cannot keep personal vows or oaths, we cannot expect
him to keep national vows. We have witnessed this in recent years.

Knowledge or intelligence (as man sees it) without honesty — a good
genius with a bad heart — is worse than an ignorant honest man because

the evil genius could find more subtle ways to rob the people of their rights. Some have argued support for certain candidates based upon their intelligence, saying: "He's so smart. We ought to elect him." Yet, if a man, no matter how smart, is reasoning from wrong presuppositions, or has bad character, he will not be a good leader.

Just and compassionate

We need rulers with firmness and resolution, yet also with compassion, tenderness, and kindness. As a "minister of God" he should imitate the "Father of mercies," but who is also just and righteous. When such a ruler inflicts punishment on offenders, he "does it, not because he takes pleasure in the misery of his subjects, but to vindicate his authority and government — to preserve order in the system, and, in the end, to promote the public good."[9]

This is the emphasis of Biblical law — restitution to the wronged and restoration of Godly order — and is in contrast to the Roman idea of law which seeks firstly the punishment of the criminal. The Roman idea is much more pronounced in our penal system today.

Humility

Jesus taught that leaders are to be servants (Matt. 20:25-28). George Washington understood this as evidenced by a letter he sent to all the Governors, on June 8, 1783, where he gave the following advice:

> I now make it my earnest prayer, that God would have you, and the State over which you preside, in his holy protection . . . that he would most graciously be pleased to dispose us all to do justice, to love mercy, and to demean ourselves with that charity, humility, and pacific temper of mind, which were the characteristics of the Divine Author of our blessed religion, and without an humble imitation of whose example in these things, we can never hope to be a happy nation.[10]

Washington was a great example of a humble leader. His response to the proposition by some officers in the army to make him king is one incident showing this.[11]

3. Faith or True Religion — " men who fear God"

The fear of God is an essential qualification for a Godly official. What are men like who fear God? "Men acting under the belief and awe of God as their inspector and judge, to whom they consider themselves accountable for their conduct and whom they fear to offend."[12]

This is not just saying "I am a Christian," simply going to church, or culturally embracing Christianity, but having a reverential fear of the Almighty. Many today think that the fear of God is of no matter for our rulers, and even see it as a negative factor. Rev. Matthias Burnet said it well:

> If God be such a being, as both reason and revelation declare him to be, an omniscient, holy, just and all-powerful being, whose eyes are in every place, beholding the evil and the good, to punish the one and reward the other according to their character and deeds, then certainly, the fear and awe of him must operate as the greatest restraint from that which is evil, and the most powerful incentive to that which is good, and he who is truly actuated by this principle, will never give his voice or influence to pervert justice or support iniquity. But the man who does not believe in the being and providence of God, or is not actuated by the fear and awe of him, has in many cases no bond or restraint upon his conduct, and therefore is not fit to be trusted with a nation's weal, which he will not scruple, whenever he can with impunity, to sacrifice to his lust or ambition.[13]

When the righteous rule the people rejoice (Prov. 29:2). The righteous are those in right standing with God — they fear God.

Rev. Robbins preached to the Massachusetts officials in 1791:

> By a man of Religion, I mean one who fears God from the heart, with a fear founded in esteem — in a supreme love implanted in the soul, by the renovating influence of the Spirit of God — one who believes in, and honors his Son Jesus Christ, as the only mediator and Saviour; and who makes conscience of conforming his temper and life to the sacred rules of the Gospel.[14]

Early Americans looked for this quality in their rulers, and most rulers were men who feared God. Men of irreligion would not be tolerated.

Irreligion in a ruler counteracts the design of the office to execute justice.

A leader who does not fear God will not make an effective governor, for if he himself disregards the laws of God, how can he effectively condemn the vice and immorality of others? If he is a slave to his lusts, how can he attempt to regulate the passions of others. In so doing, people will cry out, "Physician heal thyself." All authority will be brought into contempt. We have seen this negative effect today, with some citizens justifying lying, and many other things, in personal actions because some officials did the same thing.

Righteous rulers are called of God and have vision.

Romans 13 tells us that civil rulers are ministers of God who hold their position by His providence. It is a ministry that God will call some people to fill. We should discern if those we seek to place in power are those that God has called and "anointed" to rule. God prepares different people to perform different things. Recognizing the call of God on a person for a specific office is important. There are many examples in history of God's call on rulers, including David, Moses, Daniel, William Penn, and George Washington.

Having a Godly vision for administering God's justice in the civil realm is important for effective leadership. A Godly leader will have knowledge, Christian character, and a fear of God and will be able to impart vision, hope, purpose, and direction to a nation. This is especially true for those in executive positions like presidents, governors, and mayors. Godly rulers will use the office as a "pulpit" to raise the vision of the American people, and implant noble desires and hope for the future.

Noah Webster summarized the effect of unprincipled men in office:

> Let it be impressed on your mind that God commands you to choose for yourselves rulers, "just men who rule in the fear of God." The preservation of a republican government depends on the faithful discharge of this duty; if the citizens neglect their duty and place unprincipled men in office, the government will soon be corrupted; laws will be made, not for the public good, so much as for selfish or local purposes; corrupt or incompetent men will be appointed to execute the laws; the public revenues will be squandered on unworthy men; and the rights of the citizens will be violated or disregarded. If a republican government fails to secure public prosperity and happiness, it must be because the citizens neglect the divine commands, and elect bad men to make and administer the laws.[15]

The election of unprincipled men produces misery and tyranny, but Godly rulers bring peace, prosperity, justice, and rejoicing. If we fulfill our duty and place Godly men in office (who have knowledge, character, and faith) our future will be bright. According to 2 Samuel 23:3-4,

> The God of Israel said…He who rules…in the fear of God, is as the light of the morning when the sun rises, a morning without clouds, when the tender grass springs out of the earth, through sunshine after rain.

End Notes

1. Matthias Burnet, "Religion and Government the Foundations of Order, Peace, and Security, in Society," An Election Sermon Preached at a General Assembly of the State of Connecticut at Hartford, on the Day of the Anniversary Election, May 12, 1803.

2. Ideas on the Christian and humanistic views of law from Rousas John Rushdoony, *Law and Liberty*, Vallecito, Cal.: Ross House Books, 1984.

3. For more on this see *Watchmen on the Walls* and *Liberating the Nations*, published by the Providence Foundation.

4. "On the Cod Fishery Bill, granting Bounties," February 7, 1792, in *The Debates of the Several State Conventions on the Adoption of the Federal Constitution as Recommended by the General Convention at Philadelphia in 1787...*, In Five Volumes, by Jonathan Elliot, New York: Burt Franklin R, Vol. IV, p. 429.

5. This and the following quotes are from Edward S. Ellis, *The Life of Colonel David Crockett*, Philadelphia: The John C. Winston Co., n.d., pp. 137-156.

6. See *Liberating the Nations,* chap. 1, by Stephen McDowell and Mark Beliles, Charlottesville, Vir.: Providence Foundation, 1995.

7. Matthias Burnet.

8. Chandler Robbins, "And Also in Judah Things Went Well." A Sermon Preached before His Excellency John Hancock, Governour; His Honor Samuel Adams, Lieutant-Governour; the Honourable the Council, and the Honourable the Senate and House of Representatives, of the Commonwealth of Massachusetts, May 25, 1791, Being the Day of General Election.

9. Chandler Robbins.

10. Circular Letter Addressed to the Governors of all the States on Disbanding the Army, 1783. Old South Leaflets, no. 15.

11. See Chapter 5, and also Stephen McDowell and Mark Beliles, *In God We Trust Tour Guide*, Charlottesville, Va: Providence Foundation, 1998, pp. 70-71.

12. Matthias Burnet.

13. Matthias Burnet.

14. Chandler Robbins.

15. Noah Webster, *History of the United Sates*, New Haven: Durrie & Peck, 1833, pp. 307-308.

Chapter 14

Biblical Principles of Business
Exemplified in the Life of Cyrus Hall McCormick, a Reaper in the Kingdom

He Advanced Civilization and Destroyed Famine by Fulfilling His Kingdom Business

In the parable in Luke 19:11-27, Jesus instructs us in how we should live on the earth as we wait for, and assist in bringing forth, His kingdom. Jesus related this parable because "they supposed that the kingdom of God was going to appear immediately." Among other things, He wanted to correct their view of how the kingdom would come.

He told us to "do business with this until I come back" (vs. 13). The *this* are minas, which certainly speak of wise money usage, but in a broader sense represent the talents, skills, and abilities God has given each of us. God created us for a purpose (Gen. 1:26-28). He wants us to work as partners with Him to take dominion over the earth by using the talents He has given us. These talents express themselves in the business or work He has called us to perform. Our work is a vital part of God's plan for us and the nations. As we are faithful to labor hard and multiply what He has given us, we will be taking part in bringing forth His Kingdom on earth and being a blessing to the nations.

Those who develop and multiply their talents will also be given authority over cities (vs. 17,19) in the future kingdom (and often in this life). If we do not use the talents and abilities God has given us and give Him back a return, we are in big trouble (vs. 22-24, see also Matt. 25:30). God commands us to increase what He puts into our lives and hands.

Cyrus McCormick was a faithful servant who utilized the talents God gave him, and in so doing elevated the position of farmers and common laborers, helped provide abundant and affordable bread to the nations, and lay the foundation for the advancement and prosperity of America and many other nations. He fulfilled his Kingdom purpose.

Providential Preparation of Cyrus McCormick

His birth in America at the given time in history

Cyrus Hall McCormick was prepared by God to accomplish his specific purpose in history. God brought him forth at just the right time and place. Cyrus was born in 1809 in the Shenandoah Valley of Virginia. Just one generation before Cyrus was born, America had become a free nation unlike any the world had seen. This freedom, which was rooted in Christianity, provided the atmosphere necessary for McCormick to succeed. Such a man could not have been in any other nation. His work was dependent upon those who came before him – without the pilgrims, patriots, and founding fathers of America, there would have been no Cyrus Hall McCormick, the "reaper man." He played an important role in the advancement of man – an advancement brought about due to the spread of the gospel in history according to the plan of God.

Our founders gave us freedom. This freedom provided an environment necessary for the development of inventions, like the reaper, which allowed for the expansion of the agricultural base of America. The growth of the agriculture base led to the prosperity of our nation.

His home and upbringing

McCormick biographer Herbert Casson writes:

> Cyrus McCormick was predestined, we may legitimately say, by the conditions of his birth, to accomplish his great work. From his father he had a specific training as an inventor; from his mother he had executive ability and ambition; from his Scotch-Irish ancestry he had the dogged tenacity that defied defeat; and from the wheat-fields that environed his home came the call for the Reaper, to lighten the heavy drudgery of the harvest.[1]

Cyrus' father, Robert McCormick, had worked to invent a reaper from the time Cyrus was a child. He tried his first machine when Cyrus was seven in 1816, but it failed. Subsequent attempts also failed, and the jests of his neighbors forced Robert to carry on his experiments in secret. Robert would allow no one in his workshop except his children. Cyrus was often in his father's workshop, which helped inspire him with the vision of inventing a working reaper, one that cut and then properly handled the grain.

From his youth, Cyrus was inspired to invent, and he did. Before the invention of the reaper, he had devised a new grain-cradle, a hillside plow, and a self-sharpening plow. The back-breaking work of harvesting grain was also a great motivation for Cyrus to invent a reaper.

The Invention

Cyrus' first successful reaper was tested in July 1831 on a small patch of wheat on his father's farm. Cyrus gave a public exhibition a few days later at the nearby town of Steele's Tavern. He cut six acres of oats with his reaper drawn by two horses in an afternoon, which was an amazing feat for it was equal to the work of six laborers with scythes or 24 peasants with sickles.

In 1832, he gave a large-scale public exhibition to one hundred people in the town of Lexington. This brought a wider recognition of his invention and praise from many sources. A noted professor declared that "this machine is worth a hundred thousand dollars." No praise was more encouraging than the words of his father who said, "It makes me feel proud to have a son do what I could not do."[2]

Many other people had attempted to invent a reaper — Cyrus was the 47th person to secure a patent for a reaper — but none of them worked properly or could have developed into a successful machine for they lacked the proper operational design. His invention combined for the first time the seven mechanical elements necessary for a working reaper. Those who built their own reapers after this time copied McCormick's basic design.

Cyrus Hall McCormick is remembered as the inventor of the reaper. But he did much more than that — he also invented the business of making and selling reapers, and he did it in a Biblical manner, with Kingdom fruit. His work impacted the world. "He did more than any other member of the human race to abolish the famine of the cities and the drudgery of the farm — to feed the hungry and straighten the bent backs of the world."[3]

Building His Business

McCormick had built a successful reaper, but no one knew about it. Promoting the value and importance of the reaper was just as important as building it. He built the machine, so now he had to build the business. Cyrus worked harder and longer to build his business than he did to build his reaper. "His whole soul was wrapped up in his Reaper," said one of his neighbors.[4]

In the summer of 1832 while looking out over rolling fields of wheat the thought came to him, "'Perhaps I may make a million dollars from this Reaper.' This thought was so enormous that it seemed like a dream-like dwelling in the clouds — so remote, so unattainable, so exalted, so vision-ary."[5] For years it appeared only that, a vision. In fact, it was nine years be-fore McCormick found anyone with enough money and courage to buy a reaper from him. During that time he struggled greatly and instead of mak-ing any money toward his vision of a million dollars, he actually lost money, and even had to give up his farm to creditors. But he held on to his reaper, and his indomitable spirit would not give up on his vision.

In 1839 he opened the first of the world's reaper factories in the little log workshop near his father's house and begin to make reapers. But even so it was not until over a year later that he sold his first reaper to Abraham Smith. During those first years of failure "Cyrus McCormick hung to his Reaper as John Knox had to his Bible."[6] In the next decade as he traveled around the country and promoted his reaper, he became so identified with his invention that he was often called "the Reaper Man."

During the 1840s, he gradually begin to sell more and more reapers, but as he looked to expand his business he recognized Virginia was not the place to do it, so he traveled to the midwest and opened up a factory in Chi-cago, then a little mud-town. As he looked for ways to sell his reapers throughout the states he created "a new species of commercial organization which is by many thought to be fully as remarkable as his invention of the Reaper."[7]

His Christian Faith

Before looking at principles of his business, we should first look at his faith, for his faith and his business were inseparable. There would have been no McCormick the businessman without McCormick the Christian. In 1845 he wrote: "Business is not inconsistent with Christianity; but the latter ought to be a help to the former, giving a confidence and resignation, after using all proper means."[8] His faith was a product of the Protestant Reformation. Two fundamental ideas that supported his character sprang from the Reformation. These were the sovereignty of God and the respon-sibility of the individual.

McCormick understood that God calls people in the business realm and gives them the talents, gifts, and grace they need to accomplish His purpose for them. During one of his struggles with manufacturers who had broken their contracts, he wrote:

> If it were not for the fact that Providence has seemed to assist me in our business, it has at times seemed that I would almost sink under the weight of responsibility hanging upon me; but I believe the Lord will help us out.[9]

His belief that a man must not violate his own conscience, but be a good steward of it, gave him the strength and courage to fight many battles. He was constantly in the courts seeking to obtain protection for his invention. He also fought the Pennsylvania Railroad for 23 years when they acted irresponsibly — losing his luggage — and refused to make amends. He spent hundreds of thousands of dollars to win a settlement of about $18,000, and that came after his death.

Parental training

Cyrus' Calvinistic faith was instilled in him by his parents and grandfather from boyhood. He first learned to read from the Bible and the Shorter Catechism. His home-life, schooling, and church infused into him the faith that his forefathers had practiced for generations. His parents were strict Presbyterians, and the whole family faithfully attended the New Providence Church.

At the age of 10, Cyrus started attending the Field School in a nearby log schoolhouse where he was taught the "3-Rs", geography, and religion. About 30 boys and girls would be schooled here a few weeks out of each year using the Bible, Webster's Speller, Murray's Grammar, and a few other books. Cyrus displayed his inventive nature during this time by making a wooden globe that revolved on a metal stand. The teacher had seen nothing like it and marveled at its detail. Cyrus loved to learn and read every book he could obtain. In addition, he learned Latin from his minister. During his teen years he learned to survey, and at age 17 he made his own surveying instruments.

His public profession of faith

In 1834, when Cyrus was 25 years old, he attended a series of meetings at the church on his grandfather's farm. At the end of the four days of meetings, where three ministers preached all day, those who were not Christians or who had not made a public profession were given the opportunity to acknowledge their faith. Herbert Casson writes:

Cyrus McCormick was there, and he was not a member of the church; yet he did not stand up. That night his father went to his bedside and gently reproached him. "My son," he said, "don't you know that your silence is a public rejection of your Saviour?" Cyrus was conscience-stricken. He leapt from his bed and began to dress himself. "I'll go and see old Billy McClung," he said. Half an hour later, old Billy McClung, who was a universally respected religious leader in the community, was amazed to be called out of his sleep by a greatly troubled young man, who wanted to know by what means he might make his peace with his Maker. The next Sunday this young man stood up in the church, and became in name what he already was by nature and inheritance — a Christian of the Presbyterian faith.[10]

Biblical Principles of Business and Work Exemplified in Cyrus' Life[11]

1. Work is a holy calling and, therefore, we should love it and work hard.

Our work is a part of our calling and is a primary way we will extend God's kingdom on the earth. Work is not merely a secular activity that is unimportant in God's purposes, nor is it a necessary evil that we must endure to obtain the necessities of life. God commissioned work before the fall and shows us by His example how we should view work.

God loves to work, and so should we! Wherever He is, there is work. John 5:17 states: "But He answered them, 'My Father is working until now, and I Myself am working.'"

Heaven is not a place where we sit around the pool all day and drink lemonade. We will be working, and we will love it. Remember, those who faithfully use and multiply the talents God has given them will be put in charge of cities, now, but more so in the life to come. Work gives us the skills we need to govern well.

God has been working from the beginning of the creation. We first know of Him as the Creator. Romans 1:20 reveals that God's power, attributes, and nature are revealed through the creation — through His work! This is true for us as well.

Dennis Peacocke writes:

Work is the incarnation of my intangible "soul" out into God's Cosmos. . . . Work allows what is inside of me to be revealed in the outside world. That is why God created the concept of work and loves it so much, because what is inside God is so spectacular it must be externally revealed.

It is through His work that we see who He is! . . . No wonder so many people hate work: It is revealing externally what is inside of them.[12]

The Bible teaches that what is inside of us will come out in our words, attitudes, and actions. This is most evident in our place of work and, consequently, the real you can be seen by your boss, co-workers, or employees more easily than by your pastor. You are at church a few hours a week and are on your best behavior. You are at work 40 or more hours a week and express all your conditions. What an opportunity Christians have to minister to those at work!

The Christian religion is essential for the prosperity of a nation, for it teaches a philosophy of work and a theology of labor, unlike other religions. By precept and example, God and His Son Jesus communicate to us a love of work, a desire to be good stewards, entrepreneurship, and the principle that work is a holy calling.

Cyrus saw his work as a holy calling and, therefore, loved to work. He rarely recreated. "He was the most laborious worker I ever saw," said one of his secretaries. In his latter life, Cyrus McCormick remarked that "I expect to die in the harness, because this is not the world for rest. This is the world for work. In the next world we will have the rest."[13] His strategy for work was: one thing at a time, and the hardest thing first. "He followed the line of most resistance. If the hardest thing can be done, he reasoned, all the rest will follow."[14]

Work was so much a part of his nature, that when he lay on his death bed in 1884, some of his last words, uttered as he regained consciousness for one of the last times, were: "Work, work!"[15]

2. Business is a means of serving and blessing others.

Blessing customers

Cyrus built his business upon a number of unique ideas. One was a **written guarantee**. McCormick first "warranted the performance of the Reaper in every respect" in 1842, which helped him to sell seven of them that year. In 1848 the guarantee was printed like an advertisement and if the machine did not perform according to the written agreement, he would take the machine back and refund the total price. This idea of a free trial and refund to dissatisfied customers was new then, but quite common today. This reflected the Biblical ideas of serving and trusting the customer, seeking not chiefly personal profit, but providing the farmer with a machine that saved him labor and produced greater profit for him. He was caring for others and desired them to benefit from his invention.

A second idea he used: **Reapers sold at a known price**. Since the bargaining method was norm during his day, the seller would seek to get the highest price he could for his items. Contrary to this, Cyrus announced his price in ads, and the buyer knew exactly what he would pay beforehand and that it would be the same for everyone. He treated all men equally, showing no partiality to any.

A third idea of McCormick's business: **The customer's good-will**. Foremost of the concerns of McCormick was the well being of the farmer. While he never sought the praise of the public or other businessmen, he always stood well with the farmers. He wanted them to prosper and saw his reaper as a way to fulfill this desire. That is one reason why he extended them credit and allowed them to pay for a reaper with the money that was saved during the harvest. He said, "It is better that I should wait for the money than that you should wait for the machine that you need."[16]

This policy caused him to lose much in some instances, as when drought forced early settlers in the Dakotas to leave without being able to pay their debts. But for the most part, McCormick and the new immigrants in the mid-west prospered, thanks to his reaper and his desire to get one into the hands of every farmer. Many date their prosperity to obtaining a McCormick Reaper. One example of this follows.

> In 1855 a poor tenant farmer, who had been evicted from his rented land in Ayrshire, Scotland, arrived with his family at the banks of the Mississippi. There was then no railroad nor stage-coach, so the whole family walked to a quarter section of land farther west, not far from where the city of Des Moines stands today. The first year they cut the wheat with the cradle and the scythe, and the following year they bought a McCormick Reaper. They prospered. The father went back for a visit to Ayrshire and paid all his creditors. And the eldest son, James, became first Speaker of the Iowa Legislature, then a professor in an agricultural college, and finally the founder of the Department of Agriculture.[17]

A business will grow by caring for people and seeking to serve your customers. Another way McCormick served his customers was by servicing the machines he had sold in the past and carrying spare parts to replace any worn or broken. This was a new idea, and the spare parts business grew with the reaper sales. It began with a desire to serve.

Serving employees and co-workers

The focus of a successful and godly business will be to develop human beings — their character, talents, stewardship, etc. "Good leaders help their people become b etter stewards."[18] C hristian businesses s hould be helping workers practice stewardship and assume more responsibilities because this produces growth and self-government necessary for the production of wealth and riches. Socialism robs man of this, and so impoverishes him and his nation. In contrast, private property and free enterprise are of great benefit to man because when you give property to people to manage and steward, it develops the character in them necessary for them and the nation to prosper.

Our policies as a nation, businessman, or parent should encourage individual enterprise and should not reward non-biblical action. Our government today pays people when they have babies out of wedlock and when they do not work. If a crime is committed, instead of making restitution, criminals are put up in prison with TV, sports, and education at tax-payers expense of $25,000 per year. The stay is even nicer for white-collar crimes. This treatment is done in the name of *compassion*, but "the compassion of the wicked is cruel" (Prov. 12:10).

People should not be shielded from the rewards or penalties of their actions, for this is one way they learn reality. Those that shield others from failure in life cause those that fail to become dependent upon them instead of God. The state is doing this today and becoming god, the provider, for many. If we spare people from the consequences of disobedience, we will destroy them.

Having a servant's heart

Matthew 20:20-28 and Luke 22:25-27 reveal that kingdom businessmen should have the heart of a servant. In business we should be seeking to serve those who work for us or with us and help build in them the character and skills they need to fulfill God's plan for their lives. We should gradually give others more responsibilities, which will help to develop the skills they need to grow. If we do, everyone will benefit, including our business.

3. Business must be built on integrity and godly principles.

All that we do in our life should be done as unto the Lord. As a business leader or employee we should certainly carry out our work in a manner that reflects godly character. As everyone involved in a business, especially the leader, does this, it will provide a foundation for success. McCormick displayed many godly traits in his personal life and in his business. He also sought to provide the best product possible to his customers.

Any job Cyrus set out to do, he did with great thoroughness. He labored diligently to be exact in his labors and did not settle for second best or 90 percent. He did not seek to patent or sell his reaper for many years because he had improvements he wanted to make before doing so — he wanted it as good as possible. He exerted the same amount of labor over all his endeavors, large or small. He even took great care in writing letters to his family members, making sure that all sentences were formed correctly and that there were no misspelled words.

Cyrus' foremost character quality was his tenacity or strength of will. When he set his mind on a project, every ounce of his being would be exerted toward the endeavor. "He was so strong, so dominating, so ready to crash through obstacles by sheer bulk of will-power, that smaller men could never quite subdue a feeling of alarm while they were in his presence."[19]

Yet, if the outcome was not in his favor he was not crushed, but got up and continued on in his life. In 1877 he made a run for the United States Senate. After a long hard struggle that ended in his defeat he said: "Well, that's over. What next?"[20]

While he was strong in his will, he was kind and tender in his relations. One of his cashiers said, "I had only one brush with him in thirty-five years."[21] He always treated his parents and family with the greatest respect. His tender heart is revealed in a letter he wrote to his brother after his father's death in 1846: "Many a sore cry have I had as I have gone around this place and found no father."[22]

Cyrus required complete integrity of his employees. One young man lost his chance of promotion for he had put a two-cent stamp from the company on a private letter. Yet, once McCormick had tested a man, he trusted him completely, and they trusted him. He loved to talk of the loyalty of his agents and workmen. It was one of his favorite topics.

Once when some of his agents were pressing McCormick for higher salaries and seeking to get others to join with them, one agent in Minnesota refused saying, "I don't want to force Mr. McCormick. I have worked for him for nearly thirty years, and I know that he is a just man, and that he will do what is right."[23] Shortly after this, Cyrus showed his appreciation to this man by giving him a gift of a carriage and team of horses.

Another of McCormick's unique business ideas — **the field test** — reveals his integrity. Cyrus wanted the customer to see the product up front, to know what they were getting. As a means of bringing to the people a knowledge of the value of the reaper and allowing farmers to compare rival manufacturers, McCormick initiated the field test. People were invited to come and witness two or ten or even more machines compete against one another. His first test was in 1844 in Richmond against a practical mowing machine built by Obed Hussey. McCormick's Reaper was judged better in all ways.

4. Business growth comes from encouraging individual initiative and seeing that all involved benefit from the fruit of their labor.

As individuals grow, business will grow.

A business will grow from the inside-out. It will grow as you learn to handle problems and operate affairs properly. The process of growth produces the character necessary to support c ontinued growth. As Dennis Peacocke puts it: "Power is guarded by problems" where "power . . . [is] sharing knowledge, ability, and authority with God over some portion of His creation."[24]

Handling problems produces character, which is necessary as the foundation for long-term permanent growth. As we are faithful to persevere, work hard, be creative, solve problems, and steward our resources, we will develop the capacity to oversee growth in our business. As we develop this in others who work with us, they and the whole business will grow.

The prodigal son (Luke 15:11-32) is an example of what happens when someone gets power before they have been prepared to handle it. Power should come on the basis of faithfulness. As employees show their faithfulness and ability through handling problems, they can then be given more power and responsibility. Problems are a form of property of which we must be good stewards. Learning to handle problems produces good character, which causes all to profit.[25]

Cyrus' field representatives were partners.

A fifth unique idea McCormick built his business upon was **a responsible agent and regional warehouses**. McCormick enlisted agents who went out to the people and "flooded the country with his machines," as one of his competitors complained in an 1848 lawsuit. His agents were not mere employees, but partners who were in charge of their own area and benefitted or suffered based on their performance. They reaped what they sowed. This helped greatly in the expansion of the enterprise.

An important part in the success of a business is for the employer to seek to develop the talents of his employees and to impart to them the proper vision of business. If each person is performing the function they enjoy and are best suited for, everyone will benefit. While employees will work harder if they benefit from the fruit of their labors, they must also have a higher vision than merely making a quick profit. Cyrus sought to train responsible agents, who not only benefitted from hard work, but also had a desire to serve the customer.

Government should recognize that freedom encourages inventiveness.

The reaper was the product of a free republic. It could not have been the product of Russia or Austria for at this time farm laborers received no wages — they were serfs. The land owners had no economic reason for reapers for they could get all the free labor they needed.

In the free nation of America, various factors were forcing wages higher during the time of the growth of the reaper. Land was cheap and readily available, so few would want to work for others when they could work for themselves. Gold prospecting drew many potential workers further west. This kept the labor supply small and more costly, and limited the amount of grain a farmer could plant. When it came time to harvest the grain, it all had to be reaped within about two weeks or it would be lost. Therefore, the number of laborers greatly affected how much grain was planted. The reaper came at just the right time. A farmer could plant ten times more grain and feed not only his family, but many others as well.

Bismarck once asked why reapers could not be produced in Germany. To fully understand the answer he would have had to read the history of the United States. "He would have seen that the Reaper can be produced only in countries where labor receives a high reward, where farmers own their own acres without fear of being despoiled by invading armies, and where the average of intelligence and enterprise is as high in the country as in the city."[26]

Freedom produces new inventions and tools which produce prosperity for all.

Tools allow productivity to increase greatly. The McCormick Reaper allowed one man to cut more wheat in a day than ten men by hand. But men were still needed to bind the wheat after it was cut. The next step was a self-binding reaper. McCormick began a large scale production of these in the mid-1870s. Now one man could sit on a self-binder and harvest a whole wheat field on his own. Comparing hand-harvesting to the self-binder shows a dramatic decrease in the time cost per bushel of wheat — three hours by hand versus ten minutes by machine![27]

The nation prospered as well from foreign trade. At the beginning of the twentieth century, the reaper was the number one machine export of America. Four-fifths of all the harvesting machines in the world were made in the United States, and at least one-third of these were made in the factory McCormick had started in Chicago in 1847.

The invention of the reaper changed the life of the farmer and the nation. With one man able to produce food for many, others were able to specialize to produce other goods and services. The amount of capital and leisure time increased for everyone, and with this the people had more time to pursue education and development of other inventions, which led to more prosperity and leisure.

5. Incorporating the family into your business is a means of building wealth generationally.

The parable in Luke 19:11-27 tells us that whoever uses what he has will be given more, and he who does not will lose what he has. This is why many who inherit riches lose them, for they have not developed the capacity to multiply or even hold on to what is given them. They have not gone through the process to get the character and talents they need to produce riches. George Gilder writes: "The vast majority of American's fortunes are dissipated within two generations." This is because, "When the money is actually passed on, [much of it] ends up among large numbers of prodigal sons and daughters. . . The receipt of a legacy, it turns out, often erodes the qualities of entrepreneurship that are needed to perpetuate it."[28]

In his book, *Doing Business God's Way!*, Dennis Peacocke differentiates between riches and wealth. Riches are perishable assets and can be inherited or gotten by illegal means. Wealth is much different. Wealth is "primarily achieved through the skills, spiritual knowledge, and character developed in obeying God's way or approaching resource management."[29]

Many rich people have no real wealth. Real wealth entails having a Biblical view of life and living according to that view. It involves understanding your purpose in life. It includes relationships, good health, and material contentment. While capitalism is riches oriented, Kingdom economics is wealth oriented. Godly stewardship motives Kingdom businessmen to be productive as opposed to greed, envy, and discontent, which motivates many.

The family is the pipeline of wealth development in the earth. Genesis 12:3 tells us that through Abraham all the families of the earth would be blessed. The skills to produce wealth come primarily from the homes of a nation. If they are not produced there, they will not be produced in the schools or businesses or by the government or media. The economics of a nation is rooted in the the families of a nation.

We are to pass on our wealth to our children (i.e., develop in them what they need to accomplish God's mission for them). Proverbs 13:22 says, "a good man leaves an inheritance to his children's children."

Cyrus' family produced wealth in him who, in turn, passed it on to his family.

The atmosphere of Cyrus' family produced Cyrus the inventor and businessman. His father worked with him in his early years on the farm factory. After Cyrus started his company in Chicago, he quickly made his brothers partners with him. When his son became old enough, he was brought into the business, and after that his grandson. Cyrus and his wife passed on their wealth and riches to their children.

McCormick's son, Cyrus H., worked for years to get the leading men who made farm machinery to join together, enabling them to be more productive. He finally succeeded in 1902, when five leading manufacturers joined to form the International Harvester Company.

We Need a Biblical View of Business and Work.

Cyrus had a vision of business as a means of advancing God's Kingdom and purposes.

The reaper was essential for the advancement of civilization and the growth of the industrial age. It provided a means of harvesting a large supply of cheap food which was necessary to feed all the people who began living in cities and working in factories. It was the means of bringing prosperity to many. One of McCormick's competitors said, "It seems as though the McCormick Reaper started the ball of prosperity rolling, and it has been rolling ever since."[30]

Cyrus saw his reaper as a means of blessing and prospering others all over the world. In 1851, he traveled to Europe to introduce his machine. Beginning with England, some of the European nations had abolished serfdom; therefore, cheap labor was no longer readily available. It was the ideal time to introduce the reaper.

Over the years many reapers were sold in Europe, and McCormick received many honors for his contribution to agriculture. His significance could be summed up by the French Academy of Science, who elected him a member in 1878 for the reason that he "had done more for the cause of agriculture than any other living man."

His life work was the abolition of famine. But this was not accomplished by using resources that others produced and channeling them to the needy in the world. Rather, he set out to make all men more productive so that the total food supply would greatly increase and potentially mean an abundance for everyone. Casson writes:

> He instructed the wheat-eating races how to increase the "seven small loaves" so that the multitudes should be fed. He picked up the task of feeding the hungry masses — the Christly task that had lain unfulfilled for eighteen centuries, and led the way in organizing it into a system of international reciprocity.[31]

McCormick paved the way for a new era in the advancement of mankind. No longer would man be forced to exert most of his effort in obtaining the basic necessities of life. Much more of his time could be given to pursuing many of the noble causes God had set before him. The reaper was indispensable in the advancement of America and numerous other nations.

To McCormick, work was not a secular pursuit that had no spiritual value. Nor was it a necessary evil he had to endure in order to make money to finance the real work of God in missions and church activities. *To McCormick, his work was his calling through which he fulfilled His divine mission and manifested God's Kingdom on earth.*

You do not have to be like Cyrus McCormick and invent something great to fulfill your divine mission. But as you are providing mankind with necessary goods or services and are helping to order and maintain God's creation, then that is sacred work. This can be done as a farmer, teacher, parent, manufacturer, carpenter, doctor, store clerk, etc.

Work and business must be kept in balance with all our responsibilities.

We have responsibilities in many spheres of life besides work, including our family, church, and nation. We must not neglect any of these.

McCormick fulfilled his duties in every sphere of life.

Throughout his life, Cyrus not only was faithful to extend God's Kingdom through his business, but he also sought to bring godly change in many other spheres. In his early travels through the mid-west, he noticed many of the new settlements were rough and immoral. He wrote in 1845, "I see a great deal of profanity and infidelity in this country, enough to make the heart sick."[32] He recognized the best means to deal with this problem was to have more trained ministers available for these towns, so he resolved to help when he was able. Fourteen years later he had made enough money to contribute $100,000 to establish Northwestern Theological Seminary (later called McCormick Theological Seminary) in Chicago. Thousands of men were trained for the ministry through this college.

He did many other things to further "the cause" (as he called it) in the northwest. As another means of educating the people toward godliness, McCormick bought *The Interior* in 1872. He turned this Christian weekly into a magazine of the highest rank.

His godly vision for his nation also inspired him to enter politics. This he did with the same zeal and determination he showed in business and religious affairs. He not only actively supported others to run for government, but sought office a number of times himself. Cyrus ran as a statesmen, not as a politician. He had no time to play the game of politics. This may have been why he was never elected. He talked of "fundamental principles" and often turned a party speech into a sermon on national righteousness. He was too sincere and straightforward to follow the path that his political consultants laid out for him. If the opposition was a man of merit, he did not hesitate to publicly speak in favor of him. He arose above party interests to look down at the nation as a whole to consider what was best for it.

Cyrus gave much time and money toward godly reform in the public sector, usually with no personal reward and often with seemingly little fruit. Yet, his involvement was not motivated by personal benefit but out of a desire to serve his nation. His action was based upon the principles that governed his life. Someone once asked him why he bothered himself with political things since it brought him no glory or benefit. His response was: "I am in politics because I cannot help it. There are certain principles that I have got to stand by, and I am obliged to go into politics to defend them."[33]

As with his business, it was his faith that had shaped his view of political responsibilities. He had been trained in the views of John Knox and other preacher-patriots who saw it as their duty to fight for both civil and religious liberty.

While fulfilling his destiny through a Biblical view of business, Cyrus kept His faith.

The rise of America and the rise of McCormick's business go hand in hand. From the time of the invention of his reaper until the time of his death

(1831 to 1884), America went from an insignificant nation to a great nation. Cyrus' invention had as much to do with this as anything.

> The invention of the Reaper was the right starting-point for the up-building of a republic. It made all other progress possible, by removing the fear of famine and the drudgery of farm labor. It enabled even the laborer of the harvest-field to be free and intelligent, because it gave him the power of ten men.[34]

It also played a key role in the settlement of the west. It was said that the reaper extended the frontier fifty miles a year.

Cyrus' favorite Bible passage was Romans 8. He certainly proved to be more than a conqueror in all the trials he faced by trusting in his Lord Jesus Christ. His favorite hymn, which he sang often, begins:

O Thou in whose presence my soul takes delight,
On whom in affliction I call,
My comfort by day, and my song in the night,
My hope, my salvation, my all.

Cyrus expressed and exuded hope and optimism throughout his life, whether it involved his business or his efforts at godly reform. His last speech, given at the laying of the cornerstone of a new building at the college he helped found, reveals this.

> I never doubted that success would ultimately reward our efforts, and now, on this occasion, we may fairly say that the night has given place to the dawn of a brighter day than any which has hitherto shone upon us.[35]

His last words occurred on May 11, 1884. Early that morning he gathered his family around him where he led them in prayer and in singing several old hymns. Before lapsing into unconsciousness for the last time, McCormick quietly uttered, "It's all right. It's all right. I only want Heaven."[36] Two days later he died. The man who had faithfully done business and multiplied the talents God had given him — the man who had done so much to extend the Kingdom of God on earth and who had reaped an abundance for himself, his family, and untold multitudes was now going to reap his external reward as a good and faithful servant.

May God grant us the grace to do business with the talents He has given us and to multiply them many-fold, so as to fulfill our divine purpose in the earth, and, to prepare us to rule and reign with Him forever.

End Notes

1. *Cyrus Hall McCormick, His Life and Work*, Herbert N. Casson, Chicago: A.C. McClurg & Co., 1909, p. 25.

2. Ibid., p. 40.

3. Ibid., p. 47.

4. Ibid., p. 53.

5. Ibid., p. 54.

6. Ibid., p. 58.

7. Ibid., p. 79.

8. Ibid., p. 160.

9. Ibid.

10. Ibid., pp. 159-160.

11. Some of these principles are adapted from *Almighty & Sons, Doing Business God's Way!*, Dennis Peacocke, Santa Rosa, Cal.: Rebuild, 1995, p. 22.

12. Ibid., p. 53.

13. Casson, p. 140.

14. Ibid., p. 141.

15. Ibid., p. 187.

16. Ibid., p. 85.

17. Ibid., pp. 86-87.

18. Peacocke, p. 22.

19. Casson, p. 154.

20. Ibid., p. 151.

21. Ibid., p. 179.

22. Ibid., p. 181.

23. Ibid., p. 180.

24. Peacocke, p. 25.

25. Ibid., pp. 25-26.

26. Casson, pp. 136-137.

27. Ibid., p. 210.

28. quoted in Peacocke, pp. 37-38.

29. Peacocke, p. 32.

30. Casson, p. 230.

31. Ibid., p. 202.

32. Ibid., p. 162.

33. Ibid., p. 169.

34. Ibid., p. 190.

35. Ibid., p. 163.

36. *Cyrus Hall McCormick, Harvest, 1856-1884*, William T. Hutchinson, New York: D. Appleton–Century Co., 1935, p. 771.

Chapter 15

Education and the Kingdom of God

In the Lord's prayer, Jesus taught us to pray, "Thy kingdom come, Thy will be done, on earth as it is in heaven." His desire is for His kingdom to come to the earth. **Biblical education is a means of bringing God's kingdom on earth** as it is in heaven.

In Matthew 28:18-20 Jesus commanded us to "go and make disciples of all the nations" and tells us the way to do this is through "teaching them to observe all" that He commanded — that is, through education. According to Matthew Henry, this passage means we are to do our "utmost to make the nations Christian nations." How is this to be done? Through Biblical education.

The kingdom of God can be defined as the government (rule, direction) of God. One way that God governs in the earth is through teaching. Therefore, teaching is key for the kingdom (government) of God coming.

Education is a sowing and reaping process. Education operates like the seed principle. The kingdom of God is like a seed (Luke 13:18-19). The kingdom comes gradually from the inside out through the sowing of God's Word in individuals and nations.

While Biblical education is a means of bringing God's kingdom on earth, **present-day state education is the means of bringing man's kingdom on earth.** Godly education is rooted in the absolutes of God's Word. Man-centered, state education has a completely different foundation.

All Education Is Religious

All education is religious. This is why state education is so dangerous; it passes on the predominant religion of those in control. Some people say education is neutral, and therefore religion must be kept separate from education, which in America today translates to mean that any mention of God or Godly values must be extirpated from our public schools. But all education imparts a worldview and basic presuppositions about life which are rooted in religion. The issue is not keeping religion out of education (which is impossible); the issue is what religion forms the foundation of education.

The modern state compels everyone to be educated, and hence is compelling in the arena of fundamental beliefs, in faith or religion. Throughout most of history nations have controlled and compelled in the area of faith. Many people who came to America did so to escape this, and set an example that ended state-compelled worship.

In his *Statute for Religious Freedom*, Thomas Jefferson said to compel a man to support the "propagation of opinions which he disbelieves . . . is sinful and tyrannical." This was one argument used to end state established religion in early America. Throughout the nineteenth century this idea spread to many other nations in the western world. However, **at about the same time the western world ended compelling worship, they adopted the practice of compelling in education.**

While the modern humanist is appalled at forced worship, he does the same thing in the area of education, and since all education is religious, he is really compelling in the area of religion. We have need today for a *Statute for Educational Freedom*.

The foundational philosophy of education in a nation is of utmost importance because whoever controls the education of the nation, controls the future of the nation. As has been said, the philosophy of the schoolroom in one generation will be the philosophy of government in the next.

Foundational Principles of Modern State Education

In most nations today, the state or government is in control of education. What is the foundational philosophy of modern state education? Is it Godly? How does it compare to education that is Christian? Biblical education is rooted in the absolutes of God's Word. Man-centered, state education has a completely different foundation, which includes these components:

1. Relativism

Relativism has been defined as the conviction that "there is no such thing as truth or right, but only the varying beliefs of varying cultures, each apparently justified in its own terms; no fixed norms, but merely shifting opinions."[1]

Humanists are absolutely sure there are no absolutes (which this statement in itself reveals the fallacy of relativism). "That may be true for you but it isn't true for me," many people say today. But we know there is right and wrong. Christians know that God reveals this to us in the Bible. But all men know certain aspects of right and wrong for God has written this in our consciences as well. To murder a man is wrong, even if society says its right, and men know this within them no matter what a majority of those around us may say. (However, man can sear his conscience by continued practice of sin.)

Relativism is communicated in many spheres of life today and in many ways. Even modern dictionaries reflect this idea in word definitions. This is in direct contrast to early American dictionaries which defined words Biblically (which reflected the worldview of most Americans at that time). Take, for example, the word *immoral*. In *An American Dictionary of the English Language* (1828), under the definition for *immoral*, Noah Webster writes: "Every action is immoral which contravenes any divine precept, or which is contrary to the duties men owe to each other."[2] To Webster, divine precept was the standard to judge immorality. Today, the standard is quite different, as reflected in the definition of *immoral* in modern dictionaries. *Webster's New World Dictionary* defines *immoral* as "not in conformity with accepted principles of right and wrong behavior."[3] The standard for immoral behavior today is what the consensus of the population thinks. Man, rather than God, is the judge of right and wrong conduct. Man becomes his own god when relativism is embraced.

As educational institutions have taught moral relativism, it has not only affected individual actions, but also business, law, government, and every sphere of life, because we will reap what we sow. Consider how the view of law has changed over the years. The founders of America believed law was rooted in the absolutes of God's truth. Blackstone said any law that is contrary to God's higher law was no law at all. But as the philosophical foundation of law in America changed, this view of law changed as well. According to Charles Evans Hughs, Supreme Court Chief Justice from 1930 to 1941: "We are under a Constitution, but the Constitution is what the judges say it is."[4]

Where did such ideas come from? They were taught in the schools and law schools prior to this time. Roscoe Pound, President of Harvard Law School in the 1920s, said the old Christian legal foundations were not good enough to bring us into the modern era. According to him, we needed a new law system, where the law was rooted in the best that society had to offer—in the consensus of the society and what they deemed best for mankind. Pound said "the state takes the place of Jehovah."[5]

2. Positivism

Positivism is a second underlying principle upon which modern state education rests. According to Ronald Nash, positivism is "the belief that human knowledge cannot be extended beyond what can be discovered by use of the scientific method."[6] Nash writes:

> Many people believe that science is the only area of human study (other than mathematics and logic) that is true. Anything else can only be a matter of opinion. If some belief cannot be tested by the scientific method, it cannot be true; belief in it cannot be rational. Of course, it is interesting to ask if that claim (the positivists's own thesis) can be tested by the scientific method. Obviously, it cannot.[7]

Scientists, as the keepers of truth, have become **the** voice of reason and of what is objectively true, for many in our nation today. They have become priests for those who worship at the shrine of science.

3. Humanism

The third tenet upon which modern state education is built is humanism, or better described as secularism–naturalism–humanism.[8] Secularism is the belief "that human life can be lived and understood, in its own terms, without regard to any higher order of reality, that is, without regard to God."[9] The claim of naturalism is that "nothing exists outside the material, mechanical, natural order"[10] (which of course cannot be proved). Both secularism and naturalism are aspects of humanism. In reality, humanism is a religion in which human beings assume the place of God. Humanism is the belief that man is god; man decides what is right and wrong.

Relativism, positivism, and humanism form the foundation of state education today. These are the tenets of the religion that predominates in public schools in the western world. This is in great contrast to the foundation of education in the western world, which had its roots in Christianity. The vast majority of American colleges and universities were founded as seminaries—in fact, 106 of the first 108 colleges were founded by and for the Christian faith. Most of the early schools in this nation were started by the church, the Bible was the central text, ministers were the primary teachers, and a Biblical worldview was taught to everyone.[11]

Education today teaches actions and ideas contrary to God's truth. People can chose to do things contrary to God's law and desire, but it will be to their own hurt. A fish can be placed on land to try to live, but it is not too smart. The religion of humanism is dumb.

In the second commandment, God warns us to not make any idols for ourselves. Habakkuk tells us why it is idiotic to do so: "What profit is the idol when its maker has carved it, or an image, a teacher of falsehood? For its maker trusts in his own handiwork when he fashions speechless idols" (Hab. 2:18). Modern western man wouldn't think of making a golden calf, setting it up in his living room, and bowing down before it. What he does is much more subtle.

Humanists are sophisticated idol makers. They are like the guy who carves an idol and worships it—they trust in their own handiwork. They create their own laws, think up their own value systems, form their own governmental and educational systems, and worship them. It's as if some modern educrats say: "Oh, educational system, you are our savior. If we can get everyone to come to you, this will solve all our problems and bring peace and utopia to earth!"

Humanists trust in these things as their "god" (that which is right and true). They can do this, but it is not too smart, for if it isn't based upon God's truth (upon right principles), it will lead to ruin. Such idol worship leads to bondage, not liberty.

In Colossians 2:8, Paul contrasts the fruit of worldly and Christian philosophies: "See to it that no one takes you captive through philosophy and empty deception, according to the tradition of men, according to the elementary principles of the world, rather than according to Christ." Worldly philosophies of men produce bondage; they lead people into captivity. A Christian philosophy—of education, government, economics, etc.—produces liberty. We must provide an education for liberty. The more Christian the education, the more liberty will be produced—liberty in individuals but also in the society as a whole.

A liberal arts education in America used to prepare people for liberty, giving them an understanding of what true liberty is and how to conduct their lives in a proper way to live in liberty. Most liberal arts education today prepares people to live socialistically or humanistically. Consequently, most Americans are not knowledgeable of principles of liberty, nor have they had the character developed within them that is necessary to sustain freedom. In the new American society where humanism has become the predominate religion, state schools have become the new churches, and classrooms the modern pulpits. Unfortunately, there are many well-meaning but unknowledgeable Christian teachers who are propagating this new religion.

Components of Kingdom Education

What would be necessary for us to restore true liberal arts education to the nation? What would education that produces liberty look like? What are the components of Biblical or kingdom education? First of all, such education would look much different than most education in the world today. Following are a few general components of Kingdom education.

1. All aspects of education will be Christian

For education to be Biblical, all aspects of it should be Christian—that is, it will have a Christian philosophy, methodology, and curriculum. In brief, philosophy deals with the "why" of education, methodology with the "how", and curriculum with the "what."[12]

2. Education will be carried out by the appropriate jurisdictional sphere

Parents are primarily responsible for the education of their children. Grandparents and the church have a role as well. From a Biblical perspective, the state should be very limited in its role in education. While civil government does have an interest in the education of all its citizens, it is not appropriate for the state to control or compel in education, or even establish state schools as we know them today.[13]

3. Education will be modeled after the way Jesus educated.

Jesus was a teacher. He educated, and hence planted seeds of the kingdom of God, which have grown over the centuries. We should examine and emulate what and how He taught. First, the content of His teaching was Biblical and contained both "revelation knowledge" and "rational knowledge." We must search out truth in all areas of life in our educational endeavors (that is, obtain rational knowledge), but we must also realize that we need God to illuminate our understanding to more fully perceive that which is true (we need "revelation knowledge"). The disciples who were walking on the road to Emmaus were talking to "The Truth" but they did not perceive this until He opened their eyes to see (Luke 24:13-32). Education modeled after Jesus' example will impart both rational and revelational knowledge.

Jesus also used Biblical methods of education. There were a variety of techniques He employed as He educated his disciples and others. Some of these include:

- Demonstration (Mt. 6:9-15; Mark 6:41)

- Involvement of students in learning (Mark 6:7-12)
- Discovery (Mark 14:66-72)
- Familiar illustrations (Luke 6:4)
- Individual instruction (John 3:2-21; John 4:5-26; Luke 19:1-8)
- Lecture [formal teaching] (Luke 6:20-49; 1 Tim 4:13)
- Memorization (2 Tim. 3:15)
- Practice (Mt. 10; 1 Tim. 5:4; Luke 9, 10)
- Questions and answers (Mt. 16:13-18; Luke 6:3)
- Repetition (Mt. 16:21; 20:18-19)
- Review (Luke 24:44)
- Small group activity (Mt. 17:1-9; Mark 6:7-12)
- Visual aids (Mt. 22:19-21; Luke 13:19)
- Discipline, correction (Mk. 11:15-17)[14]

The general method Jesus used to educate or train others was that of making disciples by being a living demonstration of what He wanted to impart. He was a mentor to others. Jesus chose 12 disciples, poured His life into them, and equipped them to carry the Kingdom. Paul followed Jesus' example by making disciples. To the saints in Philippi he wrote: "The things you have learned and received and heard and seen in me, practice these things" (Phil. 4:9). He instructed Timothy to mentor others as well: "And the things which you have heard from me in the presence of many witnesses, these entrust to faithful men, who will be able to teach others also" (2 Tim. 2:2).

Parents Should Disciple Their Children

Parents can have a great effect upon society through properly training their children. The education of John Quincy Adams by his parents, John and Abigail, is a great example.[15] How parents educate their children will also have a great impact upon future generations. The ability to affect society (for good or evil) can grow exponentially with each succeeding generation. In Chapter 1 we saw how Jonathan and Sarah Edwards faithfully discipled and educated their eleven children. In turn, their children passed on to future generations the vision for advancing liberty and building up their nation. A study was done of 1400 descendants of Jonathan and Sarah. Of these 13 were college presidents, 65 were professors, 100 lawyers, 30 judges, 66 physicians, and 80 holders of public office including 3 senators, 3 governors, and a vice president of the United States. Their training not only benefitted their children, but thousands of their descendants, and the nation at large.

The seeds we plant today through education of our children (and others) have impact beyond measure in the future. After all, you can count how many seeds are in an apple, but you cannot count how many apples are in a seed.

Pastors Should Be Mentors

Just as parents can greatly impact society through educating their children in a Biblical manner, pastors and leaders in the church have the opportunity to extend God's Kingdom in all spheres of life through discipling and mentoring those in the church. One example of this can be seen in the life of the eighteenth-century minister, Samuel Davies.

Rev. Samuel Davies was a bold ambassador for Christ. In his desire to see the Kingdom of God come *on earth as it is in heaven* he served not only as a pastor but also as a lawyer, an ambassador to England, and President of Princeton College. E.L. Magoon writes that

> he had made himself a thorough master of English law, civil and ecclesiastical, and always chose to meet every persecuting indictment in the highest courts with his own plea. . . . [H]e went to England and obtained the explicit sanction of the highest authority with respect to the extension of the Toleration law to Virginia. It was during this mission that . . . George II and many of his court were in the congregation of this American Dissenter. His majesty, struck with admiration, or forgetting the proprieties of the occasion, spoke several times to those around him and smiled. Davies paused a moment, and then looking sternly at the king, exclaimed, "When the lion roars, the beasts of the forest all tremble; and when King Jesus speaks, the princes of earth should keep silence."[16]

Davies, one of the greatest orators in colonial America, served as the mentor for who Thomas Jefferson called "the greatest orator that ever lived" — Patrick Henry. When Patrick was around 12 years old his mother joined the church where Samuel Davies preached. Mrs. Henry would attend regularly and would always take Patrick, who from the first showed a high appreciation for the preacher. Each Sunday as they rode home in their buggy, Mrs. Henry and Patrick would review the sermon. This greatly influenced Patrick's thinking and the development of his oratorical skills. Patrick ever declared that Davies was "the greatest orator he ever heard."[17] But Patrick Henry also learned from Davies a sound Biblical theology, one which has produced some of the leading men in all history. William Wirt Henry writes: "His early example of eloquence . . . was Mr. Davies, and the effect of his teaching upon his after life may be plainly traced."[18]

Henry's association with dissenters by way of his mother's Presbyterian faith, caused him to greatly aid the cause of religious liberty among various groups, especially the Baptists. Henry often represented Baptist ministers when they were imprisoned for "the heinous charge of worshipping God according to the dictates of their own consciences." Henry secured the release of one minister who had been imprisoned five months on the charge of creating a disturbance by preaching. When the jailer refused to release the man until his jail fees, which were substantial, were paid, Henry secretly covered this cost out of his own pocket. The minister learned of the event over 20 years later.[19] Davies' example also produced a great effect through Patrick Henry during our struggle for independence. Henry's oratory and vocal leadership had such an impact that he became known as the "voice or orator of the American Revolution."[20]

This is a great example for Pastors today to be mentors for our youth, inspiring and equipping them to lead in all areas of life. Besides Henry, many other of America's Founding Fathers were trained by ministers, including Jefferson, Madison, and Noah Webster.

4. Biblical education will produce kingdom fruit

A primary purpose of education is to build Christian character, to shape the man both internally and externally. Noah Webster gave a Biblical definition for education: "Education comprehends all that series of instruction and discipline which is intended to enlighten the understanding, correct the temper, form the manners and habits of youth, and fit them for usefulness in their future stations."[21] The focus of education should firstly be the inner man. The fruit of education, according to Webster, is the same fruit that the Word of God will produce within an individual. Paul writes that "all Scripture is inspired by God and profitable for teaching, for reproof, for correction, for training in righteousness; that the man of God may be adequate, equipped for every good work" (2 Tim. 3:16). Webster's definition for education coincides with the fruit of the Word of God. Biblical education will build the total man (inside and out) and prepare him to fulfill his destiny ("fit them for usefulness in their future stations").

A central purpose of education is to build godly character. Whoever controls education in a nation controls the formation of character. Whoever controls the character of the people controls the form of government. America began as a constitutional republic because the Christian character necessary to support such a government was formed in Americans in the homes and churches. Rosalie Slater writes that "as we let go the control of education, we let go the control of character, and we declined from a republic into a socialistic democracy."[22]

Biblical education will not only effect individual lives, but it will also impact all spheres of life. John Witherspoon was a Kingdom educator who trained young men to be "Kingdom men". He was "the man who shaped the men who shaped America." Witherspoon was a Presbyterian minister who came from Scotland in 1768 to serve as President of the College of New Jersey. During Witherspoon's tenure there were 478 graduates of, what became, Princeton University. Of these, at least 86 became active in civil government and included: one president (James Madison), one vice-president (Aaron Burr), 10 cabinet officers, 21 senators, 39 congressmen, 12 governors, a Supreme Court justice (Brockholst Livingston), and one attorney general of the United States (William Bradford).[23]

> Nearly one-fifth of the signers of the Declaration of Independence, one-sixth of the delegates of the constitutional Convention, and one-fifth of the first Congress under the Constitution were graduates of the College of New Jersey.[24]

Here was a man who literally discipled his nation. Those today who have a vision for Biblical education, and an understanding of the components of Kingdom education, may, likewise, have an opportunity to disciple the nations.

5. Kingdom education will pass the baton to future generations

Psalm 78:1-7 reveals to us as parents and educators that we are to pass on to our posterity all of the vision, mission, principles, character, and truth that God has made known to this generation. This is to be done in such a way that they will then, in turn, teach their children, who will teach their children, "that they may arise and tell them to their children, that they should put their confidence in God and not forget the works of God" (verses 6-7).

We are in a race—not a hundred yard dash but a relay race. We will not win the race by merely running fast. We must pass the baton. Our generation was not given the baton, but had to grope around and find it in the weeds. After finding it we had to learn how to run, what the race was all about, where the track was, and how to pass the baton. We also must train our posterity to run in the race and how to receive the baton, and teach them how to pass the baton on to the next generation. We can do great things for God in this generation, but if we fail in this, we have failed to fully fulfill God's purpose for this generation.

Biblical education is the means of passing the baton (the Kingdom) to the next generation and equipping them to pass it on to their posterity. The extent to which we educate in a Kingdom manner determines, in part, the extent to which His Kingdom will come on earth. Establishing Biblical education in the nations is, therefore, of utmost importance. May God increase our understanding of how to "disciple the nations."

End Notes

1. Will Herberg, "Modern Man in a Metaphysical Wasteland," *The Intercollegiate Review*, vol. 5 (1968-69), p. 79; quoted in Ronald H. Nash, *The Closing of the American Heart*, Probe Books, 1990, p. 62.

2. Noah Webster, *An American Dictionary of the English Language*, 1828, republished in facsimile edition by Foundation for American Christian Education, San Francisco, 1980.

3. *Webster's New World Dictionary of the American Language*, David B. Guralnik, editor, Nashville: The Southwestern Company, 1969.

4. David Barton, *Original Intent*, Aledo, Tex: WallBuilder Press, 1996, p. 172.

5. Roscoe Pound, *The Spirit of the Common Law*, New York: The Legal Classics Library.

6. Nash, p. 65.

7. Nash, p. 66.

8. Nash, p. 67-70.

9. Nash, p. 67.

10. Nash, p. 68.

11. See *Restoring America's Christian Education*, by Stephen McDowell, Charlottesville: Providence Foundation, 2000.

12. This is a large topic which educators need to pursue vigorously. For more, see Providence Foundation resources: *Liberating the Nations*, ch. 7, and *The Principle Approach to Education* tape series.

13. State involvement in education is appropriate if it comes under the jurisdictional purpose of civil government to protect the righteous and punish the evil-doer; therefore, as an example, schools for police or military would be okay. For more see Providence Foundation Resources: *Liberating the Nations*, *Watchmen on the Walls*, and *Restoring America's Christian Education*.

14. Anita Simpkins, Lecture notes on the Principle Approach to Education.

15. See Chapter 9 and also "The Education of John Quincy Adams," by Rosalie J. Slater in *The Christian History of the American Revolution, Consider and Ponder*, compiled by Verna Hall, San Francisco: Foundation for American Christian Education, 1997, p. 602 ff.

16. E.L. Magoon, *Orators of the American Revolution*, New York: C. Scribner, 1857, reprinted by Sightext Publications, El Segundo, Cal, 1969, pp. 207-208.

17. William Wirt Henry, *Patrick Henry, Life, Correspondence and Speeches*, Vol. 1, first published by Charles Scribner's Sons, 1891, republished by Sprinkle Publications, 1993, p. 15.

18. Ibid., p. 16.

19. Ibid., pp. 118-119.

20. For more on Henry, see *In God We Trust Tour Guide*, Chapter 7, by McDowell and Beliles, Charlottesville: Providence Foundation, 1998.

21. Webster's 1828 Dictionary.

22. Rosalie Slater, "The Christian History Literature Program," in *A Guide to American Christian Education*, by James B. Rose, Camarillo, Cal.: American Christian History Institute, 1987, p. 328.

23. Mary-Elaine Swanson, *The Education of James Madison, A Model for Today*, Montgomery: The Hoffman Education Center for the Family, 1992, p. 53.

24. Ibid.

About the Author

Stephen McDowell is co-founder and President of the Providence Foundation. After obtaining a B.S. Degree in physics at the University of North Carolina at Chapel Hill and a M.S. Degree in geology at the University of Memphis, he was ordained for the ministry in 1978, working in the pastorate until 1984 when he assisted in establishing the Providence Foundation, and since then has served as its President.

McDowell is the editor of the *Providential Perspective* and has authored or co-authored a dozen books, videos, and training courses, including *America's Providential History, In Search of Democracy, Liberating the Nations, In God We Trust Tour Guide*, and *The Story of America's Liberty*. His books and writings have been translated into French, Spanish, German, Portuguese, Russian, Czech, and Chinese, and distributed to hundreds of thousands of people.

He has traveled to 40 states and over fifteen nations in six continents, teaching tens of thousands of people from about 100 different countries. He has consulted with numerous government officials, assisted in writing political documents, aided in establishing political parties, and helped start a number of Christian schools.

McDowell has written scores of articles for various publications, appeared on numerous TV and radio programs, and spoken to many different religious, educational, civic, and political organizations. He also periodically does historic portrayals of Thomas Jefferson. He and his wife, Beth, have four children and live in Charlottesville, Virginia.

Providence Foundation Resources

The Providence Foundation is a nonprofit Christian educational organization whose mission is to spread liberty, justice, and prosperity among the nations. This mission is accomplished primarily by assisting churches in their task of teaching and equipping people to apply the principles of a Biblical and providential worldview in their homes, businesses, schools, and political activities.

Books

America's Providential History   (B01) $16.95
How the Lord guided our nation from the very beginning. Proof from history: our nation grew from Christian principles. How to bring them back into the mainstream.

Liberating the Nations   (B02) $13.95
God's plan, fundamental principles, essential foundations, and structures necessary to build Christian nations.

Defending the Declaration   (B04) $13.95
How the Bible and Christianity influenced the writing of the Declaration.

Watchmen on the Walls   (B06) $6.95
The role of pastors in equipping Christians to fulfill their civil duties.

In God We Trust   (B03) $13.95
A Christian tour guide for historic sites in Washington D.C., Philadelphia, Jamestown, Williamsburg, Richmond, Mt. Vernon, Charlottesville, and more.

Building Godly Nations   (B14) $15.95
The mandate for building Godly nations, lessons from America's Christian history, and how to apply Biblical principles to governing the nations.

In Search of Democracy   (B07) $5.95
Foundations, framework, and historical development of biblical government and law.

Independence, Drums of War, vol. 1   (B08) $7.95
Bunker Hill, Drums of War, vol. 2   (B09) $7.95
A Captive in Williamsburg, Drums of War, vol. 3   (B10) $7.95
Drums of War is a series of historical novels for young people designed to teach in an enjoyable way the principles, events, and persons behind America's independence.

The Ten Commandments and Modern Society   (B11) $4.95
Restoring America's Christian Education   (B12) $4.95
A Guide to American Christian Education   (B13) $39.95
Hardback book by Jim Rose examines the Principle Approach to Education, including Christian philosophy, methodology, notebooks, and various subjects.

Videos/DVD/Game

The Story of America's Liberty   (VT01) $19.95
A 60-minute video that looks at the influence of Christianity in the beginning of America, examining principles and providential occurrences.

Dawn's Early Light   (VT02) $19.95
A 28-minute version of *The Story of America's Liberty* with up-dated statistics.

The Wall   (Video or DVD)   (VT03 or DVD01) $15.00
Documentary on the historical roots of "the wall of separation" metaphor.

America: the Game   (GM1) $29.95

Audios Tape Series

The Christian Roots of America (2 tapes)	(ATS05)	$13.00
Discipling the Nations (4 tapes)	(ATS04)	$19.95
Fundamentals of a Biblical Worldview (8 tapes)	(ATS06)	$40.00
In Search of Democracy (4 tapes)	(ATS02)	$19.95
The Principle Approach to Education for Home or Church Schools (24 tapes)	(ATS01)	$109.95
Liberating the Nations: Developing a Biblical Worldview (7 tapes)	(ATS03)	$39.95

Audio Tapes

America's Freedom: Founded on Faith	(AT15)	$5.95
No Cross, No Crown: Exemplified in the Life of William Penn	(AT1)	$5.95
Reforming the Nations—an Example from the Life of Webster	(AT2)	$5.95
Teaching History from a Providential Perspective	(AT10)	$5.95
The Principle Approach	(AT9)	$5.95
The Principle Approach: Teaching History & Literature	(AT19)	$5.95
God Governs in the Affairs of Men	(AT11)	$5.95
Biblical Economics	(AT7)	$5.95
Honest Money and Banking	(AT8)	$5.95
Biblical Government and Law	(AT5)	$5.95
Forming a Christian Union	(AT6)	$5.95
The Role of Women in History	(AT13)	$5.95
Fundamental Principles of Christian Nations	(AT3)	$5.95
Christ's Teaching on Public Affairs	(AT4)	$5.95
Biblical Principles of Business, Exemplified by McCormick	(AT16)	$5.95
We Hold These Truths—Governmental Principles of Founders	(AT12)	$5.95
The American Christian Revolution — Christianity: Foundation of America's Liberty	(AT14)	$5.95
Education and the Kingdom of God	(AT17)	$5.95
The Biblical Relationship of Church and State	(AT18)	$5.95
Prophetic Christian Statesmanship	(AT20)	$5.95
The Ten Commandments & Modern Society	(AT21)	$5.95
Why We Celebrate Thanksgiving	(AT28)	$5.95
Qualifications for Godly Officials	(AT27)	$5.95
Thomas Jefferson on "The Foundation of America's Liberty"	(AT29)	$5.95
Jesus: the Focal Point of History	(AT25)	$5.95
Loving God with All Your Mind	(AT24)	$5.95
Fulfilling the Cultural Mandate: How Christians Have Helped Establish God's Kingdom in the Nations	(AT23)	$5.95
Christ the King	(AT22)	$5.95

RESPONSE & ORDER FORM

I want to join the Providence Foundation in spreading God's liberty, justice, and prosperity among the nations and restoring to America's homes, churches, and schools the ideas that form the foundation of freedom by becoming a:

☐ **SPECIAL SUPPORTER**: those who contribute any amount toward the ongoing ministry of the Providence Foundation receive the *Providential Perspective* and *Reformation Report*. Enclosed is my gift of: $ _____

☐ **MEMBER**: those who contribute $100 or more per year receive our newsletters, a 30% discount on all our books, videos, and materials, plus discounts to our Seminars. I will send a regular gift of $_____ per month / quarter / year (circle one). Enclosed is my gift of: $ _____

I wish to order the following items:

Qty.	Title/Product code	Price	Total

	Subtotal
	Member disct. (30%)
Shipping & Handling: * U.S. Mail: $3.50 minimum, 10% if over $35 * UPS: $5.00 minimum, 12% if over $50. (Game orders will be sent UPS)	Sales tax (VA orders add 4.5%)
	Shipping
	TOTAL
	Contribution
☐ Please send me a Resource Catalog	**GRAND TOTAL**

Method of Payment: ☐ Check/Money Order ☐ VISA ☐ Mastercard ☐ AmEx ☐ Cash

Credit Card No.:_____ Exp. date: _____

Signature:_____

SHIP TO:

Name:_____

Address:_____

City:_____ State:_____ Zip:_____

Phone:(_____)_____

Email:_____

Make checks payable to:
Providence Foundation
PO Box 6759
Charlottesville, VA 22906
Phone/Fax: 434-978-4535

Also, order by phone or at website:
www.providencefoundation.com